T0312609

Assembly Language Programming

Assembly Language Programming

ARM Cortex-M3

Vincent Mahout

First published 2012 in Great Britain and the United States by ISTE Ltd and John Wiley & Sons, Inc.

ISTE Ltd
27-37 St George's Road
London SW19 4EU
UK

John Wiley & Sons, Inc.
111 River Street
Hoboken, NJ 07030
USA

www.iste.co.uk

www.wiley.com

© ISTE Ltd 2012

Library of Congress Cataloging-in-Publication Data

Mahout, Vincent.
 Assembly language programming : ARM Cortex-M3 / Vincent Mahout.
p. cm.
Includes bibliographical references and index.
 ISBN 978-1-84821-329-6
1. Embedded computer systems. 2. Microprocessors. 3. Assembler language (Computer program language) I. Title.
 TK7895.E42M34 2012
 005.2--dc23

2011049418

British Library Cataloguing-in-Publication Data
A CIP record for this book is available from the British Library
ISBN: 978-1-84821-329-6

Printed and bound in Great Britain by CPI Group (UK) Ltd., Croydon, Surrey CR0 4YY

Table of Contents

Preface

To be able to plan and write this type of book, you need a good work environment. In my case, I was able to benefit from the best working conditions for this enterprise. In terms of infrastructure and material, the *Institut National de Sciences Appliquées de Toulouse*, France (Toulouse National Institute of Applied Sciences), and in particular their Electrical and Computer Engineering Department, has never hesitated to invest in computer systems engineering, so that the training of our future engineers will always be able to keep up with rapid technological change. I express my profound gratitude to this institution. These systems would not have amounted to much unless, over the years, there was an educational and technical team bringing their enthusiasm and dynamism to implement them. The following pages also contain the hard work of Pascal Acco, Guillaume Auriol, Pierre-Emmanuel Hladik, Didier Le Botlan, José Martin, Sébastien Di Mercurio and Thierry Rocacher. I thank them sincerely. Two final respectful and friendly nods go to François Pompignac and Bernard Fauré who, before retirement, did much work to fertilize this now thriving land.

When writing a book on the assembly language of a μprocessor, we know in advance that it will not register in posterity. By its very nature, an assembly language has the same life expectancy as the processor it supports – perhaps 20 years at best. What's more, this type of programming is obviously not used for the development of software projects and so is of little consequence.

Assembly language programming is, however, an indispensable step in understanding the internal functioning of a μprocessor. This is why it is still widely taught in industrial computer training, and particularly in training engineers. It is clear that a good theoretical knowledge of a particular assembly language, combined with a practical training phase, allows for easier learning of other programming languages, whether they are the assembly languages of other processors or high-level languages.

Thus, this book intends to *dissect* programming in the assembly language of a μcontroller constructed around an ARM Cortex-M3 core. The choice of this μcontroller rests on the desire to explain:

– a 32-bit processor: the choice of the ARM designer is essential in the 32-bit world. This type of processor occupies, for example, 95% of the market in the domain of mobile telephony;

– a processor of recent conception and architecture: the first licenses for Cortex-M3 are dated October 2004 and those for STMicroelectronics' 32-bit flash microcontrollers (STM32) were given in June 2007;

– a processor adapted to the embedded world, based on the observation that 80% of software development activity involves embedded systems.

This book had been written to be as generic as possible. It is certainly based on the architecture and instruction set of Cortex-M3, but with the intention of explaining the basic mechanisms of assembly language programming. In this way we can use systematically modular programming to show how basic algorithmic structures can be programmed in assembly language. This book also presents many illustrative examples, meaning it is also practical.

Chapter 1

Overview of Cortex-M3 Architecture

A computer program is usually defined as a sequence of instructions that act on data and return an expected result. In a high-level language, the sequence and data are described in a symbolic, abstract form. It is necessary to use a compiler to translate them into machine language instructions, which are only understood by the processor. Assembly language is directly derived from machine language, so when programming in assembly language the programmer is forced to see things from the point of view of the processor.

1.1. Assembly language versus the assembler

When executing a program, a computer processor obeys a series of numerical orders – instructions – that are read from memory: these instructions are encoded in binary form. The collection of instructions in memory makes up the *code* of the program being executed. Other areas of memory are also used by the processor during the execution of code: an area containing the *data* (variables, constants) and an area containing the *system stack*, which is used by the processor to store, for example, local data when calling subprograms. Code, data and the system stack are the three fundamental elements of all programs during their execution.

It is possible to program directly in machine language – that is, to write the bit instruction sequences in machine language. In practice, however, this is not realistic, even when using a more condensed script thanks to hexadecimal notation (numeration in base 16) for the instructions. It is therefore preferable to use an *assembly language*. This allows code to be represented by symbolic names, adapted to human understanding, which correspond to instructions in machine language.

Assembly language also allows the programmer to reserve the space needed for the system stack and data areas by giving them an initial value, if necessary. Take this example of an instruction to copy in the no. 1 general register of a processor with the value 170 (AA in hexadecimal). Here it is, written using the syntax of assembly language studied here:

EXAMPLE 1.1.– *A single line of code*

```
MOV R1, #0xAA  ; copy (move) value 170 (AA in hexa)
               ; in register R1
```

The same instruction, represented in machine language (hexadecimal base), is written: E3A010AA. The symbolic name *MOV* takes the name *mnemonic*. *R1* and *#0xAA* are the *arguments* of the instruction. The semicolon indicates the start of a commentary that ends with the current line.

The *assembler* is a program responsible for translating the program from the assembly language in which it is written into machine language. Upon input, it receives a source file that is written in assembly language, and creates two files: the object file containing machine language (and the necessary information for the fabrication of an executable program), and the printout assembly file containing a report that details the work carried out by the assembler.

This book deals with assembly language in general, but focuses on processors based on Cortex-M3, as set out by Advanced RISC Machines (abbreviated to ARM). Different designers (Freescale, STmicroelectronics, NXP, etc.) then integrate this structure into μcontrollers containing memory and multiple peripherals as well as this processor core. Part of the documentation regarding this processor core is available in PDF format at www.arm.com.

1.2. The world of ARM

ARM does not directly produce semiconductors, but rather provides licenses for microprocessor cores with 32-bit RISC architecture.

This Cambridge-based company essentially aims to provide semiconductors for the embedded systems market. To give an idea of the position of this designer on this market, 95% of mobile telephones in 2008 were made with ARM-based processors. It should also be noted that the A4 and A5 processors, produced by Apple and used in their iPad graphics tablets, are based on ARM Cortex-Type A processors.

Since 1985 and its first architecture (named ARM1), ARM architectures have certainly changed. The architecture upon which Cortex-M3 is based is called ARMV7-M.

ARM's collection is structured around four main families of products, for which many licenses have been filed[1]:

– the ARM 7 family (173 licenses);

– the ARM 9 family (269 licenses);

– the ARM 10 family (76 licenses);

– the Cortex-A family (33 licenses);

– the Cortex-M family (51 licenses, of which 23 are for the M3 version);

– the Cortex-R family (17 licenses).

1.2.1. *Cortex-M3*

Cortex-M3 targets, in particular, embedded systems requiring significant resources (32-bit), but for these the costs (production, development and consumption) must be reduced. The first overall illustration (see Figure 1.1) of Cortex-M3, as found in the technical documentation for this product, is a functional diagram. Although simple in its representation, every block could perplex a novice. Without knowing all of the details and all of the subtleties, it is useful to have an idea of the main functions performed by different blocks of the architecture.

1.2.1.1. *Executive units*

These units make up the main part of the processor – the part that is ultimately necessary to run applications and to perform them or their software functions:

– CM3CORE: This is the core itself. This unit contains different registers, all of the read/write instruction mechanisms and data in the form of the arithmetical and

---

1 Numbers from the third quarter of 2010.

logical unit for the proper execution of different instructions. The functioning of this block will be explained in detail in Chapter 2. It is necessary to understand its mechanism in order to write programs in assembly language.

– Nested Vector Interrupt Controller (NVIC): Cortex-M3 is intended to be embedded in a μcontroller, which includes peripheral units to allow interfacing with the outside world. These units can be seen as independent micromachines. The exchanges between them and Cortex-M3 must consequently be rhythmic and organized so that the sequence of tasks complies with rules (the concept of priorities) and determinism set in advance by the programmer. NVIC plays the role of "director". It is in charge of receiving, sorting and distributing the different interrupt requests generated by the collection of μcontroller units. It also manages events that threaten the smooth running of the code being executed (reset, memory bus problem, division by 0, etc.).

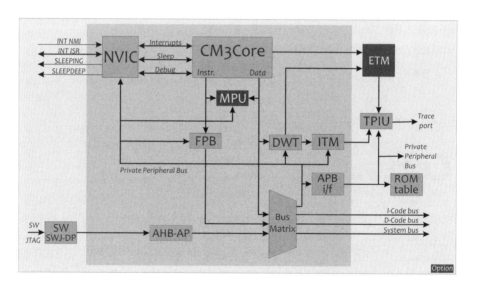

Figure 1.1. *Cortex-M3 functional diagram*

– Memory Protection Unit (MPU): This block is optional – a designer using Cortex-M3 to make their μcontroller can choose not to implement this function. This block allows the allocation of specific read and/or write privileges to specific memory zones. In this way, when different independent software tasks are executed in parallel (or more precisely in sharing the common resources of the processor), it is possible to allocate a memory zone to each task that is inaccessible to the other tasks. This mechanism therefore allows programmer to secure memory access. It usually goes hand-in-hand with the use of an operating system (real-time or otherwise) for the software layer.

– Bus matrix: This unit is a kind of gigantic intelligent multiplex. It allows connections to the external buses:

- the *ICode* bus (32-bit AHB-Lite type[2]) that carries the memory mappings allocated to the code and instructions;

- the *DCode* bus (also 32-bit AHB-Lite type) that is responsible for reading/writing in *data* memory zones;

- the *System* bus (again 32-bit AHB-Lite type), which deals with all system space access;

- the *Private Peripheral Bus* (PPB): all peripherals contained in the μcontroller are added to the Cortex-M3 architecture by the designer. ARM designed a specific bus to allow exchanges with peripherals. This bus contains 32 bits, but in this case it is the *Advanced Peripheral Bus* (APB) type. This corresponds to another bus protocol (which you may know is less efficient than AHB type, but it is more than sufficient for access to peripheral units). It should be noted that the bus matrix plays an important role in transmitting useful information to development units, which are mentioned in the next section.

1.2.1.2. *Development units*

The development of programs is an important and particularly time-consuming step in the development cycle of an embedded application. What is more, if the project has certification imperatives, it is necessary that tools (software and/or material) allowing maximum monitoring of the events occurring in each clock cycle are at its disposition. In Cortex-M3, the different units briefly introduced below correspond to these monitoring functions. They are directly implanted in the silicon of the circuit, which allows them to use these development tools at a material level. An external software layer is necessary, however, to recover and process the information issued by these units. The generic idea behind the introduction of hardware solutions is to offer the programmer the ability to test and improve the reliability of (or certify) his or her code without making any changes. It is convenient (and usual) to insert some *print ("Hello I was here")* into a software structure to check that the execution passes through this structure. This done, a code modification is introduced, which can modify the global behavior of the program. This is particularly true when time management is critical for the system, which, for

---

2 Advanced High-performance Bus (AHB) is a microcontroller bus protocol brought in by ARM.

embedded systems controlled by a μcontroller, is almost always the case. The units relating to monitoring functions in Cortex-M3 include:

– Flash Patch and Breakpoint (FPB): the FPB is the most basic function for this process. It is linked to the concept of a stopping point (breakpoint), which imposes a stop on a line of code (that is to say, an instruction in the case of assembly language) located beforehand. This unit is used to mark instructions so that when they come into effect, the processor puts itself into a particular mode of operation: *debug* mode. Development software (and other pieces of software that use it) can therefore observe the state of the processor and directly influence the running of the program in progress.

– Data Watchpoint and Trace (DWT): the concept of a "point of observation" is the counterpart to the concept of a stopping point for the data. The DWT stops the program running when it works on marked data rather than a marked instruction. This action can be in reading, writing, passing on values, etc. The unit can also send requests to the *ITM* and *ETM* units.

– Embedded Trace Macrocell (ETM): the concept of trace includes the capacity for the hardware to record a sequence of events during program execution. The recovery of these recordings allows the programmer to analyze the running of the program, whether good or bad. In the case of ETM, only information on instructions is stored in a first in, first out (FIFO)-type structure. As with the MPU unit, this unit is optional.

– Instrumentation Trace Macrocell (ITM): this unit also allows the collection of *trace* information on applications (software, hardware or time). The information is more limited than with the ETM unit but is nevertheless very useful in isolating a vicious bug. This is especially true if the optional ETM is not present.

– Advanced High-performance Bus Access Port (AHB-AP): this is an (Input/Output) port within Cortex-M3 that is designed to debug. It allows access to all records and all addressable memory space. It has priority in the arbitration policies of the *bus matrix*. This unit is connected upstream by the Serial Wire JTAG (Joint Test Action Group) port (SW/JTAG), which is the interface (with its physical layers) that connects to the outside world, equipped with its part of the JTAG probe. The JTAG protocol is a standardized protocol used by almost all semiconductor manufacturers.

– Trace Port Interface Unit (TPUI): the TPUI plays the same role in *trace* functions as the SW/JTAG plays in debug functions. Its existence is principally linked to the fact that it is necessary to sort the external world recordings collected by the ITM. There is an additional challenge, however, when an ETM unit is present, as it must also manage the data stored there. Its secondary role is therefore to combine and format this double stream of data before transmitting it to the port. In the outside world, it is necessary to use a *Trace Port Analyzer* to recover the data.

1.2.2. *The Cortex-M3 core in STM32*

As already stated, ARM does not directly make semiconductors. The μcontroller core designs are sold under license to designers, who add all of the peripheral units that make up the "interface with the exterior". For example, the STM32 family of μcontrollers, made by STMicroelectronics, contains the best selling μcontrollers using Cortex-M3. Like any good family of μcontrollers, the STM32 family is available in many versions. In early 2010, the STMicroelectronics catalog offered the products shown in Figure 1.2.

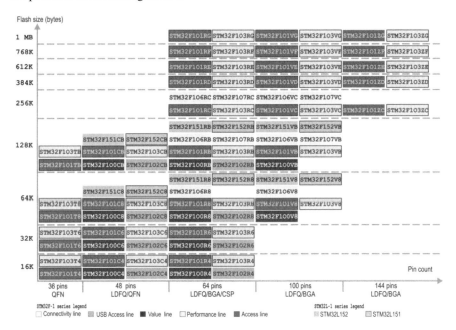

Figure 1.2. *STM32 family products*

1.2.2.1. *Functionality*

The choice of the right version of μcontroller can be a significant step in the design phase of a project: based on the needs (in terms of function, number of Input/Output, etc.) but also on the proper constraints (cost, consumption, size, etc.), each version of the processor will be more or less well adapted to the project. Again, the purpose of this book is not to go into detail on the function of the *peripheral* aspects of the μcontroller. It is, however, useful to have an overall view of the circuit that will eventually be programmed, so you are not surprised by such basic things as, for example, addressing memory. From a functional point of view, Figure 1.3 shows how STMicroelectronics has "dressed" Cortex-M3 to make a processor (the STM32F103RB version is shown here). The first important remark is that, inevitably, not all functions offered by this μcontroller are available simultaneously. Usually several units share the output pins. So, depending on the configuration that the programmer imposes, certain functions must *de facto* be unavailable for the application. Only a profound knowledge of a given processor will allow the programmer to know, *a priori*, whether the chosen version will be sufficient for the needs of the application being developed. The issue of choosing the best version is therefore far from trivial.

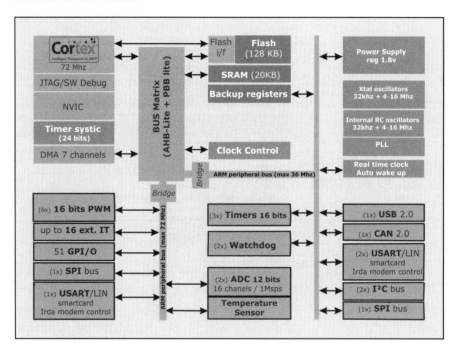

Figure 1.3. *Functional description of the STM32F103RB*

In looking at the outline of the STM32F103RB processor, we can see that it has ARM design elements in its processor core, namely:

– a power stage and so clock circuits. This makes it possible to put the processor into "sleep" mode and allow access to different frequencies (which is interesting for timer management in particular);

– the addition of *Flash* and *RAM*. The amount of memory present in the case is one of the variables that fluctuates the most, depending on which μcontroller is chosen. The STM32F103RB version has 128 KB of *Flash* memory which, to put it in perspective, can represent up to 65,000 lines of code written in assembly language (assuming that an instruction is coded on 16 bits);

– managers developed in system time, including the *Systick* 24-bit timer and an automatic wake-up system when the processor has gone into "sleep" mode. These units have an undeniable usefulness during the use of the real-time kernel.

STMicroelectronics then added the following functions:

– time and/or counting management peripherals;

– analog signal management peripherals. These are analogical/numerical converters for acquiring analog quantities, and represent the PWM (Pulse Width Modulation) managers for sending assimilable signals to the analog quantities;

– digital input/output peripherals. These 51 General Purpose Input Output (GPIO) peripherals are the TTL (Transistor-Transistor Logic) input/output ports and the other 16 signals involving digital input that can transmit an interrupt request;

– communication peripherals. Different current protocols are present in this chip for communications via a serial link (Universal Synchronous Asynchronous Receiver Transmitter (USART)), Universal Serial Bus (USB) or an industrial bus (I^2C, Controller–area network (CAN), Serial Peripheral Interface (SPI)).

1.2.2.2. *Memory space*

Memory space management is certainly the most complicated aspect to be managed when developing a program in assembly language. Fortunately, a number of *assembly directives* associated with a powerful *linker* make this management relatively simple. However, it is helpful to have a clear idea of the memory mapping in order to work with full knowledge of the facts while developing (and debugging) the program. In fact, processor registers regularly contain quantities that correspond to addresses. When the program does not behave as desired (a nasty bug, clearly!), it is helpful to know whether the quantities produced are ones that could be expected. Cortex-M3 has a 4 GB consecutive address memory space (32-bit bus). A memory address corresponds to one byte. It follows that a *half-word* occupies two addresses and a *word* (32-bits) occupies four memory addresses.

By convention, data storage is arranged according to the *little endian* standard, where the least significant byte of a word or half-word is stored at the lowest address, and we return to the higher addresses by taking the series of component bytes making up the numbers stored in memory. Figure 1.4 shows how, in the *little endian* standard, memory placement of words and half-words is managed.

The architecture is of the *Harvard*-type, which results in a division separating code access from data access. Figure 1.5 shows how this division is planned out. The other zones (*Peripheral, External,* etc.) impose the placement on the addressing space of different units, as presented in Figure 1.3.

One feature that should be noted concerns memory access – *bit banding*. This technique is found in both the *Static Random-Access Memory* (SRAM) zone (between addresses *0×20000000* and *0×2000FFFF* for the *bit-band region* and addresses *0×22000000* and *0×23FFFFFF* for the *alias*) and the *peripheral* zone (between addresses *0×40000000* and *0×4000FFFF* for the *bit-band region* and addresses *0×42000000* and *0×43FFFFFF* for the *alias*). These four zones are schematized by the hatching in the memory-mapping in Figure 1.5. This technique allows the programmer to directly modify (set or reset) bits situated at the addresses within the *bit-banding* zone.

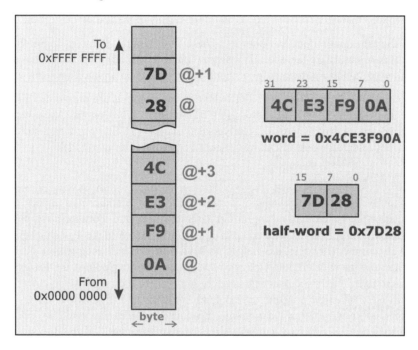

Figure 1.4. *Little-endian convention*

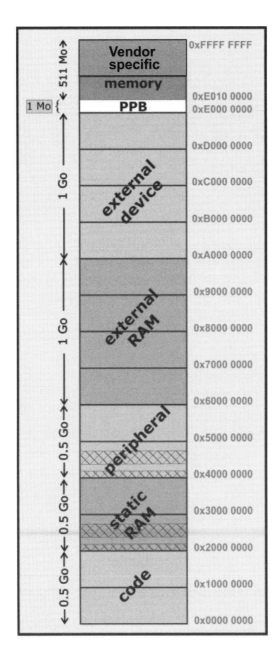

Figure 1.5. *Cortex-M3 memory mapping*

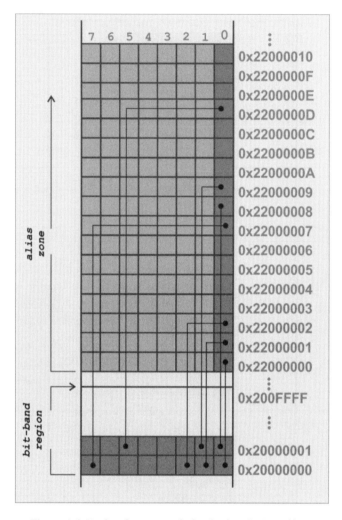

Figure 1.6. *Bit-banding principle for the first SRAM address*

What is the problem? Insofar as the architecture cannot directly act upon bits in memory, if we wish to modify a bit in a memory zone without this feature, it is necessary to:

1) recover the word from memory;

2) modify the bit (by application of a binary mask, for example);

3) rewrite the word to memory.

ARM is designed to match the address of a word (in the alias zone) with a bit (in the bit-banding zone). So when the programmer writes a value in the alias zone, it amounts to modifying the bit-banding bit corresponding to the zero-weight bit that they just wrote. Conversely, reading the least significant bit of a word in the alias zone lets the programmer know the logic state of the corresponding bit in the bit-banding zone (see Figure 1.6). It should be noted that this technique does not use RAM memory insofar as alias zones are imaginary: they do not physically correspond to memory locations – they only use memory addresses, but with 4 GB of possible addresses this loss is of little consequence.

Chapter 2

The Core of Cortex-M3

The previous chapter showed how the programmer could break down the different units present in a μcontroller like STM32 from a functional point of view. It is now time to delve a little deeper into the Cortex-M3 core, and to explain in detail the contents of the CM3CORE box, as shown in Figure 2.1.

It would be pointless to create a replica (which would be incomplete due to the simplification necessary) of the contents of the various reference manuals [ARM 06a, ARM 06b, ARM 06c] that give detailed explanations of Cortex functions. It would also be pointless, however, to claim to program in assembly language without having a reasonably precise idea of its structure. This chapter therefore attempts to present the aspects of the architecture necessary for reasoned programming of a μcontroller.

2.1. Modes, privileges and states

Cortex-M3 can be put into two different operating modes: *thread mode* and *Handler mode*. These modes combine with the privilege levels that can be granted to the execution of a program regarding access to certain registers:

– At the *unprivileged* access level, the executed code cannot access all instructions (those instructions specific to the access of special registers are excluded). It does not generally have access to all functions within the system (Nested Vector Interrupt Controller [NVIC], timer system, etc.). The concern is simply to avoid having code that, by bad management of a pointer for example, would be detrimental to the global behavior of the processor and severely disturb the running of the application.

– At the other end of the spectrum, at the *privileged* level, all of these limitations are lifted.

– *Thread* mode corresponds to the default mode in the sense that it is the mode that the processor takes after being reset. It is the normal mode for the execution of applications. In this mode, both privilege levels are possible.

– The processor goes into *Handler* mode following an exception. When it has finished processing the instructions for this exception, the last instruction allows a return to normal execution and causes the return to *thread* mode. In this mode, the code always has *privileged* level access.

Passage between these three types of functioning can be described by a state machine, see Figure 2.1 [YIU 07]. After being reset, the processor is in *thread* mode with privilege. By setting the least significant bit (LSB) of the *CONTROL* register, it is possible to switch into unprivileged mode (also called *user mode* in the ARM documentation) using software. In unprivileged mode, the user cannot access the *CONTROL* register, and so it is impossible to return to the privileged mode. Just after the launch of an exception (see Chapter 8) the processor switches to *Handler* mode, which necessarily has privilege. Once the exception has been processed, the processor returns to its previous mode. If, during processing of the exception, the LSB of the *CONTROL* register is modified, then the processor can return to the opposite mode to that which was in effect before the launch. The only way to switch to unprivileged *thread* mode, as opposed to privileged *thread* mode, is by going through an exception that expresses itself by passing into *Handler* mode.

This level of protection can appear somewhat minimalist. It is a little like the locking/unlocking of your mobile phone: it takes a combination of keys (known to all) to achieve. It is obviously no use in preventing theft, but it is still useful when the phone is in the bottom of a pocket.

This type of security can only be developed within a global software architecture including an operating system. In a rather simplistic but ultimately quite realistic manner, it is possible to imagine that the operating system (OS) has full access privileges. It can therefore launch tasks in unprivileged *thread* mode, which could guarantee an initial level of security. A second privilege level concerns the functions of the memory protection unit block mentioned previously. Each task can only access the memory regions assigned to it by the OS.

A supplementary element should be taken into account in order to understand the functioning of Cortex-M3. It concerns the internal state of the processor, which can be in either *Thumb* or *debug* state.

The term *Thumb* refers to the set of processor instructions (see Chapter 5) where the associated state (Thumb state) corresponds to normal running. The *debug* state results from a switch to development mode. The execution rate of a program does not follow the same rules (stopping point, observation point, etc.) in this mode, so it is understandable that it results in a particular state. As with any event in the internal mechanisms of a processor, the switch from one state to another is reflected (and/or caused) by switching the values of one or more bits. In this case, it involves two bits (*C_DEBUGEN* and *C_HALT*) located in the *Debug Halting Control and Status Register* (DHCSR).

REMARK 2.1.– Mastery of the different functioning options is not a prerequisite for writing your first programs in assembly language. The preceding brief explanations are only there to help you realize the capacities of the processor. They are also to help you to understand that the observation of the "step-by-step" execution of your program comes from the exploitation of specific processor resources by the development software.

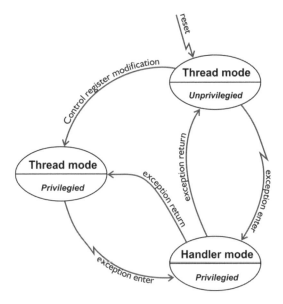

Figure 2.1. *Modes and privileges*

2.2. Registers

The first thing that should be noticed about a processor is that it is made up of various registers. This is without doubt the most pragmatic approach to the extent that modern architectures, such as those of Cortex-M3, are called *load-store* type architectures. This means that the programs initially transfer data from memory to the registers and performs operations on these registers in a second step. Finally, and when necessary, there is the transfer of the result to memory.

First we must define what a register is. A register, in the primary sense, corresponds to the location in internal memory (in the sense of a series of accessible bits in parallel) of a processor. We should, however, adjust this definition for the simple reason that, in the case of a μcontroller, although there is internal memory (20 KB of *static RAM* in the case of a standard STM32, and that is without taking into account *Flash* memory), this internal memory does not make up a set of registers. An equally inexact definition would be to think of a register as a memory location that does not take part in memory mapping. In effect, all peripherals of a controller can be programmed by means of the values that they are given by the registers; they have no fewer physical addresses that the processor can access than any other memory space. The extensive use of the term "register" in computer architecture means that this term often encompasses, in a rather vague manner, all memory spaces whose content directly affects the functioning of the processor. In this section, we will only consider the registers of the Cortex-M3 core. Their main feature is that they are accessible by the instruction set without submitting a request to the data bus. The *opcode* (which is linked to the coding of the instruction to be executed) of an instruction manipulating the contents of a register must therefore contain the information of the register to be contacted. The execution of an instruction can cause the modification of one or more of these registers without the need to activate the data bus.

Conrtex-M3 has 17 initial registers, all obviously 32-bit:

– *R0* to *R12*: 13 general usage registers;

– *R13*: a stack pointer register, also called *SP*, *PSP (SP_process)* or *MSP (SP_main)*;

– *R14*: link register (LR);

– *R15*: ordinal counter or *PC (program pointer)*;

– *xPSR:* a state register (*Program Status Register*, the *x* can be A for Application, I for Interrupt or E for Execution) that is strangely never called R16.

To these 17 registers we must add three special registers (*PRIMASK, FAULTMASK* and *BASEPRI*), which are used for exception handling (see Chapter 8). The 21st that we can add to this list is the *CONTROL* register, which has already been mentioned for its role in privilege levels but which is also a level of the R13 stack pointer.

2.2.1. *Registers R0 to R12*

These 13 registers are used, as we shall see in the passage reviewing the instruction set, as a container for storing the *operands* of an instruction and to receive the results of these operations. ARM distinguishes between the first eight registers R0 to R7 *(low registers)* and the following four (R8 to R12, the *high registers)*. The high registers have employment restrictions with respect to certain instructions. The prudent programmer will primarily use the first eight registers so that they do not have to manage these restrictions.

REMARK 2.2.– These general registers, contrary to other architectures, are only accessible in 32-bit packets. The registers can therefore not be split into two half-words or four bytes. If your application deals with bytes (chains of characters to be more precise), for example, the 24 highest weighted bits would be positioned at 0 in order for their operation to be sensible.

2.2.2. *The R13 register, also known as SP*

R13 is the SP register. As its name suggests, it points (i.e. it contains the address of a memory location) to a place that corresponds to the current location of the *system stack*. This idea of a stack will be explained in more detail later (see section 6.5.6), but for now we will just consider it as a buffer zone where the running program can temporarily store data. In the case of Cortex-M3, this storage zone is doubled, and so the SP register comes in two versions: *PSP (SP_Process)* or *MSP (SP_Main)*. It is important to note that, at any given moment, only one of the two stacks is visible to the processor. So when writing to the stack as in the following example:

EXAMPLE 2.1.– *Saving a register*

```
PUSH R14 ; PC save
         ; MSP or PSP???
```

The writing is done to the visible zone. In terms of this visibility, we can accept that, in *Handler* mode, the current pointer is always MSP. In *thread* mode, even if it can be modified with software, the current pointer is PSP. Thus, without particular manipulation, access to the system stack will be via PSP during the normal course of the program, but when there is an exception the management of the stack is subject to MSP. This division induces a much greater reliability in the functioning of the µcontroller and greater speed during context changes (not forgetting that the peripherals communicate with Cortex-M3 through interruptions and so an exception is not exceptional, etc.).

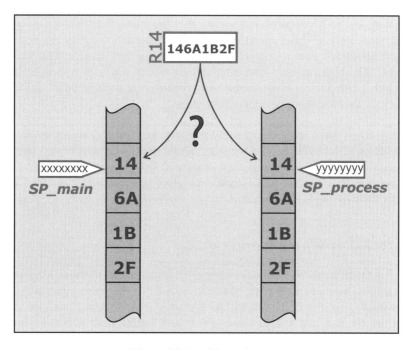

Figure 2.2. *Double stack system*

2.2.3. *The R14 register, also known as LR*

Throughout this register, there are hints of the structure of a program, which will be discussed in Chapter 7. Let us discover, through Example 2.2, one of the basic mechanisms: jumping to a subroutine.

In this example, the programmer has written two procedures (that is the term used for the concept of a subroutine): *Main* and *MyFirst*. The *Main* procedure does nothing but call *MyFirst*, which itself does nothing (the *NOP* (No Operation) instruction has no effect beyond using one machine cycle to run itself). When the processor reaches the *Branch with Link* (BL) instruction, it uses the *LR* to store the next address, where it then modifies the instruction pointer with the routine address. In a symmetrical manner, in the *MyFirst* routine with the *Branch and Exchange* (BX) instruction it will change the contents of the instruction pointer with the value contained in the *LR* and so return to where it started to continue processing the calling program. It should be noted that, despite the implication, the symbol is not exchanged but simply copied.

EXAMPLE 2.2.– *Utility of the link register LR*

```
Main      PROC
Here      BL MyFirst      ; Jump to MyFirst

          . . .

          ENDP

          . . . .

MyFirst   PROC
          NOP             ; No operation..
          BX LR           ; Return to calling program
          ENDP
```

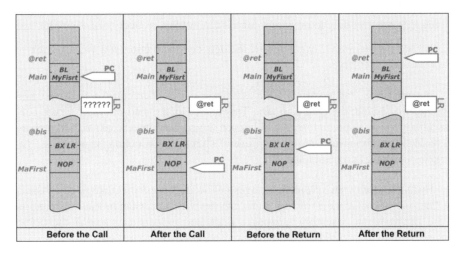

Figure 2.3. *Call to subroutine (use of the LR)*

2.2.4. *The R15 or PC register*

This register can be called "the instruction pointer", "the ordinal counter" or "the *Program Counter* (PC)" but it has a unique role: it contains the memory address where the next instruction to be executed is stored. The LSB of this register is (normally) at 0, assuming that the instructions are coded on 16 bits *(Thumb)* or 32 bits *(Thumb2)*, so they take up at least two consecutive addresses. During the running of a code sequence, the PC pointer will automatically increment itself (usually two-by-two) in order to then point and recover the rest of the code. The term ordinal counter could imply that its functioning is limited to this simple incrementation. This is not so, and things quickly become complicated, particularly when there is a break in the sequence (in the instance of Example 2.2, where the call to a subroutine caused a discontinuity in the rest of the stored code addresses). In this case, PC would take a value that was not a simple incrementation of its initial value.

The management of this pointer is intrinsically linked to the *pipeline* structure of this *Reduced Instruction Set Computer* (RISC) architecture. This technique allows the introduction of a form of parallelism in the work of the processor. At each moment, several instructions are processed simultaneously, each at a different level. Three successive steps are necessary for an instruction to be completely carried out:

– The *Fetch* phase: recovery of the instruction from memory. This is the step where PC plays its part.

– The *Decode* phase: the instruction is a value encoded in memory (its *opcode*), which requires decoding to prepare it for execution (data recovery, for example).

– The *Execute* phase: execution of the decoded instruction and writing back of the results if necessary.

In these three stages (which are classic in a *pipeline* structure) a first upstream unit must be added: the *PreFetch* unit. This unit (which is part of ARM's expertise) essentially exists to predict what will happen during sequence breaks and to prepare to recover the next instruction by "buffering" about six instructions in advance. This practice optimizes processor speed.

This simplified view of *pipeline* stages deliberately masks its complexity. Again, in line with the objectives of this book, this level of understanding is sufficient to write programs in assembly language. Interested readers can search the ARM documentation to find all of the explanations necessary to go further.

2.2.5. *The xPSR register*

This register contains information regarding the "status" or "state" of the processor. It contains important information – a kind of short report – about what has happened in the processor. It is available in three versions, although it is only one register. The distribution of significant bits, as shown in Figure 2.4, is such that there is no intersection, so it is possible to separate it into three independent subsets:

– *APSR*, with the *A* meaning *Application*: this register contains the flags of the processor. These five bits are essential for the use of conditional operations, since the conditions exclusively express themselves as a logical combination of these flags. Updating of these is carried out by most of the instructions, *provided that the suffix S is specified in the symbolic name of the instruction*. These flags are:

- indicator *C (Carry)*: represents the "carry" during the calculation of the natural (unsigned) quantities. If *C*=1, then there was an overflow in the unsigned representation during the previous instruction, which shows that the unsigned result is partially false. Knowledge of this bit allows for much more precise work;

- indicator *Z (Zero)*: has a value of 1 if the result is zero;

- indicator *N (Negative)*: copies the most significant bit of the result. If the value is signed, *N* being 1 therefore indicates a negative result;

- indicator *V (oVerflow)*: if this has a value of 1, there has been an overflow (or underflow) of signed representation. The signed result is false;

- indicator *Q (Sticky Saturation Flag)*: only makes sense for the two specific saturation instructions *USAT* and *SSAT*: the bit is set at 1 if these instructions have saturated the register used.

– *IPSR*, with the *I* meaning *Interrupt*: in this configuration, this refers to the nine LSBs containing information. These nine bits make up the exception number (*Interrupt Service Routine* or ISR) that will be launched. For example, when the ISR has a value of 2, it corresponds to the launch of a *Non Maskable Interrupt* (NMI) interruption; if it has a value of 5 then there has been a problem with memory access.

– *EPSR*, with the *E* meaning *Execution*: this register stores three distinct pieces of information:

- the 24-bit (T) to indicate whether it is in *Thumb* state – that is, if it is using the *Thumb* instruction set. As this is always the case, this bit is always at 1. We could question the usefulness of this information. As a matter of fact, it is useless in the case of Cortex-M3, but in other architectures this bit can be at 0 to show that the processor is using the *ARM* set and not *Thumb*;

- it uses bit fields [10–15] and [25–26] to store two pieces of overlapping information (the two uses are mutually exclusive): *ICI* or *IT*;

- for *ICI*, this is information that is stored when a read/write multiple (the processor reads/writes several general registers successively, but uses only one instruction) is interrupted. Upon returning from the interruption, the processor can resume its multiple accesses from where it was before;

- for *IT*, there is a particular *If/Then*[1] instruction in the instruction set. The *IT* bits in the execution of this instruction will contain the number (between 1 and 3) of instructions that will be included in an *If/Then* block and a coding of conditions for their execution.

The *EPSR* therefore has relative use for the programmer. Moreover, when we know that it cannot be changed, we can allow ourselves to forget its existence in developing our code.

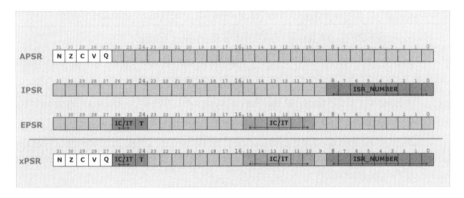

Figure 2.4. *The xPSR register*

From the point of view of assembly language, the following example shows that it is possible to access the three entities separately or to access the whole. It should be noted that this reading can only be done via a specific *MRS* (Move to Register from Special) instruction. Symmetrically, writing of these registers requires the use of a specific *MSR* (Move to Special Register) instruction.

EXAMPLE 2.3.– *Load of the status register*

```
Recup  MRS R4, APSR    ; load APSR part in R4

       MRS R5, IPSR    ; load IPSR part in R5

       MRS R6, EPSR    ; load EPSR part in R6

       MRS R7, PSR     ; load the whole PSR register in R5
```

---

1 Fortunately, this particular instruction is not the only way to write "If... If not... Then" structure in assembly language. A more systematic approach, by conditional jump, allows the construction of all kinds of algorithmic structures (see section 6.2).

Chapter 3

The Proper Use of Assembly Directives

As for any language, the syntactic aspect of a listing is of crucial importance so that the compiler (in the case of higher level language structures) or the assembler (for listings written in assembly language) understands the rest of the characters that it will read and that make up the program. If we consider the previous examples, an assembler would have trouble generating the corresponding executable code: it lacks a lot of information. Only a few instructions, without any context, were transcribed in the examples that have previously been presented. Where is the code entry point, where does the program end, where is the code located in memory, what are the constants or variables?

This chapter aims to define this context through the description of assembly directives.

3.1. The concept of the directive

An assembly directive is a piece of information that appears word-for-word in the listing and which is supplied by the assembler to give the construction rules of the executable. These lines in the source file, though an integral part of the listing and necessary for its coherence, do not correspond directly to any line of code. These pieces of information will therefore not appear during the disassembly of the code and will be also be missing if a *hacker* tries to reverse engineer it. Disassembly is a process that consists of converting the code (that is, the collection of words read in memory) into the corresponding symbols and, if necessary, the operands (numeric or register). The coding of an instruction being biunivocal, there is no particular problem in re-transcribing a code extracted from memory into primitive assembly language. The symbolic layer does not give an understanding of that which is programmed – it will still be quite incomprehensible! For example, the disassembly of the code in Example 2.2 gives the following lines:

EXAMPLE 3.1.– *Example of disassembly*

```
0x080001A0      BL.W 0x080001A8

0x080001A4      B 0x080001A4

0x080001A6      NOP

0x080001A8      NOP

0x080001AA      BX LR
```

In this example, the first column indicates the value of the address where the instruction is stored. By glancing at these addresses, we can see that an instruction is coded on either two bytes (Thumb-type code) or four bytes (Thumb-2 type code). The second column corresponds to the decoding of the read instruction and the third to the accompanying potential arguments.

3.1.1. *Typographic conventions and use of symbols*

In the following text, the following typographic conventions have been adopted:

– *slim italics* denote a sequence of characters that you must choose;

– words written in CAPITALS are compulsory. We write them in capitals to make them obvious, but they can also be written in lower case;

– ***bold italics*** indicate a field where the value is to be chosen from a set list;

– the areas not written in brackets { } are compulsory. The other fields are thus optional, but we never write the brackets.

In order to write your programs, you will need to define the symbols (a constant, a label to identify a line of code, a variable, etc.). We can also use the term identifier for these user-defined names. A symbol will always be associated with a numerical value by the assembler and the linker: in the same way as the directives defined above, a symbol will never be explicitly included in the final code. The readability of your programs, by nature very low in assembly language, is therefore directly linked to the semantics of your symbols. It is consequently better to be generous with characters in order to make it more explicit. From a syntactic point of view, a symbol must also obey the following rules if it is to be accepted by the assembler:

– the name of a symbol must be unique within a given module;

– the characters may be upper or lower case letters, numbers or "underscores". The assembler is case-sensitive;

– *a priori*, there is no maximum length;

– the first character cannot be a number;

– the key words (mnemonics, directives, etc.) of the language are reserved;

– if it proves necessary to use a palette of more important characters (in order to mix your code with a compiler, for example), it is possible to do this by surrounding the symbol with | (these do not become part of the symbol). For example |*.text*| is a valid symbol and the assembler will memorize it (in its symbol table) as *.text*.

3.2. Structure of a program

Writing a program in assembly language, in its simplest form, implies that the user can, in a source file (which is just a text file and so a simple series of ASCII characters):

– define the sequence of code instructions, so that the assembler will be able to translate them into machine language. This sequence, once assembled and given Cortex-M3 Harvard structure, will be stored in CODE memory;

– declare the data it will use, by giving it an initial or constant value, if necessary. This allows the assembler to give orders to reserve the necessary memory space, by initializing everything that is predestined to fill the DATA memory, when appropriate.

REMARK 3.1.– A third entity is required for the correct running of a program: the system stack. This is not fixed in size or memory location. This implies that somewhere in the listing there is a reservation for this specific area and at least one instruction for the initialization of the stack pointer (SP) responsible for its management. In using existing development tools, this phase is often included in a file (written in assembly language) that contains a number of initializations. Indeed, the μcontroller hosting Cortex-M3 must also undergo a number of configuration operations just after a reset; the initialization of the stack in this file is consequently not aberrant. The advanced programmer will, however, have to verify that the predefined size of the system stack is not under- or over-sized relative to its application.

3.2.1. *The AREA sections*

A program in assembly language must have at least two parts, which we will refer to as sections, that must be defined in the listing by the *AREA* directive:

– one section of code containing the list of instructions;

– one section of data where we find the description of the data (name, size, initial value).

REMARK 3.2.– Unlike in higher level languages where the declaration of variables can be more or less mixed with instructions, assembly language requires a clear separation.

From the point of view of the assembler, a section is a contiguous zone of memory in which all of the elements are of the same logical nature (instructions, data, and system stack).

The programmer uses the AREA directive to communicate with the assembler in order to show the beginning of a section. The section naturally terminates at the beginning of another section, so there is no specific marker for the end of a section.

The body of a section is made up of instructions for the *CODE* part or of various place reservations (whether initialized of not) for the *DATA* section.

The general definition syntax of a section, as it must be constructed in a source file, is:

> AREA   *Section_Name*   *{ ,type } { ,attr }* ...
>
> ...   Body of the section:
>
> ...   definitions of data
>
> ...   or instructions, according to the case

So let us explain the four fields:

– AREA: the directive itself;

– *Section_Name*: the name that you have given to the section in keeping with the rules set out earlier;

– *type*: *code* or *data*: indicates the type of section being opened;

– a suite of non-compulsory options. The principal options are:

- *readonly* or *readwrite*: indicates whether the section is accessible to read only (the default for CODE sections) or to read and write (the default for DATA sections),

- *noinit*: indicates, for a DATA section, that it is not initialized or initialized at 0. This type of section can only contain rough memory reservations or reservations for data initialized at 0, and

- *align* = *n* with a value between 0 and 31. This option indicates how the section should be placed in memory. The section will be aligned with a 2^n modulo address, or in other terms it signifies that the least significant *n* bits of the first address of the section would be at 0.

There are other options which, if they need to be put in place, show that you have reached a level of expertise beyond the scope of this book.

In a program, a given section can be opened and closed several times. It is also possible that we might like to open different sections of code or data that are distinct from each other. Finally, all of these various parts combine automatically. That is the role of the linker, which should therefore take into account the various constraints so that it can assign memory addresses for each constituent section of the project.

3.3. A section of code

A section of code contains instructions in symbolic form. One instruction is written on one line, according to the following syntax:

> *{ label } SYMBOL { expr }{ ,expr }{ ,expr} { ; comment}*

The syntax of all assembly language is rigorous. At most, we can place one instruction on one line. It is also permitted to have lines without an instruction containing a label, a comment or even nothing at all (to space out the listing in order to make it more readable). Finally, please note that a label must always be placed in the first column of the line.

3.3.1. *Labels*

A label is a symbol of your choice that is always constructed according to the same rules. The label serves as a marker, or an identifier, for the instruction (or the data). It allows us to go to that instruction during execution by way of a jump (or branch).

Below is an example of a piece of program of limited algorithmic interest, but that contains a loop and consequently a label. With each loop, the program increments the *R3* register by a value contained in *R4*. The number of loops carried out is also calculated by an incrementation (unitary in this case) in register *R0*. The loop is carried out as long as it does not exceed the capacity (so as long as the flag *C* of register *xPSR* remains at 0).

EXAMPLE 3.2.– *Jump to a label*

```
        MOV    R0,#0       ; Initialization of the counter

        MOV    R3, #4      ; Initial value

        MOV    R4, #35     ; Incrementation

Turnal  ADD    R0,#1       ; Incrementation of the loop counter

        ADDS   R3,R4       ; Incrementation of the value

        BCC    Turnal      ; Conditional branch

Inf     B      Inf
```

The symbol # denotes an immediate addressing, i.e. it precedes a constant to use as it is (in this case for loading the register). The last instruction (*BCC*) is a conditional jump. The *B* signifies a *Branch* request and the suffix *CC* means *Clear Carry*. Therefore the processor only carries out the jump if the previous operation (addition with flag allocation) does not cause an overshoot and the switching of flag *C* to 1. The rendezvous point (*Turnal*) is the operand that follows the *BCC* instruction and corresponds to the label positioned a few lines higher.

A version of a jump without conditions is present in the last line of this example. The instruction jumps to the label that marks that same instruction. This therefore corresponds to an infinite loop.

When we place a label on an empty line, it serves to mark the first instruction (or piece of datum) that follows it. For the assembler, **labels are equivalent to addresses**. The numerical value of a label is the value of the address that it represents. This label can also be the address of an instruction or a piece of data.

REMARK 3.3.– In all assembly languages, the concept of label or constant has been expanded: it is possible to attribute a value to a label thanks to the equals (EQU) directive, which we will talk about in Chapter 4. It is the equivalent of a #define in C language. The label takes on the meaning of a numerical size written in symbolic form, which is not necessarily an address.

3.3.2. *Mnemonic*

We use *mnemonic* to mean the symbolic name of an instruction. This name is set and the series of mnemonics makes up the instruction set.

In the ARM world, since the ARMV4 version of the architecture, there have been two distinct instruction sets: the ARM set (coded in 32 bits) and the Thumb set (coded in 16 bits). The size for coding with the Thumb set being smaller, this set offers fewer possibilities than the full ARM set. The advantage that can be drawn from this compression is a more compact code. For many ARM processors, there is the option to make them work in Thumb or ARM mode, according to the needs and appropriate constraints of the project.

Since architecture version ARMV6, ARM has introduced a second subtlety by introducing a Thumb-2 version for the instruction set. In this second version of the Thumb appellation, the 16-bit set is expanded with some 32-bit instructions to combine performance and density, as shown in Figure 3.1[1].

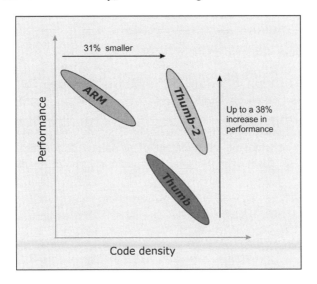

Figure 3.1. *Performances and density of the different instruction sets*

Cortex-M3 exclusively uses the Thumb-2 set. It is therefore impossible to switch to ARM mode (this is why the bit T in the *Execution Program Status Register* [EPSR] (see section 2.3.5) is always set to 1).

---

1 This diagram is extracted from ARM commercial documents, and is thus to be understood as such.

The Thumb-2 set understands 114 different mnemonics (excluding communication instructions with a potential coprocessor). A quick classification allows us to pick out:

– 8 mnemonics for branch instructions;

– 17 for basic arithmetic instructions (addition, comparison, etc.);

– 9 for logical shift;

– 9 for multiplication and division;

– 2 for saturation instructions;

– 4 for change of format instructions (switching from eight to 16 bits, for example);

– 10 for specific arithmetic instructions;

– 2 for *xPSR* register recovery;

– 24 for unitary read/write memory operations;

– 12 for multiple read/write memory operations;

– 17 for various instructions (*WAIT*, *NOP*, etc.).

REMARK 3.4.– Be careful not to make a mistake regarding the complexity of operations. These are all operations that only handle integers (signed or unsigned). The novice should not be surprised to not find, with these processors, capabilities for handling floating point numbers, for example. Similarly, for everything related to the algorithmic structure or management of advanced data structures, it will be necessary to break down even the smallest operation in order to adapt to assembly language.

3.3.3. *Operands*

Instructions act on and/or with the operands provided. An instruction can, depending on the case, have zero to four operands, separated by commas. Each operand is written in the form of an expression *Expr* that is assessed by the assembler. Generally, arithmetic and logical instructions take two or three operands. The case with four operands is relatively rare in this instruction set. In the case of the Thumb-2 set, apart from read/write instructions, the operands are of two types: immediate values or registers. For read/write instructions, the first operand will be a register and the second must be a memory address. Different techniques exist for specifying these addresses; such techniques correspond to the idea of *addressing mode*, which will be explained later (see section 4.3). It is therefore necessary to bear in mind that, because of the load/store architecture of Cortex-M3, this address will always be stored in a register. All memory access will require prior recovery of the address of the target to be reached in a register.

Let us amend the previous program so that the initial value corresponds to the contents of a byte labeled *Bytinit*. As it is now known, let us add the declaration of sections to this program.

EXAMPLE 3.3.– *The memory operand*

```
;*******************************************************************
; DATA Section
;*******************************************************************

   AREA MyData, DATA, align = 2
Bytinit DCB 0x124

;*******************************************************************
; CODE Section
;*******************************************************************

   AREA MyCode, CODE, readonly, align = 3

;- - - - - - - - - - - - - - - - - - - - - - - - - - - - - - - - -
; main subroutine
;- - - - - - - - - - - - - - - - - - - - - - - - - - - - - - - - -

main    PROC
        LDR R6,=Bytinit      ; Address load ①
        MOV R0,#0            ; Initialization of the counter
        LDRB R3, [R6]        ; Load of the initial value ②
        MOV R4, #35          ; Incrementation
Turnal  ADD R0,#1            ; Incrementation of the loop counter
        ADDS R3,R4           ; Incrementation of the value
        BCC Turnal           ; Conditional branch
Inf     B Inf
;*******************************************************************
```

In this example (see also Figure 3.2), we can see that in order to modify *R3* with the stored value of the memory block named *Bytinit*, it is necessary to pass through an additional register (*R6*). This code recovers, in a first step (①), the address of the variable (*LDR R6,=Bytinit,*). Then in a second step (②) with "indirect addressing", it loads *R3* with the stored value (*LDRB R3, [R6]*). Register *R6*, once initialized, acts like a pointer to the memory zone to be read. We can also note in passing that only the least significant byte is copied, as the *LRDB* instruction carries out the transfer of one byte. On the other hand, the instruction concerns the whole of the *R3* register, so the 24 most significant bits of this register are set to zero during the transfer. The final content of the 32-bit *R3* register is effectively equivalent to the unsigned numbers stored on a byte in *Bytinit*.

REMARK 3.5.– It is important to note that the label *Bytinit* is not in itself the data. It is merely a marker of the data – its address.

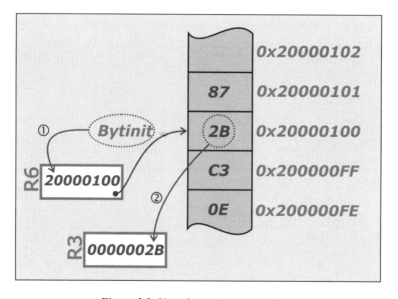

Figure 3.2. *Use of a register as a pointer*

3.3.4. *Comments*

A comment must begin with ; (a semicolon), even if it is the only thing on the line. It always finishes the code at the end of the line. If we want to write a comment requiring several lines, each line must begin with ; (a semicolon). Comments can be placed anywhere in the program, provided that they are at the end of the current line. It is worth remembering that a listing is more often read than written... even by those who wrote it. It is thus particularly useful when revisiting code written several weeks, months, years, etc., earlier for it to have comments, so do not hesitate to provide them!

3.3.5. *Procedure*

In the assembly language presented here, all instructions must be written inside a procedure. It is therefore normal that the first line following the opening of a section looks like a line where the mnemonic is replaced by *PROC*, as in the following example.

EXAMPLE 3.4.– *The declaration of a procedure*

```
        AREA New_Section, CODE, readonly, align = 2

MyFunct PROC

        ...        ; body of the procedure (instructions)

        ...

        ENDP
```

We call a sequence of instructions a "procedure". We can distinguish it from a subprogram (or subroutine) when the last instruction allows us to return to a calling program. We will return to the details of how to write and use procedures in section 7.1, but for now let us focus on the basics: the call to a procedure.

The most generic form for the call is a *Branch and Link* (*BL MyFunct*), with the return corresponding to a re-allocation of the instruction pointer by the instruction *BX LR* (Brach and eXchange), as shown in Example 2.2.

As with C language, there is a *principal procedure*, the first to be launched after a μcontroller initialization sequence known as the *main*. It is not standard, as it is in C language. It is perfectly possible to replace the standard initialization library with your own library, making the initialization work. This new library could then make the call to the entry point of the application program – the entry point whose name could then be freely chosen by the programmer.

REMARK 3.6.– It is possible to replace the PROC/ENDP pair with the FUNCTION/ENDFUNC pair, knowing that the language makes no distinction between procedure and function, unlike certain higher-level languages.

3.4. The data section

A set of directives allows us to reserve memory space that will be used by the program to store data. It is also possible assign such space an initial value, if needed. This manipulation seems simple but it needs to be looked at more closely.

3.4.1. *Simple reservation*

This just means reserving a memory space and optionally giving it a name.

> *{ label }* SPACE *expr*

expr is the amount (expressed as a number of bytes) of memory that we wish to allocate. This zone will be set at 0 by default.

The numerical expressions are the quantities that are presented directly to the assembler. In the case we are considering here, it is the number of bytes being reserved but later it may be an initial value, an immediate value to be given to a register, etc. This quantity can be expressed in different bases:

– decimal base: the default base, as neither a prefix nor a suffix is required;

– hexadecimal base: as in C language, this base is selected when the quantity is prefixed with 0x (for example, the value 255 would be 0x00FF). An alternative is to use the &;

– any base (between 2 and 9): the syntax is base_digits, where base is the chosen base and digits are the characters (from 0 to *base*-1) representing the characters. (For example in base 5: 5_1213 represents the value $183 = 1 \times 5^3 + 2 \times 5^2 + 1 \times 5^1 + 3 \times 5^0$). This possibility turns out to be interesting for the binary base, in which the programmer can easily express a value (of a register, for example) for which he or she knows the bits to locate. For example, to put the three- and five-weighted bits of a byte at 1, the programmer must specify: $2\_00101000 = 2\_101000 = 0x28 = 40$;

– ASCII "base": it is not useful to learn the ASCII table by heart. By surrounding a single character with single inverted commas ('), the assembler will understand that it must take the ASCII value of that character as the value of the expression. It is also possible to construct a chain of characters (to create a message, for example) by placing them within double inverted commas ("). Example 3.6 illustrates this technique with the declaration and initialization of the variable *Chain*.

Note that this expression can be a simple literal calculation. For example *LotsOfWords SPACE 12*4+3* would reserve 51 bytes. The calculation is obviously done by the assembler (and so the processor of the development host computer) when generating the code (and not at any time by Cortex-M3!). The principal arithmetic operators (+, -, *, /, >> (right shift), << (left shift), & (and), | (or), etc.) allow us to construct these literal expressions. The advanced user will find an exhaustive and detailed list of existing operators and their precedence level (relative priority), knowing that brackets are allowed, in the technical documentation [ARM 10].

3.4.2. *Reservation with initialization*

Different directives exist to create memory zones containing specific values (initialized variables). Below is the list with the possible arguments:

> *{ label1 }*   FILL expr {,value{,valuesize} }
>
> *{ label2 }*   DCB expr1 {,expr2}{,expr2}...
>
> *{ label3 }*   DCD{U} expr1 {,expr2}{,expr3}...
>
> *{ label4 }*   DCW{U} expr1 {,expr2}{,expr3}...
>
> *{ label5 }*   DCQ{U} expr1 {,expr2}{,expr3}...

The reservation for *FILL* is the counterpart of the directive *SPACE* but with initialization. We specify that we want to reserve *expr* initialized bytes with the value *value*, which is coded on *valuesize* bytes. For it to be completely consistent, the size of the reservation (*expr*) must be a multiple of the value of *valuesize*.

REMARK 3.7.– All unsigned values can be stored in a larger format than that which is strictly necessary for their size; just add 0 in front of the useful bits. The assembler cannot know *a priori* in what size it must code the information.

The other four directives specify the size of the variable with the last letter of the mnemonic: B = byte, W = half-word (2 bytes), D – word (four bytes) and Q = double word (8 bytes). The data are aligned by default: a type W datum starts on an even address (least significant bit at 0), and type D and Q data are on modulo 4 addresses (the two least significant bits at 0).

The number of reservations therefore corresponds to a number of given initial values. The first initialization is compulsory. Any following this are optional. The following example uses these different directives with different bases and several forms of literal expressions. Figure 3.3 shows the memory mapping resulting from this example, taking 0x20000000 as the base address.

EXAMPLE 3.6.– *Reservations with initialization*

```
Bytinit DCB 0x24,2_0111

Chain   DCB "toto",'*',10,13

HalfW   DCW 47, 12+3

Word    DCD 3,0xFFFF * 3

Byte    DCB 0xAB >> 2        ; two right shifts

Danger  DCWU 0x1234
```

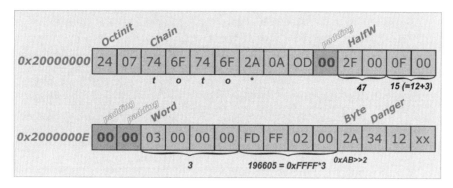

Figure 3.3. *Mapping of the example of reservations with initialization*

In the example, three padding bytes are added by the assembler to allow proper alignment of the data. A byte was placed at 0x20000009 because *HalfW* was placed at an even address (0x2000000A) and two bytes were added at 0x2000000E because the two least significant bits of the *Word* address were at 0 (0X20000010). In contrast, the half-word *Danger* finds itself unaligned at 0x20000019, since the directive *DCWU* was used to create it.

The U option means that the alignment is unnecessary, but that can be excessively dangerous! In fact, the assembler aligns its reservations on an even address for half-words and a doubly even (divisible by four) address for words. However, this alignment is not strictly necessary. Cortex-M3 allows unaligned memory accesses. Such accesses are not at all optimized, since they will need to make two reading (or writing, depending on the direction of the instruction) cycles.

It is primarily for the sake of optimality that alignment is in force at the level of memory reservations by the assembler. However, ARM has provided the option to prohibit unaligned access, physically speaking. This is done by setting the weight three bit (UNALIGN_TRAP) in the *Configuration Control Register* to 1. Thus positioned, any access to a half-word on an odd address, or a word at a non-doubly even address, would cause a *usage fault* (see section 8.2.1.4). If your processor is configured in this state, it becomes essential to manage it rigorously (notably, regarding the alignment of its pointers).

3.4.3. *Data initialization: the devil is in the details*

What happens in the life of an initialized variable? In a normal development cycle, we can imagine that this variable is born in the loading of the program to memory. The *loader* (program in charge of the transfer from the development toolchain to the target containing Cortex-M3) will write the planned initial value to the memory address corresponding to this variable. Then, if the variable is "variable", it will change and no longer be equal to its initial value. Let us now suppose that the user restarts the target (*RESET*). The program restarts without going through the *loader* step. What guarantees that the initial value will be re-transcribed? *A priori* in assembly language, nothing; however, it turns out that in the majority of cases (because it is often paired with a C compiler) the assembler has anticipated this. The mechanism put in place is based on a doubling of initialization zones: a first random access memory (RAM)-type address space for the variables themselves and a duplicate in read-only memory (ROM)-type (usually just after the code) containing the initial values. It is then enough to have a routine at its disposal that recovers the tables of different zone addresses and then operates a copy of one over the other. A slight adaptation of this method also allows us to reinitialize the variables at zero. These maneuvers, although very useful, may not appear very clearly. So in the case of the ARM-MDK (Microcontroller Development Kit), this is done through the use of a dynamic library in the code, which is accomplished by adding a nice but nevertheless obscure *IMPORT||Lib$$ Request$$armlib||* to the main file header. This initialization mechanism is revisited in detail in Chapter 9.

3.5. Is that all?

Obviously not. There are also certain directives for the assembler that are not completely explained in this chapter. Some of them (*EQU*, *RN* and *LTORG*) are discussed in the next chapter as they deal mainly with data manipulation (and thus operand management). Others concern the sharing (*IMPORT, EXPORT*) of variables or procedures, which is the subject of Chapter 9. Yet others will not be mentioned here because interest in their use is somewhat limited (INFO, TTL, etc.).

Those that are left are listed below. They are more specific (in the sense that their use is not generally necessary in producing an executable) but they can be very useful.

3.5.1. *Memory management directives*

ALIGN {expr}

where *expr* must be a value of any power of 2 (from 2^0 to 2^{32}). If *expr* is not specified, its value is taken to be 2. *ALIGN* is used to position data (or instructions) that follow this directive on a modulo *expr* aligned address. This directive inserts zeroes (in the DATA zone) or *NOP* instructions (in the CODE zone) in order to align the code. Its usefulness is clear for resolving potentially fatal memory unalignment problems. The use of an ALIGN 1 is possible but presents no interest. *ALIGN* can take other optional arguments to insert an additional offset alignment.

A typical example of the use of this directive is that of the reservation of memory space in order to make a user stack (also known as a *heap*). The reservation is carried out by the *SPACE* directive, which does not manage alignment. If access to this stack is only used for reading/writing on 32 bits, it is fine to position the base address of the stack on a doubly even value. Example 3.7 shows how this reservation can be done using a forced alignment.

EXAMPLE 3.7.– *Reservation for an user stack*

```
Dim             EQU 64

Variable        DCB 0         ; unused reservation just for creating
                              ; an unalignment in the memory

                Align 4       ; Forcing of alignment for

                              ; the next reservation

MyStack         SPACE 4*Dim   ; reservation of Dim words

Summit_Stack                  ; label on the top of the stack
```

COMMON symbol{,size{,alignment}}

This directive allows us to reserve (marked by the name *symbol*) a common memory zone of the size *size* (always in bytes) and aligned following the same syntax as that indicated for the use of *AREA* for the *alignment* option. The memory spaces thus created will be reserved by the linker in a zone set to 0 and pooled. This means that in the end the linker will only reserve a single communal zone within which the most important *COMMON* zone will be included. One of the advantages of having this directive is to optimize memory management in sizable projects, particularly for the allocation of memory dynamic in an operating system.

> {label} DCI{.W} expr{,expr}

This directive allows us to reserve memory locations with initialization (*expr*), as with directives *DCB, DCD*…, but in the *CODE* zone rather than the *DATA* zone. We can, for example, use this directive to create jump tables to carry out indexed accesses to a set of procedures (see section 6.2.4).

> REQUIRE8 {bool}
> PRESERVE8 {bool}

Here, *bool* can have a value of *TRUE* or *FALSE*. The absence of *bool* would be equivalent to *TRUE*. These two directives allow us to specify to the assembler that we want to get or retain a modulo 8 alignment for the system stack. It is of little use in assembly language. The programmer manages his or her own stacks on the stack system, and does not have to worry about this 8-byte alignment. The usefulness of this directive becomes apparent when the code written in assembly language is interfaced with code written in C language. The compiler can, in some cases (use of floating-point numbers, for example), "require" this functional principle for the system stack. It is therefore normal to find a way to specify such a systematic alignment and thus to have the directives that it produces.

3.5.2. *Project management directives*

The *ROUT* directive allows the management and limitation of the visibility of local labels. This is useful for avoiding interference between two similar labels. A local label is a label with the form *n*{*name*}, where *n* is a number (between 1 and 99) that is normally forbidden because theoretically a label must start with a letter. Consequently, we reference the label as %*n*{*name*}. As the name is optional, the label may just be a number. The *ROUT* directive, then, is used to position the visibility border of local labels.

EXAMPLE 3.8.– *Use of local labels*

```
Procedure1      ROUT                  ; ROUT doesn't mean routine ! !

                ...                   ; Code

3Procedure1     ...                   ; Code

                ...                   ; Code

                BEQ %4Procedure1      ; No ambiguity

                ...                   ; Code

                BGE %3                ; The target is 3Procedure1

                ...                   ; Code

4Procedure1     ...                   ; Code

                ...                   ; Code

Others          ROUT                  ; Border of visibility

                BEQ %3                ; The target is now 3Others

                ...                   ; Code

3Others         ...                   ; Code

                ROUT                  ; Border but without the option [name]

                ...                   ; Code

3               ...                   ; Code    Possible too...

                ;                          ... but not very readable

                B %3                  ; Branch to the label 3 ...
```

GET filename
INCBIN filename

This allows us to insert (GET) the file *filename* into the current file. In the case of INCBIN, the file is assumed to be binary (either raw data or a type .obj executable file).

KEEP { symbol }

indicates to the assembler that it should keep the symbols of the referenced label in its symbol table. In effect, without this notice, the assembler does not keep track of local markers and only retains the most significant elements such as, for example, the addresses of procedures.

The following directives allow us to set conditions for the inclusion of parts of the listing in a project. What does this mean? Let us suppose that you were to develop some code that can be developed into several versions for a system. Let us assume that 90% of the code is common to all versions, and that the remaining 10% corresponds to options. How can we manage this? Either you have as many versions of the project as you have versions of the system, or you have only one project in which some parts are only included if, during the assembly phase, you indicate which version it is.

EXAMPLE 3.9.– *Use of conditioned assembly*

```
        GBLS Version           ;Declaration of a key (global string)

Version SETS ? ? ?             ; with ? ? ? "Classic" or "Design"

        AREA MyCode, CODE      ;Opening of a CODE section

main    PROC

        ...                    ;Common part of the code

        BL Function1

Infinity B Infinity            ;end of the program


        AREA MyCode, CODE      ;Opening of a CODE section

;ooooooooooooooooooooooooooooooooooooooo

IF Version = "Classic"

Function1 PROC

        ...                    ; code for this first version

        ENDP

;ooooooooooooooooooooooooooooooooooooooo

ELSEIF Version = "Design"

Function1 PROC
```

```
        ....                        ; code for this second version

        ENDP

ENDIF

; OOOOOOOOOOOOOOOOOOOOOOOOOOOOOOOOOOOOO
```

In Example 3.9, the function *Function1* exists in two versions. It is clear that, if nothing is added to the code, the linker will be confused to find two identical references to the same function, and would not know which to choose to finish the instruction *BL Function1*. As the inclusion of one or other of the two versions is conditioned by the structure *IF..ELSEIF..ENDIF*, however, the assembler will test to find out which part of the code should be included in the project. The other part is simply ignored. Be careful not to get confused: Cortex-M3 will never see these algorithmic structures. Likewise, it will never know of the existence of the *Version* assembly key that allowed the selection to take place. Only the assembler knows of this key, which should therefore not be confused with the idea of a variable (we could talk about environmental variables, but that term can be confusing). The programmer must, when generating the software version that he or she wants to provide, supply the key and replace the ??? with *Classic* or *Design*.

There are various types of assembly keys: Boolean (*L*), arithmetic (*A*) and string (*S*). Their creation is carried out by a *GBLx* directive (with $x = L$, A or S) for a global creation (which is true for all files in the project) or a *LCLx* directive for a local creation (true for only the current file). A *SETx* directive allows us to modify the value of this key. In the rest of the code, the conditioning is located inside the following structure:

```
        IF Logic_Exp
        ...                  ; code to include if Logic_Exp is true

        ELSE

        ...                  ; code to include when Logic_Exp is false

        ENDIF
```

3.5.3. *Various and varied directives*

```
        ASSERT Logic_Exp
```

The above directive allows us to display a message (such as an error message) during the second assembly phase (an assembler takes several passes to carry out its work). If *Logic_Exp* is false:

> name CN expr

allows us to rename a register in a possible coprocessor:

> { label } DCFSU fpliteral{,fpliteral}...

which allows us to reserve initialized memory space for floating points. This implies that the program has access to floating-point calculation libraries and/or that a floating-point arithmetic unit type coprocessor is attached to the Cortex-M3 structure.

> ENTRY

The above defines the entry point of the program. This directive is essential if you create all of the code. If you use a processor initialization library, it will integrate entry point management. In this case, you should avoid using this directive.

> IMPORT   EXPORT

The two directives above allow us to share a symbol (name of a procedure, of a variable, etc.) between several files of a single project. Their advantages and uses will be elaborated on in section 9.1.5.

Chapter 4

Operands of Instructions

Chapter 3 showed us how a program written in assembly language is formed. Let us now look at techniques in this language for accessing and manipulating data. This involves defining what an operand is. First, let us specify that this processor has a load/store type structure. It is therefore only possible to access memory zones in the *Data* section by using specific instructions. For these instructions, one of the operands will necessarily be the address of a memory location where it will need to read or write. The way to describe this address corresponds to the term *addressing mode* and will be covered at the end of this chapter.

For other instructions, the operands are explicitly given values (immediate operand), contents of registers, or labels in the case of branch instructions. In order to specify which operands a programmer wants to use to carry out the operation, he or she writes an expression made up of numbers and symbols.

When the instruction takes two or three operands, as in the following example:

```
Instr op1,o2{,op3}
```

op1 is called the *destination* operand. It is this operand that receives the result of the operation or assignment. Operands *op2* and *op3* are called *source* operands, as they serve to supply the instruction.

REMARK 4.1.– For read (LDR (LoaD Register), etc.) and write (STR (STore Register), etc) instructions (see section 5.7), the meanings of destination and source operands are reversed. This is a source of error when writing a source program in assembly language, even if at the instruction level we can see a certain logic.

4.1. The constant and renaming

In section 3.1.1, we explained the rules for constructing a symbol as well as those for expressing numerical values (with or without literal expression), see section 3.4.1. The simplest way to use a combination of these two is the declaration of a constant. A constant is a symbol with which we associate a fixed value. So each time the assembler encounters this symbol, it knows that it should simply replace the symbol with the associated value. You would do as well if you use the *Find/Replace* function in your usual text editor. Using a constant in a listing has two major advantages. The first is that it makes the listing easier to read (which should not be considered a luxury) and the second is that it allows us, when the constant is used several times in the file, to carry out a modification of the value in only one place in the listing. The maintenance or development of the program is thus made much easier.

The *EQU* (EQUivalent) directive allows us to define these constants. Here are some examples:

EXAMPLE 4.1.– *Use of the EQU directive*

```
Loop    EQU 12          ; Basic version
TRUE    EQU 0xFF        ; The value is expressed in hexadecimal base
FALSE   EQU #0          ; Insert a # for immediate access
Twice   EQU Loop        ; Double equivalence...why not!
Begin   EQU main        ;  The equivalence is a label
Char_G  EQU 'G'
Msg     EQU "Hello"     ; IMPOSSIBLE => assembly error!
```

The *EQU* declaration has no local consequence, so long as the third field is an expression that corresponds to a 32-bit integer constant[1]. A string like the one in the last line of the example is impossible. It is necessary to be vigilant when using a constant in the rest of the listing, particularly if it concerns access to immediate values, such as those we will deal with in the following section. Indeed an instruction such as *MOV R0, TRUE*, where *TRUE* is the constant declared in Example 4.1, risks causing serious problems, which we will come back to.

---

1 A label, as in the fifth line, corresponds to an address and therefore has a 32-bit determined value.

The directive *RN* (ReName) can also make the listing more readable (although):

> name RN n

where *n* is a number between 0 and 15 and serves to identify the general register that is the target of this directive. The directive allows us to rename the target register with a proposed *name*. So *Counter RN 0* allows us to use the symbol *Counter* instead of the symbol *R0* in the rest of the listing. This makes sense even if, in the end, the disappearance of the name of a general register in the listing can confuse a programmer. You can also definitively discourage future readers by writing *XV34_Z RN 1* and *R_4 RN 2*. Register *R2* would become *R_4* and register *R1* would become *XV34_Z*. In terms of readability, this does not seem like an improvement[2]!

4.2. Operands for common instructions

By common instructions, we mean the set of instructions other than the read/write instructions.

4.2.1. *Use of registers*

4.2.1.1. *General registers*

In most instructions (and the examples presented here follow this approach), the programmer will mainly use the general registers *R0* to *R12* to store the values with which he or she carries out the common instructions. As such, the registers could be considered local variables. General registers are thus the most common operands that we come across in a program. They can contain quantities that express values of very different natures (an 8-bit integer for the ASCII code of a character, an unsigned 16-bit integer for an array index, a signed integer for a relative displacement in the program, etc.). Whatever the case, the 13 registers will always be seen by the processor as a quantity coded on 32 bits. The programmer is faced with mastering the entire contents of a register when the information that he or she is dealing with only holds a half or a quarter of it.

From the coding point of view, it can be interesting to see what the code generated by the assembler looks like. Let us take the simple addition instruction *ADD R0,R1* as an example. This adds together the value contained in the two registers and stores the result in *R0*. This result is *a priori* of the Thumb type. Its coding (and so what will be stored in the CODE memory) is on 16 bits and its

---

2 Not all registers are allowed! For example, R3 RN 4 is impossible.

hexadecimal value is 4,408. Let us look at what the ARM documentation specifies for the coding of this instruction (see Figure 4.1).

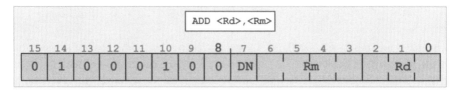

Figure 4.1. *16-bit encoding of the ADD instruction*

The 8- to 15-weight bits correspond to the opcode of the instruction. Those of 3- to 6-weight code the register number Rm, which must correspond to *R1* for us. We can therefore expect to find that *Rm* = 1 (or 0001 in binary). The DN as the most significant bit combined with the three least significant bits of Rd gives the number of the second register, *R0* in our case and so 0000 in binary. When reconstructing this code, we must therefore have 01000100|0|0001|000 = 0100010000001000 = 0X4408, which matches up well with the code proposed by the assembler.

The coding of instructions is a little more complicated than that which we have just presented. Fortunately the programmer does not need to go on dissecting the coding of the instructions in order to correctly write the program. A precise repository of different instruction possibilities will, happily, be amply sufficient.

It is interesting to realize how the choice of registers can influence the size of the code. Let us take the instruction that causes a logical *or* with flag assignment as an example: *ORRS Rx,Ry*. In *Thumb* version, the register numbers are coded on three bits (see Figure 4.2). Also, the use of registers *R0* to *R7* can be fitted into 16-bit encoding without any problem. In contrast, the use of registers *R8* to *R12* can no longer be coded on 3 bits. The assembler is therefore forced to choose Thumb-2 encoding, and the instruction will thus be coded on 32 bits. In this case, the coding becomes more complex and *ORRS R1,R9* (while doing the same thing) will become *ORRS R1,R1,R9*. The three registers used are coded on four bits (and so there are no more restrictions) and the fields *imm3* and *imm2* and *type* are used for coding a hypothetical offset (shift), as we shall see at the end of this section.

Going from 16- to 32-bit code, an arithmetic operation only really represents an additional load of two bytes to the memory, but it also means a 100% increase in the size of the code. If we are trying to optimize memory usage, it can be useful remember this and to avoid carrying out operations that use registers *R8* to *R12* as much as possible.

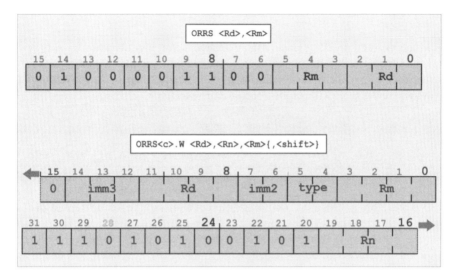

Figure 4.2. *16-bit and 32-bit encoding of the ORRS instruction*

4.2.1.2. *Other registers*

In most cases registers *R13* and *R14* act as operands, like the other general registers. These two are different, however, as they correspond directly to the stack pointer (*SP*) and the link register (*LR*). We should therefore handle them with caution.

As for the *R15* register (the instruction pointer), most instructions refuse to work with it (as it is too dangerous) and the assembler will throw up an error when it comes across such a use. In any case, the only reasonable use of this register is to assign it to execute subroutines. For this, the instruction set has all the jump options (*B, BL, BX*...) to cover our needs, so there is no need to play with fire.

As for the *xPSR* register, we have already seen in Example 2.3 that two specific instructions (*MRS* (Move from Special to Register) and *MSR* (Move to Special Register)) allow us to access the *xPSR*. Again, there is no reason to want to do anything else.

That just leaves all the other registers that we may encounter in a μcontroller (i.e. everything but the processor core), and there are plenty! In Cortex-M3 they belong to the outside world; all of this memory space is only accessible by *load/store* instructions. We will see in a few sections how to access it. Such registers will never be operands for common instructions.

4.2.1.3. *Shift*

In the instruction set, at least in the extended 32-bit part (Thumb-2), there is the option to impose a shift on the last source operand. In Example 4.2, a logical *AND* is carried out: $R0 \leftarrow R1$ & $(R2 \ll 3)$. Note that the suffix S in the instruction just shows where the flags will be positioned for the execution.

EXAMPLE 4.2.– *Logical AND a little bit complex*

> ### ANDS.W R0,R1,R2,LSL #3

It is therefore possible[3] to introduce different shifts, to the left or right of the last source operand. What can appear to be a subtle trick is in fact widely used by compilers. Remember that a right shift of *n* bits is equivalent to multiplying by 2^n (for a left shift, it would be equivalent to dividing by 2^n). Used well, this can save a lot of computing time.

In the case of three operands, the syntax is as follows:

Instr Ri, Rj , Rk, LSL #n	; logical left shift of n bits
Instr Ri, Rj , Rk, LSR #n	; logical right shift of n bits
Instr Ri, Rj , Rk, ASR #n	; arithmetic left shift of n bits
Instr Ri, Rj , Rk, ROR #n	; rotate right to n bits
Instr Ri, Rj , Rk, RRX	; rotate right including the flag C

In each case, the indices *i*, *j* and *k* are integers between 0 and 12, and *n* is an integer between 1 and 31. The logical shift introduces zeros to the right or the left. The arithmetic shift reintroduces the most significant bit (so the sign bit) in order to prevent the loss of the signed representation of a number. Rotation copies bit[0] onto bit[31] with each turn. Finally, *RRX* makes a single 33-bit rotation, the 33rd being the *C* flag.

REMARK 4.2.– The previous example actually only shows three operands. In fact, R2,LSL#3 is only really considered to be one operand. This observation is of minor semantic interest.

---

3 This possibility is limited to the 16 following arithmetic instructions: ADC, ADD, AND, BIC, CMN, CMP, EOR, ORN, ORR, RSB, SBC, SSAT, SUB, TEQ, TST and USAT.

4.2.2. *The immediate operand*

4.2.2.1. *A classic case*

The transfer instruction *MOVS R5,#0x11* is made up of two different types of operands. It will modify the first operand (register *R5*) with the second operand (the value *17=0x11*). This second operand is an *immediate operand*. This means that it is an integral part of the instruction: the immediate operand will be included in the instruction code, as shown in the coding of this instruction (see Figure 4.3). The assembler gives us the hexadecimal code 2511.

Let us look at the ARM documentation here: the five most significant bits code the opcode, bits 8 to 10 code the register number (16-bit coding is only possible for registers *R0* to *R7*) and the immediate value is coded on the 8 least significant bits. By taking 101 as the code for *R5*, we find the expected code, knowing that 0010010100010001 = 0x2511.

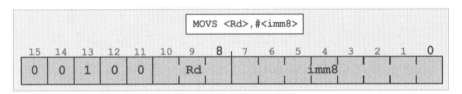

Figure 4.3. *16-bit encoding of MOVS with immediate operand*

4.2.2.2. *An awkward case*

What happens if the immediate value, which we assume is unsigned in this example, exceeds 255? Initially, as for the coding of a register number for the example of a logical OR (see Figure 4.2), the assembler will switch to 32-bit encoding. Consulting the documentation shows that it is also possible to specify an immediate operand coded on 16 bits.

Let us go even further. As register *R5* is 32-bits, it must be able to be initialized with an immediate value coded in 32-bits. Try the following example.

EXAMPLE 4.3.– *A problematic immediate operand*

```
MOV R5,#0X1FF400                    ; => Assembly ERROR
```

Failure! It now faces Cortex-M3's Reduced Instruction Set Computer (RISC) architecture. The assembler will return a friendly message of discontentment, stating that the operand exceeds the representation capacities of an immediate operand. The instructions are coded in 16 or 32 bits and it is not possible to depart from this. It is therefore perfectly understandable that an operand cannot use all of the space provided for the instruction code set.

ARM provides two solutions to this problem. The first partial solution involves using register shifts. For example, adding R0 to the immediate value 0xff100 is impossible. It is, however, possible to load *R1* with 0xFF10 and to add *R0* to *R1*<<4.

The second approach is more systematic, but it is only valid for loading a register and relies on the use of the *LDR* instruction. As we will see in the next section, *LDR* allows us to load a register with the contents of a memory for which the address is given in the argument. Let us take our previous line of code and replace it with the following example.

EXAMPLE 4.4.– *A less problematic pseudo-operand*

> LDR R5,=0x1FF400   ; => OK for the assembler

Now there is no problem on the assembler's side. We think we can, with slightly different syntax, use an immediate operand. In fact the *true* code loaded for this instruction, meaning that which we would find in a disassembly operation, looks something like Example 4.5.

EXAMPLE 4.5.– *but where is the immediate operand passed?*

> LDR R5,[PC,#18]   ; => OK for the assembler

[PC,#18] means that the processor must fetch the contents of the address located 18 addresses above the current address of the instruction pointer (*program counter or PC*). The value 18 is set here as an example. This offset is usually an even *n* number. Let us leave aside indirect addressing for the moment (recognizable by the use of []), and just look at the principle. Schematically the placement of containers and contents is implemented as shown in Figure 4.4.

An instruction such as *LDR R$_i$ =expr*, where *expr* is a literal value expressed in some base or other, is a pseudo-instruction. Depending on the value of *expr*, the assembler will generate different coding:

   – if *expr* can be coded on 8 bits, the instruction will be *MOV R$_i$, #expr*;

– if *expr* can be coded on 16 bits, the instruction will be *MOV.W R_i, #expr*; otherwise

– *LDR R_i{PC, #offset]*, where the *offset* is a relative displacement with respect to the current position of instruction *PC* pointer, allowing us to reach the *literal pool* where the value will be created.

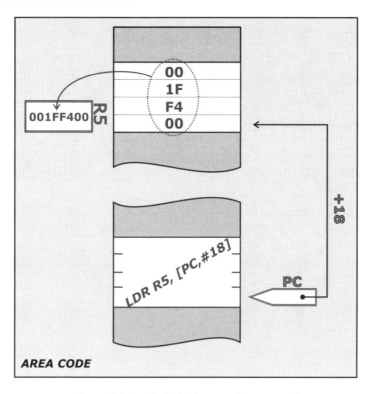

Figure 4.4. *Load of a 32-bit immediate operand*

4.2.2.3. *Literal pool and the LTORG directive*

On its own initiative, when necessary the assembler will create memory zones to store immediate values that cannot be directly included in the instruction code. These zones are called *Literal Pools*. They are created by default at the end of each CODE section. This relative proximity prevents the relative displacement that must be added to the PC pointer from reaching too large a value. In fact, this *offset* must be smaller than 4,096 (in the ideal scenario for 32-bit encoding). When the pseudo-instruction *LDR Rd, =expr* needs to place an immediate value in a *Literal Pool*, the assembler first verifies that this value has not previously been created; if it has, the assembler determines whether it can be reached (relative displacement <4,096) so that it can be used. If these two conditions are not met, it creates this constant in the next *Literal Pool.*

EXAMPLE 4.6.– *Use of the LTORG directive*

```
;*****************************************************************
;
; CODE SECTION
;
;*****************************************************************

 AREA MyCode, CODE, readonly, ALIGN=6

;- - - - - - - - - - - - - - - - - - - - - - - - - - - - - - - -
;
; Principal Procedure
;
;- - - - - - - - - - - - - - - - - - - - - - - - - - - - - - - -


main            PROC                    ; Beginning of the program

                LDR R5,=0x1FFFF         ; Load of an immediate value

                BL DoNothing            ; Call to the procedure DoNothing

inf             B inf                   ; Infinite loop


                LTORG                   ; Opening of a literal pool


DoNothing       PROC

                NOP                     ; Do nothing...

                BX LR                   ; ... and go back

                ENDP

EmptyResa       space 5000              ; reservation "to move away"

                                        ;                the section end

                ENDP

;*****************************************************************
```

However it is still possible for the end of the section to be too far away to consider this implicit manipulation. There is also the option of forcing the creation of a storage zone using the *LTORG* directive.

In Example 4.6, the *LTORG* directive is placed between the *main* procedure and the *DoNothing* function. The storage area would thus be inserted at this location. We could also note that the instruction *LDR R5, =0x1FFFF* in this configuration corresponds to *LDR R5,[PC,#8]*. Without using this directive, the assembler would have been failing as the 5,000 byte reservation of the *EmptyResa* label in the same code section implies that the following *Literal Pool* is too far away to be reached with an *offset* that is <4,096.

4.3. Memory access operands: addressing modes

It is clear that all not of the data in a program can be entirely contained in the registers. It is therefore necessary during the running of a program to fetch source operands (read) or to deposit destination operands (write) in memory. These are *load/store* operations. Many variations of these instructions can be used, but overall they can be sorted into two operation types:

> LDR **R**$_i$, {expr}
>
> STR **R**$_i$, {expr}

{expr} is an expression that allows us to calculate the address where the value to be set as the value of R_i will be read (*LDR*) or where the value contained in register R_i will be stored (*STR*). Some important notes about this syntax:

– this expression always contains at least a general register. It is usually called the base register because it will define a base address from which memory access will occur;

– the usual concept and meaning of source/destination operands for common instructions does not apply here;

– the base register can change (incrementation or decrementation) with the execution of the instruction. The different possibilities of these changes reflect the addressing modes;

– the use of these instructions is necessary in the course of a program but they are the ones that cause the most trouble. In fact, if following a bad manipulation, the base register contains an incorrect value and a bug is guaranteed;

– the different variations will correspond to different mnemonics but will always contain the radical *LDR* or *STR*. We can especially distinguish:

- those that authorize the reading or writing of a byte (*LDRB, STRB*), a half-word (*LDRH, STRH*), and even those that cause several readings/writings (*LDRD, STRD, LDM, STM*, etc.),

- those that allow us to specify whether a datum to be read is signed (*LDRBS, LDRSH,* etc.), and finally

- those that are linked with privileges or memory access protection (*LRDEX, LDRBT,* etc.);

– *there is no direct memory access* (unlike in other assembly languages, such as those of Intel, Motorola, MicroChip, etc.);

– it is therefore always necessary to proceed in two steps: one for recovering the address in a register and a second for accessing to memory via this register;

– the syntax *LDR Ri,=val* is fictitious. It will always be translated as either *MOV Ri,#val* or *LDR Ri, [PC,#n]*.

4.3.1. *The pointer concept*

{expr} contains at least one register that contains the base address. Therefore here we find the concept of a pointer that we could find in a higher level language structure. In assembly language, we will most often use indirect addressing terms. The principle has already been illustrated through the *LDRB R3,[R6]* instruction presented in Figure 3.2. *R6* is a pointer that therefore (by the very definition of a pointer) contains an address at which the processor can read an instruction in order to modify the destination operand (*R3* in this example). The use of square brackets ([and]) around the register name allows us to indicate to the assembler that we are interested in the contents of the address stored in the register, rather than contents of the register itself. The mnemonic *LDRB* was used in this example; the processor will therefore only read one byte that it considers to be unsigned (*LDRSB* allowed it to take the sign into account). In this manner, the three most significant bytes would be set to 0 so that the 32-bit value eventually contained in *R3* corresponds to the 8-bit value contained in the source address. In this case, we are talking about unsigned promotion (in signed promotion, the most significant bit would be copied in the 24 most significant bits of the register so that the values in 8-bit and 32-bits correspond to the same signed quantity).

One detail remains to be settled: how was the address contained in *R6* specified? Talking in terms of structured language: how was the pointer initialized? Simply using the syntax detailed in section 4.2.2: *LDR R$_i$, =imm32*. In the previously cited example, *R3* was initialized by *LDR R3,=Bytinit*. With this instruction formulation, as mentioned in this section, we are dealing with immediate addressing. The immediate value is the 32-bit address of the variable *Bytinit*. The assembler therefore expects the storage of this immediate information in the *Literal Pool* and the embedded code will correspond to a *LDR R3,[PC,#offset]*, where *offset* is the relative value that allows us to reach the target zone of the *Literal Pool*. Thus we implicitly have a first indirect access in order to read the address of the variable where we found our datum.

Schematically, the two lines of code (① and ②) in this example therefore involve double pointing, as summarized in Figure 4.5. It is the only way to access the contents of a variable.

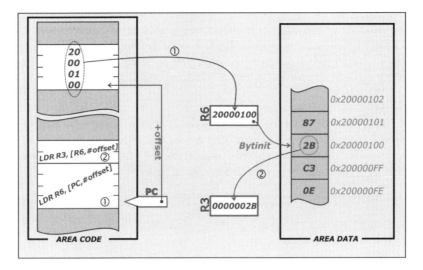

Figure 4.5. *Initialization and use of a pointer*

4.3.2. *Addressing modes*

When using simple indirection *[R$_i$]*, the target address for the transfer is explicitly contained in the *R$_i$* register.

The simplest syntax for executing the reading of a half-word in memory, "pointed" to by register *Rn* and transferring into register *Rn* therefore corresponds to the following syntax:

```
LDRH Rt, [Rn]
```

There are three other addressing modes, however, for which this link is less direct. As for the syntax presented above, the explanation of these addressing modes is illustrated through the instruction to load a half-word to a register, but these modes are also for writing (*STRH*) and for the different variations of the mnemonics *LDR* and *STR*.

4.3.2.1. *Indirect addressing with displacement*

In this addressing mode, we add an additional displacement (*offset*) to the address contained in the base register. The syntax is:

LDRH Rt, [Rn, #±offset]

The principle of this transfer is shown in Figure 4.6a. We should note that the value of the *offset* is in most cases limited to 4,096, but for some special forms (*LDRHT*, for example) the maximum value can be lower. This quantity, like any immediate value in an instruction, can also influence the size of the coding (16 or 32 bits).

One of the main uses of this addressing mode is to access data structures. Only the address of the structure is known. This can be deposited in the base register. To then access other constituent fields of the structure, we must use the *offset* to specify the relative displacement to be imposed in order to reach this field (see section 6.5).

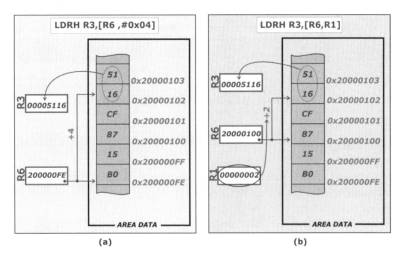

Figure 4.6. *Transfer: (a) with immediate offset; (b) with index*

4.3.2.2. *Indirect addressing mode with index*

In this mode, the address is made up of the addition of two registers. The syntax is as follows:

```
LDRH Rt, [Rn, Rm]
LDRH Rt, [Rn, Rm {, LSL #<imm2>}]    ; alternative with left shift
```

With this mode, it is quite easy to code an algorithm using a table: all we have to do is put the table address in the Rn register and the table index in the Rm register.

A line of C code like Local = [index] would translate into assembly language as the line LDRH R3, [R6, R1] (see Figure 4.6).

REMARK. 4.3.– When we wish to access the nth element of a typical table, it is convenient to use the shift operator as presented in the syntax above. So, for a table containing long integers coded on four bytes, by placing R6 at the address of this table and putting a value k in R1, the instruction LDR R3, [R6, R1, LSL#2] allows us to read the kth element of the table.

4.3.2.3. *Indirect addressing mode with post-modification*

In the two previous modes, the base register was not modified by the instruction. This practice is quite compatible with the management of tables or data structures for which the addresses are always fixed.

In this third mode (and for that which will be presented in the following section), the value of the base register will be modified by the instruction. This management corresponds perfectly to the pointer concept found in the high-level languages: when we use the pointer, the base register can evolve. Consequently it is intrinsically a variable quantity.

In this first mode, the modification of the register happens just after the execution of the transfer, using the following syntax:

```
LDRH Rt,[Rn], #±imm8
```

Thus, the execution has two successive effects: the assignment of the register Rt with the contents of the address stored in the register Rn, then the modification of the pointer itself as follows: Rn ← Rn ± imm8.

REMARK 4.4.– The syntax is quite similar to that used for indirect addressing with offset. Only the position of the immediate term (inside or outside brackets) changes, which can be a source of confusion, especially when re-reading the listing.

In the example in Figure 4.7, the value of the offset is positive (+4). We should note that the modification of the pointer is not only obligatorily unitary, but that it may also be negative. It must be between -127 and +128

4.3.2.4. *Indirect addressing with post modification*

In this case, the modification happens before the transfer:

> LDRH Rt, [Rn #±imm8] !

The execution also occurs in two steps (see Figure 4.7). In the first step, we get modification of the base register Rn ← Rn ±imm8. In the second step, the new target quantity is transfered to register Rt.

REMARK 4.5.– It is important to choose a good font for your text editor so you do not miss the "!" that follows the brackets.

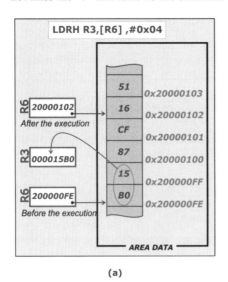

(a)

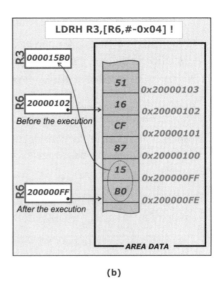

(b)

Figure 4.7. *Transfer: (a) with post-modification; (b) pre-modification*

Chapter 5

Instruction Set

Reading an instruction set is anything but pleasant. In their first reading of this chapter, readers will just skim through, but in the end, this is definitely the chapter that the user will return to the most often to find out what the processor can do and above all how he or she can make it do that (i.e. with which operands).

5.1. Reading guide

A certain number of conventions, omissions or implicit rules govern the compilation of the explanations of the instruction set. It is therefore necessary to read these sections while taking into account the following remarks:

– some instructions are only mentioned (at the end of the chapter) and are not explained. They are advanced instructions for the processor and so are directed at advanced programmers who would not, in any case, be satisfied with this single book;

– the majority of instructions are in a 16- or 32-bit version. The assembler, according to its own implicit rules and functional limits (the size of the immediate operands, for example) will choose one or the other. It is, however, possible to force the desired code size by adding the .W for a 32-bit or .N for a 16-bit extension. In doing so, this may lead to greater mastery of the code fabrication process but at the expense of failure in the event that it is impossible to code the instruction in the code with the suffix <q>. In this book we will only indicate the possible sizes (16, 16/32 or 32 bits) for each instruction, it being understood that forcing is only reasonable if the size is not fixed.

REMARK 5.1.– W means *word* but sometimes (like in this chapter) it means a 32-bit quantity and sometimes (as for the DCW directive) a 16-bit quantity. Elsewhere the 16-bit quantity can be characterized by the use of an H (*half-word*) or by the use of .N as explained above. It is not horribly complicated but it is terribly inconvenient and a source of particularly annoying small errors:

– for many instructions it is possible to add on a suffix that then allows us to condition the execution of the instruction. The option to add this suffix is shown in the table by the symbol <c>. The addition of this suffix is not without consequences for the code generated by the assembler because this amounts to inserting an *IT* instruction in front of the instruction itself. It is therefore necessary to remember this, especially during development sequences where this instruction can appear even if the programmer has not explicitly written it. It is also necessary to remember that the conditioning is relative to the state of the flags, which are themselves generally assigned by the previous instruction that must itself be conditioned. The list of suffixes is given in the Table 5.1 with the conditions and the logical combination of flags relating to each condition;

– for several instructions, it is necessary to make the distinction between the least significant and most significant bits of the operand. For the sake of compactness, the abbreviations *LSB* (least significant bit) and *MSB* (most significant bit) have been used to make this distinction;

– for common instructions, the first operand is often presented as being optional. In the following tables describing the different instructions, this is generally shown by a *{Rn}* for the recipient operand. If the recipient operand is not explicitly given, however, the first operand behaves as both the source and the destination at once. For example, in *ADD R0,#2*, the register *R0* is both the source and destination and this instruction means $R0 \leftarrow R0+2$.

The general registers are indiscriminately denoted by *Rd, Rn, Rm* or *Ra* for common instructions. It is not necessary, however, for an instruction to verify $d \neq n \neq m \neq a$ and *a priori* with, $a, d, m, n \in$:

– [0…15]. Thus, the instruction *ADDS.W R1,R1,R1* is quite allowable and shows that *R1* will receive double its contents and that the flags (suffix S) will be updated;

– for read/write instructions, the base register is *Rn* and the register that receives/supplies the data is called *Rt*;

– the expression $M_{32}(Rn)$ signifies the 32-bit contents of the address pointed at by *Rn* and the following three addresses;

– the <*shift*> operator appears (optional operator for most instructions) to impose a bit shift on the last operand in the list. The list of possible shifts is the same as that presented in section 4.2.1.1.

5.1.1. *List of possible "condition" suffixes*

Table 5.1 corresponds to the possible substitutions for the symbol $<c>$. It should be noted that this also applies to jump instructions (*B, BL, BX,* etc.) which are then conditioned. In the case of these branch instructions, the instruction *IT* is not inserted before the jump.

Suffix	Condition	Flags
EQ	EQual	Z = 1
NE	Not Equal	Z = 0
CS HS	Carry Set Higher or Same	C = 1
CC LO	Clear Carry LOwer	C = 0
MI	MInus	N = 1
PL	PLus	N = 0
VS	oVerflow Set	V = 1
VC	oVerflow Clear	V = 0
HI	unsigned HIgher	(C = 1 AND Z = 0)
LS	unsigned Lower or Same	(C = 0 OR Z = 1)
GE	signed Greater than or Equal	N = V
LT	signed Less Than	N ≠ V
GT	signed Greater Than	Z = 0 AND N = V
LE	signed Less than or Equal	Z = 1 OR N ≠ V

Table 5.1. *List of possible conditions*

When we implement different algorithmic structures, it is often necessary to program conditioned jumps following a comparison of the two quantities. Depending on whether the quantities are signed or unsigned, and whether we want a strict comparison or not, the mnemonic changes. Table 5.2 resumes the list of possible conditions to enable coding of the conditioned branch that will follow a *CMP x,y* without too many questions.

CMP x,y ... B ? ?		
	x,y signed	x,y unsigned
=	EQ	EQ
<	MI	LO
≤	LE	LS
>	GT	HI
≥	GE	HS

Table 5.2. *Use of condition suffixes for the comparison of two integers*
(see Table 5.1 for an explanation of the abbreviations)

Now for the long and tedious list of instructions. These are sorted into large families to facilitate searching by theme. Appendix A is an abridged version of this chapter, but the instructions are sorted into alphabetical order.

Let us start with a first unclassifiable instruction:

NOP	16/32	**No OPeration**
NOP<c>		Do nothing
Serves no purpose other than to use a little CPU time. *Note the surprising subtlety: NOP can be conditioned* *so that it does not "do nothing" if the condition is false!*		

5.2. Arithmetic instructions

ADC	16/32	**ADdition with Carry**
ADC{S}<c> {<Rd>,} <Rn>, #<const>		Rd ← Rn + const + flag C
ADC{S}<c> {<Rd>,} <Rn>, <Rm> {,<shift>}		Rd ← Rn +shift(Rm) + flag C
The use of the SP register makes a call to a specific encoding; *this is why it explicitly appears in this list. It does not,* *however, have specific constraints as to its use.*		

ADD	16/32		**Simple ADDition**
ADD{S}<c> {<Rd>,} <Rn>,#<const>			Rd ← Rn + const
ADD{S}<c> {<Rd>,} <Rn>, <Rm> {,<shift>}			Rd ← Rn + shift(Rm)
ADD{S}<c> {<Rd>,} SP, #<const>			Rd ← SP + const
ADD{S}<c> {<Rd>,} SP, <Rm>{,<shift>}			Rd ← SP + shift(Rm)

MLA	32	**MultipLication and Addition**
MLA<c> <Rd>, <Rn>, <Rm>, <Ra>		Rd ← (Rn * Rm) + Ra
Addition becomes an accumulation when Rd = Ra *(see instruction SMLAL for a 64-bit accumulation).*		

MLS	32	**MultipLication and Subtraction**
MLS<c> <Rd>, <Rn>, <Rm>, <Ra>		Rd ← Ra - (Rn * Rm)

MUL	16/32	**MULtiplication – 32-bit results**
MUL{S}<c> {<Rd>,} <Rn>, <Rm>		Rd ← Rn * Rm
Be aware that the result only contains the 32 LSB bits. *It does not take into account the sign of the result.* *The instruction therefore only makes sense if the source operands* *are 16 bits. We must use SMUL to get a 64-bit result.*		

RSB	16/32		**Reverse SuBtraction**
RSB{S}<c> {<Rd>,} <Rn>, #<const>			Rd ← -Rn + const
RSB{S}<c> {<Rd>,} <Rn>, <Rm> {,<shift>}			Rd ← -Rn + shift(Rm)
See also the SUB instruction with regard to subtractions.			

SBC	16/32	**SuBtraction with Carry**
SBC{S}<c> {<Rd>,} <Rn>, #<const>		Rd ← Rm – const + flag C
SBC{S}<c> {<Rd>,} <Rn>, <Rm> {,<shift>}		Rd ← Rm - shift(Rm) + flag C
Coding of the version with "const" is always in 32 bits.		

SDIV	32	**Signed DIVision**
SDIV<c> {<Rd>,} <Rn>, <Rm>		Rd ← Rn ÷ Rn
Integer division of 32-bit operands: the remainder is lost!		

SMLAL	32	**Signed MuLtipLication and 64-bit Addition**
SMLAL<c> <Rd$_{lsb}$>, <R$_{msb}$>, <Rn>, <Rm>		$[Rd_{msb} : Rd_{lsb}] \leftarrow Rn * Rm + [Rd_{msb} : Rd_{lsb}]$
$[Rd_{msb} : Rd_{lsb}]$ is a 64-bit pseudo register made up of two 32-bit registers. It is a very useful instruction for signal processing.		

SMULL	32	**Signed MULtipLication – 64-bit results**
SMULL<c> <Rd$_{lsb}$>, <Rd$_{msb}$>, <Rn>, <Rm>		$[Rd_{msb} : Rd_{lsb}] \leftarrow Rn * Rm$
This instruction complements MUL for 32-bit operands.		

SSAT	32	**Signed SATuration**
SSAT<c> <Rd>,#<imm5>,<Rn>{,<shift>}		if (Rn < 0) Rd ← $\min(-2^{(imm5-1)}, shift(Rn))$ if (Rn >0) Rd ← $\max(2^{(imm5-1)} - 1, shift(Rn))$
The Q flag is set to i if there has been saturation, otherwise it stays unchanged. The Q flag can be set to 0 before the operation in order to exploit this information. Saturation is an important operand for algorithms working on the representation of a fixed point.		

SUB	16/32	Simple SUBtraction
SUB{S}<c> {<Rd>} ,<Rn>,#<const>		Rd ← Rn - const
SUB{S}<c> {<Rd>} ,<Rn>, <Rm> {,<shift>}		Rd ← Rn - shift(Rm)
SUB{S}<c> {<Rd>} ,SP,#<const>		Rd ← SP - const
SUB{S}<c> {<Rd>} ,SP,<Rm> {,<shift>}		Rd ← SP - shift(Rm)

See also the RSB instruction regarding subtractions. The use of the SP register calls for the use of a specific encoding. This is why it explicitly appears in this list.

UDIV	32	Unsigned DIVision
UDIV<c> {<Rd>,} <Rn>, <Rm>		Rd ← Rn ÷ Rm

UMAL	32	Unsigned MuLtipLication and 64-bit Addition
UMLAL<c> <Rd$_{lsb}$ >, <Rd$_{msb}$>, <Rn>, <Rm>		$[Rd_{msb} : Rd_{lsb}] \leftarrow Rn*Rm$ $+ [Rd_{msb} : Rd_{lsb}]$

[Rd$_{msb}$: Rd$_{lsb}$] is a 64-bit pseudo-register made up of two 32-bit registers.

UMULL	32	Unsigned MULtipLication – 64-bit results
UMUL<c> <Rd$_{lsb}$ >, <Rd$_{msb}$ >, <Rn>, <Rm>		$[Rd_{msb} : Rd_{lsb}] \leftarrow Rn*Rm$

[Rd$_{msb}$: Rd$_{lsb}$] is a 64-bit pseudo-register made up of two 32-bit registers.

USAT	32	Unsigned SATuration
USAT<c> <Rd>,#<imm5>,<Rn>{,<shift>}	Rd ← $\max(2^{(imm5-1)} - 1$, shift(Rn))	

The Q flag is set to i if there has been saturation, otherwise Q stayed unchanged. The Q flag can be set to 0 before the operation in order to exploit this information. Saturation is an important operand for algorithms working on the representation of a fixed point.

5.3. Logical and bit manipulation instructions

AND	16/32	**Logical AND**
AND{S}<c> {<Rd>,} <Rn>, #<const>		Rd ← Rn AND const
AND{S}<c> {<Rd>,} <Rn>, <Rm> {,<shift>}		Rn ← Rn AND shift(Rm)

ASR	16/32	**Arithmetic Shift Right**
ASR{S}<c> <Rd>, <Rm>, #<imm5>		$Rd ← Rm >>_{imm5}$
ASR{S}<c> <Rd>, <Rn>, <Rm>		$Rd ← Rn >>_{Rm}$
The shift reintroduces the left signed bit. The last bit leaving to the right modifies the Carry C flag.		

BFC	32	**Bit Field Clearing**
BFC<c> <Rd>, #<lsb>, #<Nb>		Rd[lsb+Nb-1 : lsb] ← 0
lsb = 0 ... 31 and Nb = 1 ... 32. *This instruction does not have a flag-modifying version.*		

BFI	32	**Bit Field Copying**
BFI<c> <Rd>,<Rn>, #<lsb>, #<Nb>		Rd[lsb+Nb-1 : lsb] ← Rn[Nb : 0]
lsb = 0 ... 31 and Nb = 1 ... 32. *This instruction does not have a flag-modifying version.* *The symmetrical instruction allows the copying of a given bit field in which the LSBs of Rd do not exist.*		

BIC	16/32	**Clearing BIts by AND mask**
BIC{S}<c> {<Rd>,} <Rn>, #<const>		Rd ← Rn AND NOT(const)
BIC{S}<c> {<Rd>,} <Rn>, <Rm> {,<shift>}		Rd ← Rn AND NOT (shift(Rm))
lsb = 0 ... 31 and Nb = 1 ... 32.		

CLZ	32	**Countdown MSBs to 0 before the first bit at 1**
CLZ<c> <Rd>, <Rm>		Rd ← CLZ(Rn)

Rd gets a value between 0 (Rd = 0xFFFFFFFF) and 32 (Rd = 0).
This is a potentially interesting instruction for algorithms
working on the representation of a fixed point.

EOR	16/32	**Exclusive OR**
EOR{S}<c> {<Rd>,} <Rn>, #<const>		Rd ← Rn XOR const
EOR{S}<c> {<Rd>,} <Rn>, <Rm> {,<shift>}		Rd ← Rn XOR shift(Rm)

This is a useful instruction for inverting bit fields.

LSL	16/32	**Logical Shift Left**
LSL{S}<c> <Rd>, <Rm>, #<imm5>		Rd ← Rm <<$_{imm5}$
LSL{S}<c> <Rd>, <Rn>, <Rm>		Rd ← Rn <<$_{Rm}$

The shift introduces zeros on the right.
The last bit leaving to the left modifies the Carry C flag.

LSR	16/32	**Logical Shift Right**
LSR{S}<c> <Rd>, <Rm>, #<imm5>		Rd ← Rm >>$_{imm5}$
LSR{S}<c> <Rd>, <Rn>, <Rm>		Rd ← Rn >>$_{Rm}$

The shift introduces zeroes on the left.
The last bit leaving to the right modifies the Carry C flag.

MVN	16/32	**Logical complement to 1**
MVN{S}<c> <Rd>, #<const>		Rd ← NOT(const)
MVN{S}<c> <Rd>, <Rm> {, <shift>}		Rd ← NOT(shift(Rn))

NEG	16/32	NEGative (complement to 2)
NEG<c> {<Rd>,} <Rm>		Rd ← -Rm
NEG is equivalent to RSB with 0. There is no particular encoding for this mnemonic.		

ORN	16/32	Complemented logical OR
ORN{S}<c> {<Rd>,} <Rn>, #<const>		Rd ← Rm OR NOT(const)
ORN{S}<c> {<Rd>,} <Rn>, <Rm> {,<shift>}		Rd ← Rm OR NOT(shift(Rm))

ORR	16/32	Logical OR
ORR{S}<c> {<Rd>,} <Rn>, #<const>	Rd ← Rm OR const
ORR{S}<c> {<Rd>,} <Rn>, <Rm> {,<shift>}	Rd ← Rm OR shift(Rm)

RBIT	32	BIT transposition
RBIT<c> <Rd>, <Rm>	Rd[31-k] ← Rm[k] with k = 0 ... 31

REV	16/32	REVersal of MSBs and LSBs
REV<c> <Rd>, <Rm>		Rd[31 : 24] ← Rm[7 : 0] Rd[23 : 16] ← Rm[15 : 8] Rd[15 : 8] ← Rm[23 : 16] Rd[7 : 0] ← Rm[31 : 24]
The Arithmetic and Logic Unit only works in 32 bits. It is often necessary to carry out this kind of transfer to work on smaller representations.		

REV16	16/32	**REVersal of MSBs and LSBs by a half-word**
REV16<c> <Rd>, <Rm>		Rd[31 : 24] ← Rm[23 : 1]
		Rd[23 : 16] ← Rm[31 : 24]
		Rd[15 : 8] ← Rm[7 : 0]
		Rd[7 : 0] ← Rm[15 : 8]
See the remark on the REV instruction.		

REVSH	16/32	**Signed REVersal by Half-word**
REVSH<c> <Rd>, <Rm>		Rd[31 : 8] ← Signed promotion (Rm[7 : 0])
		Rd[7 : 0] ← Rm[15 : 8]

ROR	16/32	**Right ROtation**
ROR{S}<c> <Rd>, <Rm>, #<imm5>		Rd ← rotation(Rm, imm5 bits)
ROR{S}<c> <Rd>, <Rn>, <Rm>		Rd ← rotation(Rn, Rm bits)
The rotation reinserts bit 0 on bit 31 with each turn. *There is no rotation of n bits to the left as this* *would be a rotation of 32-n bits to the right.*		

RRX	32	**EXtended Right Rotation**
ROR{S}<c> <Rd>, <Rn>, <Rm>		Rd ← rotation([Rn,C], Rm bits
This uses the same principle as ROR, but with flag C in the 33rd bit to the *right. There is no form with immediate operand for this instruction.*		

SBFX	32	**32-bit Signed eXtend of a Bit Field**
SBFX<c> <Rd>, <Rn>, #<lsb>, #<Nb>		Rd[Nb-1 : 0] ← Rn[lsb+Nb-1 : lsb]
		Rd[31 : Nb] ← Rd[lsb+Nb-1]
See UBFX for the unsigned version.		

SXTB	16/32	**32-bit Signed eXTend of a Byte**
SXTB<c> <Rd>, <Rm> {, <rotation>}		Rd ← rotation32(Rn)[7 : 0] Rd[31 : 8] ← Rd[7]
See UXTB for the unsigned version. The rotation (which is optional) can be ROR #8, ROR #16 or ROR #24. It allows us to choose which of the four bytes in the register to promote.		

SXTH	16/32	**32-bit Signed eXTend of a Half-word**
SXTH<c> <Rd>, <Rm> {, <rotation>}		Rd ← rotation_{32}(Rn)[15 : 0] Rd[31 : 8] ← Rd[15]
See UXTH for the unsigned version Rotation (which is optional) can be ROR #8 or ROR #16 or ROR #24. It allows us to select the two consecutive bytes of the register to be promoted.		

UBFX	16/32	**Unsigned 32-bit eXtend of Bit Field**
UBFX<c> <Rd>, <Rn>, #<lsb>, #<Nb>	Rd[Nb-1 : 0] ← Rn[lsb+Nb-1 : lsb] Rd[31 : Nb] ← 0
See SBFX for the signed version.	

UXTB	16/32	**32-bit Unsigned eXTend of a Byte**
UXTB<c> <Rd>, <Rm> {, <rotation>}		Rd ← rotation32((Rn)[7 : 0] Rd[31 : 8] ← 0
See SXTB for the signed version. Rotation (which is optional) can be ROR #8 or ROR #16 or ROR #24. It allows us to select the two consecutive bytes of the register to be promoted.		

UXTH	16/32	**32-bit Unsigned eXTend of a Half-word**
UXTH<c> <Rd>, <Rm> {, <rotation>}		Rd ← rotation32((Rn)[15 : 0] Rd[31 : 8] ← 0
See SXTH for the signed version. Rotation (which is optional) can be ROR #8 or ROR #16 or ROR #24. It allows us to select the two consecutive bytes of the register to be promoted.		

5.4. Internal transfer instructions

The concept of internal transfer encompasses transfers that do not call memory locations. They are therefore transfers between registers or register assignments with immediate values.

ADR	16/32	**Loading of CODE ADdRess**
ADR<c> <Rd>, <label>		Rd ← Label address
It allows us to load an address in a CODE zone using a relative shift in the program counter (PC, with a maximum of 4,096). The label can correspond to a Literal Pool zone and must be local to the module.		

MOV	16/32	**Internal register transfer**
MOV{S}<c> <Rd>, #<const>		Rd ← const
MOV{S}<c> <Rd>, <Rm>		Rd ← Rm
MOVW replaces MOV if const cannot be coded on 11 bits. It may be desirable to carry out a MOV with a shifted source register but this is equivalent to the direct use of ASR, LSR, LSL, etc. For example: MOV <Rd>,<Rm>,ASR #<n> ⟺ ASR <Rd>,<Rm>,#<n>.		

MOVT	16/32	**Allocation of the 16 LSB bits of a register**
MOVT<c> <Rd>, #<imm16>		Rd[16 : 31] ← imm16
The 16 LSBs are unchanged.		

MRS	32	**Reading of a special register (Move Special to Register)**
MRS<c> <Rn>,<spec_reg>		Rn ← spec_reg
The special registers are: APSR, XPSR, IPSR, EPSR, PSP, MSP, PRIMASK, BASEPRI, FAULTMASK, CONTROL, BASEPRI_MAX and CONTROL. The use of this instruction requires Cortex-M3 to be configured with a privileged access level (see section 2.2).		

MSR	32	Writing to a special register (Move to Register from Special)
MSR<c> <spec_reg>,<Rn>		spec_reg ← Rn
The special registers are: *APSR, XPSR, IPSR, EPSR, PSP, MSP, PRIMASK, BASEPRI, FAULTMASK, CONTROL, BASEPRI_MAX and CONTROL.* *The use of this instruction requires Cortex-M3 to be configured with a privileged access level (see section 2.2).*		

5.5. Test instructions

For the most part, instructions can be linked to conditions, i.e. to a logical combination of flags. In Chapter 6, different algorithmic structures will be explained, all clearly based on the expression of condition and so ultimately on programming tests. The instructions presented in this section are those that have no result other than flag modification.

CMN	16/32	Addition without allocation – Flag modification (CoMpare Negative)
CMN<c> <Rn>, #<const>		Flags ← test(Rn + const)
CMN<c> <Rn>, <Rm>{,<shift>}		Flags ← test(Rn + shift(Rm))
Rn may be the SP register.		

CMP	16/32	Subtraction without allocation – Flag modification (CoMpare)
CMP<c> <Rn>, #<const>		Flags ← test(Rn - const)
CMP<c> <Rn>, <Rm>{,<shift>}		Flags ← test(Rn - shift(Rm))
Rn may be the SP register. *This is the most frequently used instruction for performing tests.* *Indeed, a ≤ b is not directly useable. It is unlike its equivalent* *(a − b) ≤ 0 because flags N and Z will contain the result.*		

TEQ	32	Exclusive OR without allocation – Flag modification (Test EQuivalence)
TEQ<c> <Rn>, #<const>		Flags ← test(Rn XOR const)
TEQ<c> <Rn>, <Rm>{,<shift>}		Flags ← test(Rn XOR shift(Rm))
Rn may be the SP register.		

TST	16/32	Logical AND without allocation – Flag modification (TeST)
TST<c> <Rn>, #<const>		Flags ← test(Rn AND const)
TST<c> <Rn>, <Rm>{,<shift>}		Flags ← test(Rn AND shift(Rm))
Rn may not be the SP register.		

5.6. Branch instructions

Branch instructions, along with test instructions, allow us to realize the different algorithmic structures of a program. This is also the way to call procedures.

All instructions are coded in 16 or 32 bits. To respect the principle of alignment, the address of an instruction must at least be even. However, consider Example 5.1.

EXAMPLE 5.1.– *LSB of the address of a jump*

```
        LDR R0,=Label  ; Loading an address...
        BX R0              ; ...and jump to the address contained in R0
        ...
Label   ...                ; Rendez-vous point
```

Observation of the contents of *R0* will show that the LSB is 1, leading us to believe that the rendezvous point is at an odd address. More surprising still, if we use a debugger to force the LSB to be 0, it will launch a *Memory Management Fault* exception (see section 8.2.1).

This curiosity comes from the successive developments of the ARM architectures, and particularly from the introduction of the *Thumb* set. It is in fact possible to make some ARM processors work with either the complete 32-bit *ARM* set or with the reduced *Thumb* set. This technique is termed *interworking* in the ARM documentation. The bit[0], then, is useful in managing these switches. In the case of Cortex-M3, there is no such thing, as only Thumb (and its extension Thumb2) exists. Five instructions, however, require bit[0] to be 1 to function correctly. These are the instructions *BLX, BX, LDR, POP* and *LDM*, the latter three only being concerned when they modify the PC. During the execution of these instructions, and so during the allocation of the instruction pointer, the LSB will be cleared and so the rendezvous address will become even.

Again, there is no need to worry; everything is completely transparent in the programming phase. The assembler and the link editor will know how to calculate the best values to produce perfectly executable code. In the development phase, however, this information may be important in order to avoid being surprised by a difference between the target address and the actual address.

B	16/32	**Simple Branch**
B<c> <label>		PC ← label
Equivalent to a simple assignment of the instruction pointer.		

BL	32	**Branch with Link**
BL<c> <label>		LR ← return @ PC ← label
The return @ is the current value of the PC+4 with bit[0]=1.		

BLX	16	**Branch and eXchange with register link**
BLX<c> <Rm>		LR ← return @ PC ← Rm
This uses the same principle as BL. *The calling address is contained in the Rm register.* *It allows the management of "jump tables" or function pointers. The X of the mnemonic means eXchange,* *but in no case does Rm receive the previous value of PC.*		

BX	16	**Branch and eXchange by register**
BX<c> <Rm>		PC ← Rm
This instruction allows the return of procedure when the register is LR. X means the same as it does in BLX.		

CBZ, CBNZ	16	**Conditional Branch on the Nullity of a register**
CBZ<c> <Rm> <label>		PC ← label if (Rm = 0)
CBNZ<c> <Rm> <label>		PC ← label if (Rm≠0)
This instruction does not modify the flags and allows us to carry out a conditional branch without carrying out the prior test. The jump must be "forward" and limited to 126 bytes (containing a maximum of 62 instructions).		

The following two instructions allow the implementation of basic algorithmic structures (alternative structures). Even if they are particularly interesting in their compactness and their speed of execution, they still have limited use, due to the number of instructions supported following a condition. In section 6.2, we will see how a systematic modular program allows us to free ourselves from these limitations and to process in any case.

IT	16	**Condition and If...Then jump**
IT{x{y{z}}} <firstcond>		Fixes the execution of the following instruction blocks (that number four at most).
firstcond determines the condition for the first instruction x,y,z, fixes the conditions for the second, third and fourth instructions of the block. x,y,z are relative to firstcond with T (Then = TRUE) or E (Else = FALSE). Be aware that the instructions of the block must take the suffix <c>, which denotes the condition or tells us that it is coded opposite in IT. IT can be omitted but the assembler will automatically insert it if you condition one of more instructions.		

EXAMPLE 5.2.– *Example of IT instruction use*

```
        CMP R4,R2        ; Modify the flags

        ITTE EQ          ; 3 conditioned instructions TRUE TRUE FALSE

        ADDEQ R4,R1      ; Instruction carried out if R4 = R2

        LSREQ R2,#2      ; Instruction carried out if R4 = R2

        SUBNE R4,R2      ; Instruction carried out if R4 ≠ R2

        LSR R4,#1        ; Instruction always carried out

        CMP R4,R2

        IT LT            ; => Assembly error

        ADDGE R4,R2      ; The code conditions are different
```

TBB, TBH	32	Relative jump TaBle (Byte or Half-word)
TBB<c> [<Rn>, <Rm>] TBH<c> [<Rn>, <Rm>, LSL #1]		$PC \leftarrow PC + Rn[Rm]$ $PC \leftarrow PC + Rn[shift(Rm)]$

Here, Rn contains the address of a table and Rm specifies the index in the table. The table contains the number of half-words that must be jumped to reach the cases to be handled. The table contains a piece of jump information relative to the position of the TBB or TBH instruction being used.

EXAMPLE 5.3.– *Example of TBB instruction use*

Table		
	DCB 0	; First case following TBB instruction
	DCB (case2-case1)/2	; Number of bytes to jump to reach case 2
	DCB (case3-case1)/2	; Number of bytes to jump to reach case 3
	...	
	ADR R4,Table	; Recovery of table address
	TBB [R4,R1]	; We assume the index is stored in R1
case 1	ADD R5, R8	; Case 1: addition
	B Finish	; Equivalent to break in C
case 2	SUB R5, R8	; Case 2: subtraction
	B Finish	; Equivalent to break in C
case 3	SBC R5, R8	; Case 3: inverted subtraction
	B Finish	; Equivalent to break in C
Finish	...	; Result of program

5.7. Load/store instructions

5.7.1. *Simple transfers*

Simple transfers consist of transferring a byte, a half-word (two bytes) or a word (four bytes) from memory to register (reading) or from register to memory (writing). Table 5.3 summarizes the mnemonics for the different transfers.

Data type	Read (load)	Write (store)
Word (32 bits)	LDR	STR
Signed half-word (16 bits)	LDRSH	STRH
Unsigned half-word (16 bits)	LDRH	STRH
Signed byte (8 bits)	LDRSB	STRB
Unsigned byte (8 bits)	LDRB	STRB

Table 5.3. *The mnemonics for different transfers*

This table shows that reading differentiates between signed and unsigned numbers. In fact, as all 32 bits of a register are systematically allocated during loading (reading), it is necessary for the processor to know how it should fill the 16 (LDRH or LDRSH) or 24 (LDRB or LDRSB) most significant bits of the register. The filling technique differs according to whether the number represents a signed quantity (when we say signed promotion, the sign bit is copied onto the most significant of the bits to be promoted) or an unsigned quantity (the unsigned promotion fills these bits with zeros). In writing, this problem does not appear as the eight, 16 or 32 bits of the register are copied as they are and occupy the same space in memory as they occupied in the register.

The detailed outline of mnemonics below is only given for the transfer of a word (*LDR* and *STR*). The different possible syntaxes for other transfers are, at the dimensions of the data transferred, strictly identical.

LDR	**LoaDing a Register with a memory word**
LDR<c> <Rt>, [<Rn> {, #±<imm>}]	$Rt \leftarrow M_{32} (Rn \pm imm)$
LDR<c> <Rt>, [<Rn>, #±<imm>] !	$Rn \leftarrow Rn + imm$ then $Rt \leftarrow M_{32}(Rn)$
LDR<c> <Rt>, [<Rn>], #±<imm>	$Rt \leftarrow M32 (Rn)$ then $Rn \leftarrow Rn + imm$
LDR<c> <Rt>, <label>	$Rt \leftarrow label$
LDR<c> <Rt>, [PC, #±<imm>]	$Rt \leftarrow M_{32} (Pc \pm imm)$
LDR<c> <Rt>, [<Rn>, <Rm> {LSL,#<shift>}]	$Rt \leftarrow M_{32} (Rn + shift(Rm))$
Register Rn can be the stack pointer (SP) or the instruction pointer PC.	

STR	Unloading a register to a memory word
STR<c> <Rt>, [<Rn> {,#±<imm>}]	M_{32} (Rn±imm)←Rt
STR<c> <Rt>, [<Rn>, #±<imm>] !	Rn←Rn+imm then M32(Rn)←Rt
STR<c> <Rt>, [<Rn>], #±<imm>	M_{32} (Rn)←Rt then Rn←Rn+imm
Register Rn can be the SP. *There is no such thing as relative writing to PC (it does not make sense).*	

5.7.2. *Multiple transfers*

With a single instruction, it is possible to order the simultaneous loading (or unloading, respectively) of several registers from (or, respectively, to) a base address. For this we must specify a list of registers in a brace, the address of the base being stored in a register (indirect access).

REMARK 5.2.– Braces in this syntax, unlike in the rest of the instructions, do not indicate an optional characteristic. It is the required syntax for the register list. Another, more unstoppable, trap is in the LDM, STM, LDMDB and STMDB instructions, where the Rn register behaves like a pointer but it is not necessary to put it in square brackets ([Rn]). With regard to the instruction this is not illogical (it is not possible to fill a register with the contents of several registers), but for the programmer this requires plenty of mental flexibility.

The register containing the base address cannot be part of the list of registers. It can, however, be the *SP*. This is quite useful when performing a context save/restore while handling an interrupt, for example. The *PC (R15)* register can be included in the list, which is not without consequence during loading as this is equivalent to carrying out a jump. It is therefore to be used with great caution.

LDM 16/32	Multiple loading from ascending addresses
LDM<c> <R$_k$>,{R$_i$-R$_j$}	R_k← M_{32}(Rn + 4 * (k − i)) with k = i...j
LDM<c> <R$_k$>!,{R$_i$-R$_j$}	R_k← M_{32}(Rn + 4 * (k − i)) with k = i...j then Rn← Rn + 4 * (j − i)
Rn points to the reading address. ***Beware***: *in this case the ! does not mean pre-displacement but modification of the register after the transfer and so post-incrementation. This instruction also uses the mnemonics LDMIA and LDMFD.*	

LDMDB	32	**Multiple loading from descending addresses**
LDMDB<c> <R_k>,{R_i-R_j}		$R_k \leftarrow M_{32}(\text{Rn-4*}(k-i+1))$ with $k=i...j$
LDMDB<c> <R_k>!,{R_i-R_j}		$R_k \leftarrow M_{32}(\text{Rn-4*}(k-i+1))$ with $k=i...j$ then Rn$\leftarrow$ Rn - 4 * $(j-i)$

*Departure Rn contains the first address following the storage zone. There is therefore a pointer decrementation before reading. This instruction is adapted for the management of the pre-decrementation stack. **Beware**: in this case the ! does not mean pre-displacement but modification of the register after the transfer and so post-decrementation. This instruction also uses the mnemonic LDMEA.*

LDRD	32	**Double loading**
LDRD<c> <Rt>, <Rt2>, <literal>		Rt$\leftarrow M_{32}(\text{literal})$ Rt2$\leftarrow M_{32}(\text{literal+4})$
LDRD<c> <Rt>, <Rt2>, [PC, #±<imm>]		Rt$\leftarrow M_{32}(\text{PC+imm})$ Rt2 $\leftarrow M_{32}(\text{PC+imm+4})$
LDRD<c> <Rt>,<Rt2>,[<Rn>{,#±<imm>}]		Rt$\leftarrow M_{32}(\text{Rn+imm})$ Rt2$\leftarrow M_{32}(\text{Rn+imm+4})$
LDRD<c> <Rt>,<Rt2>,[<Rn>,#±<imm>] !		Rn$\leftarrow$Rn+imm then Rt$\leftarrow M_{32}(\text{Rn+imm})$ and Rt2$\leftarrow M_{32}(\text{Rn+imm+4})$
LDRD<c> <Rt>,<Rt2>,[<Rn>],#±<imm>		Rt$\leftarrow M_{32}(\text{Rn+imm})$ Rt2$\leftarrow M_{32}(\text{Rn+imm+4})$ then Rn$\leftarrow$Rn+imm

Here literal is a label in the Literal Pool *zone so the first two forms are therefore equivalent.*

STM	16/32	**Multiple unloading to ascending addresses**
STM<c> <R_k>,{R_i-R_j}		$M_{32}(\text{Rn+4*}(k-i))\leftarrow R_k$ with $k=i...j$
STM<c> <R_k>!,{R_i-R_j}		$M_{32}(\text{Rn+4*}(k-i))\leftarrow R_k$ with $k=i...j$ then Rn$\leftarrow$ Rn + 4 * $(j-i)$

*Here Rn points to the address where the writing will take place. **Beware**: in this case the ! does not mean pre-displacementbut modification of the register after the transfer and sopost-incrementation. This instruction also usesthe mnemonics STMIA and STMEA.*

STMDB 32	**Multiple unloading to descending addresses**
STMDB<c> <R_k>,{R_i-R_j}	M_{32}(Rn-4*($k-i$+1))←R_k with $k=i...j$
STMDB<c> <R_k>!,{R_i-R_j}	M_{32}(Rn-4*($k-i$+1))←R_k with $k=i...j$ then Rn← Rn - 4 * ($j - i$)

*In this instruction, Rn points above the address where the writing will take place. **Beware**: in this case the ! does not mean pre-displacement but modification of the register after the transfer and so post-decrementation. This instruction also uses the mnemonic STMFD.*

STRD 32	**Double unloading**
STRD<c> <Rt>,<Rt2>,[<Rn>{,#±<imm>}]	M_{32} (Rn+imm)←Rt M_{32} (Rn+imm+4)←Rt2
STRD<c> <Rt>,<Rt2>,[<Rn>,#±<imm>] !	Rn←Rn+imm then M_{32}(Rn+imm)←Rt and M_{32}(Rn+imm+4)←Rt2
STRD<c> <Rt>,<Rt2>,[<Rn>],#±<imm>	M_{32} (Rn+imm)←Rt M_{32} (Rn+imm+4)←Rt2 then Rn←Rn+imm

5.7.3. *Access to the system stack*

It is in fact possible to achieve read/write access to the system stack (pre-decrementation evolution) using the instructions *LDMDB* and *STM*. There are two specific mnemonics (in the totality of assembly languages) for carrying out this type of transfer. It should, however, be noted that the code generated will often be identical.

POP 16/32	**Loading from the system stack**
POP<c> {R_i-R_j}	R_k ←M_{32}(SP+4*($k-i$))with $k=i...j$ then SP← SP + 4 * ($j - i$)

This is equivalent to LDM SP !, {R_i-R_j}.
It is possible to unstack PC but not LR.

PUSH	16/32	**Storing to the system stack**
PUSH<c> {R_i-R_j}		M_{32}(SP-4*(k−i+1))←R_k with k=i...j then SP← SP - 4 * (j − i)
This is equivalent to STM SP !, {R_i-R_j}. *It is possible to stack LR but not PC.*		

5.8. "System" instructions and others

Instructions described here as "system" instructions allow us to act on the state of the processor. The "others" include instructions using a hypothetical coprocessor or managing debugging sequences. In any case, they are only useful in a detailed approach to the functioning of the Cortex-M3 core and consequently are outside the scope of this book. A simple list is given here. The advanced user will find complete information in the reference manuals [ARM 06a, ARM 06c].

System...	
BKPT #<imm8>	Calls for a *Debug* exception
CPD,CPD2	Launches an instruction on a coprocessor
CLRX	Suppresses the exclusivity rights of the processor
CPS <effect>,<flags>	Changes the state of Cortex-M3 by modifying PRIMASK and FAULTMASK
DBG<c> #<option>	Launches a *Debug* or *Trace* request
DMB<c> #<option>	Setup of a memory access barrier
DSB<c> #<option>	Setup of a memory access barrier with synchronization
ISB<c> <opt>	Empties the processor pipeline
LDC, LDC2 ...	Read (memory of) a coprocessor register
LDRBT,LDRHT,LDRT	Write (unsigned) memory in unprivileged mode
LDRSBT,LDRSHT	Read (signed) memory in unprivileged mode
STRBT,STRHT,STRT	Write (unsigned) memory in unprivileged mode
STRSBT,STRSHT	Write (signed) memory in unprivileged mode
LDREX,LDREXB,LDREXH	Read (unsigned) memory in exclusive mode
STREX,STREXB,STREXH	Write (unsigned) memory in exclusive mode
MCR, MCR2	Write to a coprocessor register

MCRR, MCRR2	Write to a (64-bit) coprocessor register
MRC, MRC2	Read a coprocessor register
MRRC, MRRC2	Read a 64-bit coprocessor register
PLD, PLDW	Preload data
PLI	Preload instructions
SEV	Send a signal (situation in multiprocessor)
STC, STC2	Read (memory) of a coprocessor register
SVC (or SWI)	Generate a supervisor call
WFE	Wait for an event
WFI	Wait for an interrupt
YIELD	Send signal (multitask situation)

Chapter 6

Algorithmic and Data Structures

6.1. Flowchart versus algorithm

Assembly language uses labels and jumps, which can be conditional or not. This naturally leads to a geographic vision of a program, where we represent the route plan (route map) of the instructions in the form of a flowchart, with agreed symbols to represent the conditional diversions (switches), among others. Such use of flowcharts was abandoned long ago, however, in favor of writing structured algorithms for various reasons. Here are some of them:

– the design and maintenance of a flowchart is laborious;

– the debugging of programs is also laborious: if there is a problem in the execution of an instruction, it is not obvious which route in the flowchart we took to reach this point;

– it is very difficult to test just part of a program;

– it is also very difficult to extract part of a program from a flowchart in order to reuse it in a subsequent program.

We therefore prefer to encourage a tree analysis, known as modular analysis, in which every program is exclusively made up of a succession of cellular elements, generically called modules, each module itself being a series of sub-modules, etc. At the most basic level, we arrive at the idea of a structured language made up of instructions that, like the modules, only have one entry point and one exit point. In this way it is possible to obtain structured language when we program correctly.

In assembly language, we have at best transposed these concepts: the program can be written to different files (called "modules" in the jargon used elsewhere by assemblyists), which make up what is known as external modularity. Each file is made up of procedures, which themselves call subroutines, etc. This is known as internal modularity. Each module or procedure represents a piece of the program: it must be able to be tested separately, and to be reused later in another program. At the deepest level of this ideal tree structure, we find the instruction. In noting that each module only has one entry point and one exit point, the instruction must also only have one entrance and one exit. There is a catch with assembly language, however, since assembly language is not a structured language! Some instructions, such as conditional instructions, for example, have two exits. Despite this, we approach programming in assembly language in a structured manner: we get around the problem with so-called systematic programming. The lowest level modules are first described with a structured algorithm. Then, for each structured instruction in the algorithm, we systematically transcribe it into assembly language according to a model prepared in advance. Each structured instruction then corresponds to a block made up of lines of instructions in assembly language. This block has only one entry point (the first instruction) and one exit point. If there are labels in this block, we must consider them specific to this block, and inaccessible to other external blocks. The only label accessible to the outside world is the entry label, which is posted on the first instruction of the sealed block. In this chapter, we will show how each structured instruction can be transformed into a block of assembly language instructions. For each block of instructions presented, we will use the labels *Entry_Point* and *Exit_Point* to show the entry and exit points of the block. Structured instructions in algorithmic language use the following conventions:

- *cond* represents a Boolean condition;

- *not(cond)* is the logical opposite of *cond*;

- *treatment* is a sequence of instructions to be executed;

- *variable* is an integer datum.

It should be noted that, for the sake of readability of an assembly language program, it is strongly recommended that each block contains a maximum of about 10 lines. Treatment can then be made up of several simple instructions, or else calling procedures. We should note that the label names have been chosen to correspond as closely as possible to those that appear in the algorithms, but we should also be aware that these names or this method of choosing labels in a real program would be a very bad idea.

REMARK 6.1.– In this chapter we will present the different algorithmic structures, purposely omitting an instruction peculiar to the ARM assembler: IT (InTerrupt) (meaning the option to condition most arithmetic and logical instructions). This choice is motivated by the fact that the IT instruction can only condition a maximum of four instructions, so it is not a definitive response to the problem. What is more, it does not allow us to deal with structural problems, which is necessary in order to move towards a systematic method of programming. It is nevertheless true that using the IT instruction can be an effective response that is quick to put in place and efficient in terms of code size and so should not be completely forgotten.

6.2. Alternative structures

6.2.1. *Simple (or shortened) alternative*

The simple alternative decides whether or not to carry out the treatment, so it is not accompanied by an *else* clause:

```
If (cond)
        Then Treatment
End If
```

The block of instructions translating this algorithmic structure uses one of the four test instructions (see section 5.5) of which the only goal is to position the flags. The conditioned jumps that follow one of these tests then use the state of the flags to carry out the jumps (if appropriate). As it is most directly understandable in this context, the applied examples presented later will be based on the use of the *CMP* (CoMPare) instruction, immediately followed by a conditional jump.

To start with, let us take a generic version of the simple alternative (see Example 6.1).

Reading this reduced listing leads to the formulation of several comments:

– we use *not(cond)* rather than *cond*: this method is common to all assembly languages. The conditional jump only takes place if the complement of *cond* is true. Thus this instruction provides the possibility of preventing the treatment being carried out;

– the labels *Entry_Point* and *If* mark the same instruction, *CMP*;

– the label *Exit_Point* marks the first instruction of the next block.

In this example, the labels *If* and *Lab_Then* have an informative and didactic function only. This is a roundabout way to comment on your code. Only the label *Exit_Point* is essential, because it is referenced by a jump.

EXAMPLE 6.1.– *Generic version of the simple alternative*

```
Entry_Point

IF              CMP Val_One,Val_Two

                B** Exit_Point  ; ** correspond to non(cond)

Lab_Then        ...                   ; Instructions

                ...                   ;     for

                ...                   ;        the treatment

Exit_Point      ...
```

APPLIED EXAMPLE 6.1.– Take the absolute value of a signed (32-bit) integer contained in the R1 register:

```
If Integer < 0

        Then Integer ← -Integer

End If
```

Study of the condition: *cond* is "< signed", that is *LT*, so *not(cond)* is "≥ signed", or *GE* (Signed is Greater Than or Equal to). We can code this as follows:

EXAMPLE 6.2.– *Example of the simple alternative*

```
Entry_Point

                CMP R1,#0

                BGE Exit_Point     ; Comparison to 0

Lab_Then        NEG R1             ; R1←-R1

Exit_Point      ...
```

6.2.2. Complete alternative

The complete alternative introduces an Else clause into the simple form presented in Example 6.2:

```
If (cond)

        Then Treatment_Then

Else

        Then Treatment_Else

End If
```

This shows the case of exclusive treatment. To represent this algorithmic structure, we can use *not(cond)* just as well as we have seen for the simple alternative, *cond*.

As it is usually preferable for the readability of the code to use *not(cond)*, this is what we will do here. In effect, with this choice the treatment block *Treatment_Then* is placed before the *Treatment_Else* block, which makes reading alongside the algorithm easier.

EXAMPLE 6.3.– *Generic version of the complete alternative*

```
Entry_Point

            IF CMP Val_One,Val_Two

            B** Exit_Point          ; ** correspond to non(cond)
Lab_Then    ...                     ; Instructions

            ...                     ;    for

            ...                     ;       Treatment_Then

            B Exit_Point            ; Necessary to avoid else block
Lab_Else    ...                     ; Instructions

            ...                     ;    for

            ...                     ;       Treatment_Else
Exit_Point  ...
```

This assembly language block uses a conditional branch to provide the possibly of jumping *Treatment_Then* in order to reach *Treatment_Else*. Note the essential presence of the unconditional jump at the end of *Treatment_Then* so that the program does not carry out *Treatment_Else*!

APPLIED EXAMPLE 6.2.– We use a display procedure that takes the address of the message (i.e. the set of bytes corresponding to the ASCII codes of the characters), in register *R0*, to be displayed as an argument. It is therefore possible to create two messages that allow us to display whether an integer stored in R4 and coded on 16 bits is positive or strictly negative. The discrimination is then made by an If…Else structure:

If Integer < 0

        Then R0 ←@ negative message

Else

        Then R0 ←@ positive message

End If

Display(R0)

A possible encoding of this algorithm gives:

EXAMPLE 6.4.– *Example of complete alternative*

```
;*****************************************************************
; DATA SECTION
;*****************************************************************
      AREA MyDATA, DATA, ALIGN=0
;*****************************************************************
Message_Pos DCB "It is strictly positive ", 10,13,0
Message_Neg DCB "It is negative or null", 10,13,0


;*****************************************************************
; CODE SECTION
;*****************************************************************
      AREA MyCode, CODE, readonly, ALIGN=2
;*****************************************************************
            . . .
Entry_Point
Lab_If        SXHT R3,R4            ; 32-bit signed extend
              CMP R3,#0             ; Comparison at 0
              BGT,Lab_Else
Lab_Then      LDR R0,=Message_Neg   ; R0 ← @ Message_Neg
              B Exit_Point          ; Avoidance of the Else block
Lab_Else      LDR R0,=Message_Pos   ; R0 ← @ Message_Pos
Exit_Point    BL DispStr            ; Call to the display procedure
            . . .
```

Passing through register *R3*, the extention of the signed integer to be tested onto 32 bits could be avoided by using a 16-bit right shift or by testing (*TST* instruction) only the signed bit (weight 15) of the integer.

REMARK 6.2.– The preceding coding underlines the fact that work on a datum coded on a byte or half-word can quickly become tedious because the Arithemtic and Logic Unit (ALU) of Cortex-M3 only works on 32-bit words.

6.2.3. *Special case of the alternative*

Quite often we can reduce a complete alternative, which is more tiresome to program, to a simple alternative that is easier to re-read. This simplification relies on an *a priori* choice that is made on the alternative (for example, the Else case). We carry out this choice in advance and test (the simple alternative) whether it has been confirmed. If this is not the case, we carry out the dual alternative. This practice assumes that the two alternatives are mutually exclusive (which is normally the case in a complete alternative) and that the realization of one of the alternatives modifies neither the test nor the elements necessary for the execution of the blocks.

Let us return to the previous example. It can be transformed like this:

> Then R0 ←@ positive message
>
> If Integer < 0
>
>   Then R0 ←@ negative message
>
> End If
>
> Display(R0)

The coding is then modified like this:

EXAMPLE 6.5.– *The simplification of a complete alternative to a simple alternative*

```
                  ...
Entry_Point
                  LDR R0,=Message_Pos    ; R0 ← @ Message_Pos
Lab_If            SXHT R3,R4             ; 32-bit signed extend
                  CMP R3,#0              ; Comparison at 0
                  BGT,Exit_Point
Lab_Then          LDR R0,=Message_Neg    ; R0 ← @ Message_Neg
```

```
Exit_Point
              BL DispStr            ; Call to the display procedure
              ...
```

6.2.4. *Multiple choice*

Multiple choice corresponds to the algorithmic structure According To. Whether it is called case (as in *Ada*), switch (as in *C*), or even on...goto (as in *Basic*), it allows the user to program a treatment based on the value of an integer or listed variable. We will limit ourselves to integer values.

Switch Case (variable)

       value_0 :Treatment_0

       value_1 : Treatment _1

       value_2 : Treatment _2

       (...)

       Other value: Treatment _default

End Switch Case

The intuitive (and non-optimal) method of programming this structure in assembly language consists of a chain of If...Then structures. The algorithm becomes:

If variable = value_0

       Then treatment_0

       Else If variable = value_1

          Then treatment_1

          Else If variable = value_2

             Then treatment_2

(...etc.)

          Else default_treatment

For reasons of clarity and without losing the intended generality, in the assembly language implementation presented, each treatment will be subjected to a call to procedure. We will also limit ourselves to three selection values.

EXAMPLE 6.6.– *Switch case structure treated as a chain of If...Then structures*

```
Entry_Point    ...
               MOV R4,ref_variable
Lab_Switch     CMP R4,#value_0
               BNE See_One               ; cond = EQ, so non(cond) = NE
               BL treatment_0
               B Exit_Point              ; End of Treatment => exit !
See_One        CMP R4,#value_1
               BNE,See_Two
               BL treatment_1
               B Exit_Point              ; End of Treatment => exit !
See_Two        CMP R4,#value_2
               BNE,See_Default
               BL treatment_2
               B Exit_Point ;            End of Treatment => exit !
See_Default
               BL default_treatment
Exit_Point     ...
```

The unconditional jump *B Point_Exit* that ends each *Then* clause allows us to get out of the *Switch Case* structure: the equivalent instruction in *C* is *break*.

Such a sequence of identical structures is long and tedious to write if more than a few values have been included in the *Switch Case* structure. It is also inconvenient to modify if another case has to be added. What is more, the selection time for execution depends on the position of the value in the list.

A second method, which is more appropriate for assembly language, consists of using jump tables. A first version of this type of structure corresponds to the use of the *TBB* (Table Branch Byte) or *TBH* (Table Branch Halfword) instructions. An example of this type of use was given during the explanation of these instructions (see section 5.6). The use of *TBB* or *TBH* implies that the jump table is a relative jump table with regards to a reference address, and so can quickly become very limiting.

A slightly more generic version (i.e. directly transposable for another instruction set that does not have an equivalent to *TBB* or *TBH*) is presented below. This second version is based on an absolute jump table: the treatment address of the case is directly stored in the table. Beforehand, each treatment must be marked with a label, which is preferably encapsulated within a procedure. The address of each treatment procedure is then placed in a table (in *C*, there appears to be a table of function pointers). We use the value of the selection variable, the integer, as an index in this table. This means that the value 0 must cause the execution of *treatment_0*, 1 must cause the execution of *treatment_1*, etc. It is therefore sufficient to call the procedure indirectly, as shown Example 6.7, where we simply consider selection values from 0 to 6, and where only values 0, 2 and 6 are subject to a specific treatment:

EXAMPLE 6.7.– *Switch case structure using a jump table*

```
        AREA MyCode, CODE, readonly, ALIGN=2
;****************************************************************
Entry_Point
                LDR R9, = Jump Table    ; R9 pointer on Jump_table
                LDR R2,[R9,R6,LSL #2]
                BLX R2
Exit_Point    ...
;****************************************************************
; PROCEDURES OF TREATMENT
;****************************************************************
Treatment_0    PROC
                ...
                BX LR                   ; return
Treatment_0    ENDP
Treatment_2    PROC
                ...
                BX LR                   ; return
Treatment_2    ENDP
Treatment_6    PROC
                ...
                BX LR                   ; return
Treatment_6    ENDP

Treatment_Default PROC
```

```
            . . .
            BX LR                      ; Return to caller
Treatment_Default ENDP
;****************************************************************
; DATA SECTION
;****************************************************************
    AREA MyData, DATA, ALIGN=0, READONLY
;****************************************************************
Jump_Table    DCD Treatment_0, Treatment_Default        ; for 0 and 1
              DCD Treatment_2, Treatment_Default        ; for 2 and 3
              DCD Treatment_Default, Treatment_Default  ; for 4 and 5
              DCD Treatment_6                            ; for 6
;****************************************************************
```

In this example, we assume that register *R6* contains the (integer) selection value between 0 and 6, resulting from a previous test. The table is filled with elements that are the addresses of procedures (in each case, this is actually the address of the procedure's first instruction). The jump is effected by the *BLX* (Branch with Link and eXchange) instruction, where *R2* contains the address of the procedure to be reached. All that remains is to understand how this address, and thus the allocation statement *R2 : LDR R2,[R9,R6,LSL #2]*, is calculated. This involves reading by indirection and indexing: *R2 ← Jump_Table[R6 * 4]*.

The *Jump_Table* base address is stored beforehand in *R9*: this is indirection (use of brackets). The index is stored in *R6*, but as indirection works directly on the memory addresses and as each procedure address occupies 32 bits of memory the elements of the table each occupy four bytes. The index is therefore multiplied by four to take this into account. This multiplication by four is easily coded by a 2-bit left shift, which corresponds to the use of *LSL#2* as a supplementary operator applied to *R6*.

The adopted mechanism therefore uses **double indirection**: *R9* points to an element, which itself points to a procedure! The advantages of this solution are the simplicity of its structure and a constant selection time. It does, however, have two disadvantages: it is first necessary to obtain a selection value in the form of a natural integer; second, it is then necessary to ensure that the selection value belongs to the interval of the predicted values. This requires the inclusion of the *Switch Case* structure in a complete alternative:

> If Selection_Value >6 (unsigned)
>
>> Then default_treatment
>>
>> Else Switch Case (variable)…
>>
>> End Switch Case
>
> End If

The *Jump_Table* is placed in a data section where the access is restricted to reading (READONLY option). The structure presented here is strictly static and it is not intended that the procedure addresses change. It therefore seems cautious to ensure the durability of this data by blocking all access (even and above all accidental) for writing. A dynamic formulation of such a structure, where the jump table can change during the execution of the program, remains possible, in which case the READONLY option would be removed.

6.3. Iterative structures

Iterative structures, as opposed to selective structures, are blocks of instructions that are intended to be executed several times. The number of iterations is conditioned (this condition can be the number of iterations to be reached, as in the case of a *For* loop) and this number can be zero.

6.3.1. *The Repeat…Until loop*

The generic form of this structure is:

> Repeat
>
>> Treatment
>
> Until (cond)

In this structure, the evaluation of the condition follows a conditional jump carried out after the treatment, which gives the following general form:

EXAMPLE 6.8.– *Generic form of the Repeat..Until structure*

```
Entry_Point

Repeat          ...              ; Instructions

                ...              ;   of

                ...              ;      Treatment

                CMP Val_1,Val_2

                B** Repeat       ; ** correspond to non(cond)

Exit_Point      ...
```

Once again, the jump decision is established by *(not)cond*. We can overcome this, however, by expressing the algorithm as a *Repeat...While*. The jump condition then becomes the same as the text condition. What is important in identifying this structure is that the test is done at the end of the structure. Consequently, the treatment is carried out at least once.

APPLIED EXAMPLE 6.3.– The return of a memory zone made up of half-words (16 bits) to zero, where we know the start address and the end address. We will assume that there is at least one element in the table. The algorithm presented below uses the concept of a pointer and uses the *C* symbols of in explanation. Thus, the operator @ allows the recovery of the address and the operator *(Ptr)* allows us to see the contents of the address pointed by the pointer *Ptr*:

```
Ptr ← @Table

Ptr_end ← @End_Table

Repeat

        *(Ptr) ← 0

Ptr ← Ptr + 2

Until (Ptr ≥ Ptr_End)
```

In the following proposed code, we assume that the register *R0* corresponds to the pointer *Ptr*, and register R5 to *Ptr_End*:

EXAMPLE 6.9.– *A Repeat...Until structure*

```
;****************************************************************
; DATA SECTION
;****************************************************************
      AREA MyData, DATA, ALIGN=0
;****************************************************************
Table fill 24,0xff,2          ; Filling of 12 half-words
                              ;       initialized to 255
End_Table                     ; Simple label to
                              ;       mark the end of the Table
;****************************************************************
; CODE SECTION
;****************************************************************
      AREA MyCode, CODE, readonly, ALIGN=2
;****************************************************************
              LDR R0, =Table        ; Load of Ptr
              LDR R5, =End_Table     ; Load de Ptr_End
              MOV R2,#0              ; Local variable for cleaning
Entry_Point
Repeat        STRH R2,[R0]          ; Deletion of current
                                    ;       pointed value
              ADD R0,#2             ; Incrementation of pointer
              CMP R0,R5             ; Test of non(cond)
              BLT Repeat            ; Jump if Table_end not reached
Exit_Point    ...
;****************************************************************
```

The suggested code can be optimized. In effect a single indirection was used to carry out the deletion. It therefore assumes a "manual" incrementation of the pointer, yet the instruction set has a post-displaced addressing mode. The first two lines of the *Repeat...Until* structure can therefore be replaced by a single line that integrates the incrementation of the pointer: *STRH R2,[R0],#2*.

Let us take another example. This one involves changing the sign of the first 10 elements of a byte table. The number of loops is therefore fixed and known in advance.

Ptr ← @Table

Counter ← 10

Repeat

        (Ptr) ← -((Ptr))

        Ptr ← Ptr + 1

        Counter ← Counter - 1

Until (Counter ≤ 0)

A classic encoding in assembly language (we use *R11* for the counter and *R0* for *Ptr*) gives:

EXAMPLE 6.10.– *Second example of a Repeat...Until structure*

```
;*****************************************************************
; DATA SECTION
;*****************************************************************
      AREA MyData, DATA, ALIGN=0
;*****************************************************************
Table  DCB 12,0x23,-3,24    ; Reservation of 12 bytes
       DCB -56,0xAB,0,0     ;      initialized with various values
       DCB 1,2,5,9
       FILL 10,0XE4,1       ; Followed of 10 bytes
                            ;         initialized to 0XE4
;*****************************************************************
; CODE SECTION
;*****************************************************************
      AREA MyCode, CODE, readonly, ALIGN=2
            LDR R0, =Table             ; Load of Ptr
            MOV R11, #10               ; Initialization of counter
Entry_Point
Repeat      LDRB R2,[R0]    ; Recovering of the current pointed value
            NEG R2,R2       ; Sign inversion
            STRB R2,[R0],#1 ; Write back with post-displaced
            SUBS R11,#1     ; Decrementation of counter
                            ;         with Flag assignment
```

```
                BGT Repeat      ; Jump if less than 10 treatments
Exit_Point    ...
;*************************************************************
```

This encoding uses post-incrementation. An equivalent version would be to use indirection with indexing in reading **and** writing:

EXAMPLE 6.11.– *Modified version of Example 6.10*

```
        ...
        LDR R0, =Table          ; Load of Ptr
        MOV R11, #9             ; Initialization of counter
Entry_Point
Repeat LDRB R2,[R0,R11]         ; Recovering of the current pointed value
        NEG R2,R2               ; Sign inversion
        STRB R2,[R0,R11]        ; Write back with indexation
        SUBS R11,#1             ; Decrementation of counter
                                ;         with Flag assignment
        BGE Repeat              ; Jump if less than 10 treatments
Exit_Point    ...
```

In this second version, the order of reading/writing of the table is reversed: we recover the tenth element first. This implies that the counter must cover values 9 to 0 inclusive. The initialization of the counter and the jump condition are therefore modified in this sense (the conditioned jump passes from *BGT* to *BGE*).

6.3.2. *The While…Do loop*

This structure is rather similar to the previous one. The main difference lies in the fact that the test is performed before the treatment. There is therefore no longer the obligatory passage in the treatment block.

The generic form is:

While (cond) Do

      treatment

End While

It is possible to construct an *Until...Do* loop using *not(cond)*. In this case, by expressing the algorithm as *Until (cond)...Do* it is possible to construct assembly coding with the same assembly language test as that set out in the algorithm.

EXAMPLE 6.12.– *Generic form of the While...Do structure*

```
Entry_Point

Lab_While      CMP Val_1,Val_2

               B** Exit_Point  ; ** correspond to non(cond)

               ...             ; Instructions

               ...             ;    of

               ...             ; Treatment

               B Lab_While

Exit_Point     ...
```

The unconditional jump at the end of the treatment always leads to the evaluation of the comparison.

APPLIED EXAMPLE 6.4.– In Example 6.4, the programmer calls a *DispStr* procedure to display a message. If we look at the messages, they are composed of a set of ASCII characters and end with "10", "13" and "0".

"10" and "13" correspond to the characters *Line Feed* and *Carriage Return*. They allow us (on a classic alphanumerical terminal) to move the display cursor to the start of the next line. The "0" indicates the end of the string. We can therefore expect that the algorithm of this display procedure searches for this terminal character as follows:

```
While ((Current_Charac= *(Ptr)) ≠ NUL ) Do

        PostChar(Current_Charac)

        Ptr ← Ptr +1

End Until
```

A coding solution for this algorithm is given here:

EXAMPLE 6.13.– *A While...Do structure*

```
;*****************************************
;
;* Display Procedure of a String
;* Entry : Pointer on the String : R0
;* Exit : None
;* Use the DispChar Procedure
;*****************************************

DispStr        PROC
               PUSH {LR}
               PUSH {R1}


Lab_While      LDRB R1,[R0],#1 ; Recovering of the current pointed value
               CMP R1,#0
               BEQ End_Disp    ; Test of non(cond)
               BL DispChar     ; Call to the DispChar Procedure
               B Lab_While     ; Loop


End_Disp       POP {R1}
               POP {PC}


               ENDP
```

In this encoding, the *R1* register acts as a local variable for the storage of the current character. This recourse to a general register as soon as we want to carry out the smallest operation on a variable in the memory (here a simple comparison) is the cost of using Load/Store architecture. We will see that this register is saved on the system stack (*PUSH* on entry and *POP* on exit – the functioning of the stacks will be detailed in section 6.5.6), which allows the programmer who wants to use this routine to ignore what happens in it (he/she must still know where he/she has to specify the string address).

REMARK 6.3.– Systematic saving of registers altered by a procedure is a strategic choice. In effect, it allows us to secure our code to the extent that the "calling procedure" only has to respect the rules of a possible passage of arguments and does not have to envisage any safeguard of registers before the call. There is a cost, however, in terms of memory use and execution speed, since it requires a PUSH/POP series for implementation.

Another register is saved: the link register (*LR*). In fact, as this routine also calls a procedure (*BL Dispchar*) this register will be erased by the new call. It is therefore necessary to save it ourselves. This happens in the initial *PUSH*. On the other side there is no symmetrical equivalent, namely *POP LR*. Nor is there a *BX LR*. These two lines are replaced by *POP PC*, which allows us to carry out both the restoration and the return at the same time. We will return to this specific point in Chapter 9.

A second encoding is proposed below. For this version, two major modifications are introduced with the aim of optimizing the code and using the best points of the instruction set.

The test is reported at the end of the loop. In order for this to be allowed to be carried out at the start of the loop, an unconditional jump begins the structure. The advantage of this is that we can obtain encoding starting with a *cond* test rather than *not(cond)*. This results in a slight loss of readability, since the test is positioned after the structure even if it takes place before it.

The two stackings are compressed into a single instruction by *PUSH {R1,LR}*. Symmetrically the two unstackings are replaced by *POP{R1,PC}*. Be aware of the order in which you specify the list of registers!

EXAMPLE 6.14.– *Second version of the While...Do example*

```
DispStr      PROC
             PUSH {R1,LR}
             B Lab_Cond

Lab_While    BL DispChar    ; Call to the DispChar Procedure
Lab_Cond     LDRB R1,[R0],#1 ; Recovering of the current pointed value
             CMP R1,#0
             BNE Lab_While  ; Test of(cond) : jump if R1 ≠0

End_Disp     POP {R1,PC}
             ENDP
```

6.3.3. *The For... loop*

In algorithmics, we commonly use the *For* loop in the generic form:

For Var going from Val_0 to Val_1, increment k

      Treatment

End For

Such a structure can easily be reduced to a *While ...Do* structure:

$Var \leftarrow Val_0$

While $(Var \neq Val_1)$ Do

      Treatment

      $Var \leftarrow Var + k$

End Until

This form was used for Example 6.10.

REMARK 6.4.– Does the For loop exist? In algorithmics, certainly! In assembly language, this is less obvious because, here in any case, it is transformed into a While...Do loop. There are other processors (those of Intel or Freescale for example), however, that have an integrated instruction which decrements a register and jumps to a label if the decrementation does not give a zero result, allowing the direct coding of a For structure.

6.4. Compound conditions

The structures and examples we have dealt with up to now have always had single conditions. In practice, it is often necessary to switch to compound conditions such as, for example:

If ((Number > 0) AND (Cond_End = False)) Then…

We will note in passing that in this situation, the *IT* instruction (which we should remember corresponds to putting an instruction under a direct condition) is no longer sufficient.

It is impossible (and useless) to deal with all possible forms of combinations, but in mastering the technique for handling Boolean conditions made up of two terms or factors and by extrapolating to a larger number of terms, everything is possible and, finally – with a minimum amount of rigorousness – quite easy.

6.4.1. *Alternative with AND*

An AND combination corresponds to:

> If (cond_A AND cond_B)
>
>   Then Treatment
>
> End If

In assembly language, we separate the evaluation of *cond_A* from that of *cond_B*, and we link the decisions as follows:

> If (cond_A)
>
>   Then If (cond_B)
>
>   Then Treatment
>
>   End If
>
> End If

REMARK 6.5.– This comes back to what we call a progressive AND in C: if *cond_A* is false, the second condition is not evaluated. In a higher-level language, this can cause setbacks for the programmer, so in some languages such as Ada, Boolean evaluations are complete unless we use a compilation option or an *ad hoc* operator.

The following is the block of instructions corresponding to this structure:

EXAMPLE 6.15.– *Generic AND compound condition*

```
Entry_Point
Lab_If        CMP Var,Val_A      ; Evaluation of cond_A
              B** Exit_Point     ; ** correspond to non(cond_A)
Lab_Then_A    CMP Var,Val_B      ; Evaluation of cond_B
              B** Exit Point     ; ** correspond to non(cond_B)
```

```
Lab_Then_B    ...                    ; Instructions
              ...                    ;  of
              ...                    ;    Treatment
Exit_Point    ...
```

6.4.2. *Iteration with AND*

Let us look at the case of a *Repeat...Until* case using a compound Boolean condition.

```
Repeat
    Treatment
Until (cond_A AND cond_B)
```

The following is the framework of the corresponding block in assembly language:

EXAMPLE 6.16.– *Repeat...Until loop with an AND compound condition*

```
Entry_Point
Repeat                              ; Instructions
            ...                     ;    of
            ...                     ;       Treatment
            CMP Var,Val_A           ; Evaluation of cond_A
            B** Exit_Point          ; ** correspond to non(cond_A)
            CMP Var,Val_B           ; Evaluation of cond_B
            B** Exit_Point          ; ** correspond to non(cond_B)
            B Repeat                ; Loop on Repeat Label
Exit_Point ...
```

The code can be optimized by compressing the last two tests:

EXAMPLE 6.17.– *Modified version of the Repeat…Until loop with an AND compound condition*

```
        ...

        CMP Var,Val_A      ; Evaluation of cond_A

        B** Exit_Point     ; ** correspond to non(cond_A)

        CMP Var,Val_B      ; Evaluation of cond_B

        B** Repeat         ; ** correspond to cond_B

                           ;         ⇒ Loop on Repeat if cond_B
```

REMARK 6.6.– the exit condition of the loop can, in this case, be just as well expressed as While [not(cond_A) OR not(cond_B)].

6.4.3. *Alternative with OR*

Composition with a logical OR:

```
If (cond_A OR cond_B)
   Then Treatment
End If
```

can also be expressed as a sequence of evaluations:

```
If (cond_A)
   Then Treatment
Else If (cond_B)
   Then Treatment
End If
```

Direct and literal encoding of this algorithm is quite inefficient, since it would require the duplication of treatment instructions. A more adaptive translation into assembly language consists of using the evaluation of *cond_A* first, then that of *not(cond_B)*.

EXAMPLE 6.18.– *Generic OR compound condition*

```
Entry_Point
Lab_If          CMP Var,Val_A      ; Evaluation of cond_A
                B** Treat          ; ** Correspond to (cond_A)
Lab_Else        CMP Var,Val_B      ; Evaluation of cond_B
                B** Exit_Point     ; ** correspond to non(cond_B)
Treatment
                ...                ; Instructions
                ...                ;    of
                ...                ;       Treatment
Exit_Point
```

In this case, the second test is not systematically carried out. If *cond_A* is verified, *cond_B* is not evaluated.

REMARK 6.7.– We should note that with this composition it is direct and natural that we test cond_A and not its opposite. This effort does not last long, since not(cond_B) comes behind just as naturally.

6.4.4. *Iteration with OR*

As has been shown for composition with AND, let us see how an OR composition fits into a *Repeat...Until* loop:

```
Repeat

    Treatment

Until (cond_A OR cond_B)
```

As in the previous case, we use *cond_A* with *not(cond_B)*. The following is the framework of the corresponding block in assembly language:

EXAMPLE 6.19.– *Repeat...Until loop with an OR compound condition*

```
Entry_Point
Repeat          ...          ; Instructions
                ...          ;    of
                ...          ;       Treatment
        CMP Var,Val_A        ; Evaluation of cond_A
        B** Exit_Point       ; ** correspond to (cond_A)
        CMP Var,Val_B        ; Evaluation of cond_B
        B** Repeat           ; ** correspond to non(cond_B)
Exit_Point
```

REMARK 6.8.– Boolean algebra shows us that Until (cond_A OR cond_B) = While [(not(cond_A) AND not(cond_B)].

6.5. Data structure

The assembly language of a 32-bit processor allows us to easily exploit data on one, two or four bytes considered as components of elementary structures: records, tables, queues and stacks. Assembly language, unlike higher-level languages, does not use an assembly directive that allows us to directly declare or define one of these structures. It is therefore up to the programmer to construct them explicitly with the help of *SPACE* reservation directives or the reservation-initialization directives *FILL*, *DCB*, *DCW* and *DCD* (at least for that which concerns permanent data, because dynamic data created during the execution of a program pose other problems). If the data must be written or read on more than four bytes, the treatment of each data presents an additional challenge to the programmer (working in multiple precision).

6.5.1. *Table in one dimension*

Also called a vector, a table is made up of data with identical nature placed in consecutive memory positions. For simple data, byte, half-word or word, we can easily explore such a table by using indirect addressing modes. It is sufficient to assign the Rn register with the address of the table and to modify this pointing value before ([*Rn,#±<imm>*]!) or after access ([*Rn,#±<imm>*]!).

To directly access a datum in the table (direct access), it is also possible to use an index stored in an *Rm* auxiliary register (*{Rn, Rm, LSL #<shift>}*). The *Rm* index will contain the number of the element to be reached and the left shift by *LSL* allows us to automatically calculate the offset to be added to the base address to reach this element (*LSL#1* for 16-bit tables and *LSL#2* for 32-bit tables, …etc).

REMARK 6.9.– Assembly language gives the programmer total freedom regarding the method of placing elements in memory. The method presented above is arch-classic and simple, but the algorithm used can sometimes be more easily programmed if the data are arranged in the opposite order in memory (highest index element at the lowest address) or even if they are muddled up in a more subtle manner, for example, according to the sequence "first – last – second – second to last – etc"! Efficiency is the primary motivation when writing in assembly language – efficiency during execution but also during the re-reading of programs, so it is very useful to intelligently comment on these "exotic" solutions.

6.5.2. *Tables in multiple dimensions*

A table that has multiple dimensions, which we denote with the symbol `Tab`, must be arranged in memory in a linear form. Let us take the example of a two dimensional table, with Nb_Col columns and Nd_Row rows. It is possible for the elements of `Tab` to be arranged either row-by-row or column-by-column. It is usual (and this simplifies things when we think in terms of storage) to say that the index `Ind_Row` of the row is between 0 and `Nb_Row-1`, and that of the column `Ind_Col` is between 0 and `Ind_Col-1`. To reach the element `Tab (Ind_Row, Ind_Col)`, we first calculate what we call the linear index : `Relative_Place`. This index can then be used in indirect addressing with index, as in the case of the one-dimensional table. Here we have:

– Row-by-row arrangement:

```
Relative_Place = Ind_Row x Nb_Col + Ind_Col
```

– Column-by-column arrangement:

```
Relative_Place = Ind_Row + Ind_Col x Nb_Row
```

Let us illustrate this with the case of a matrix with three rows and four columns:

$a_{0,0}$	$a_{0,1}$	$a_{0,2}$	$a_{0,3}$
$a_{1,0}$	$a_{1,1}$	$a_{1,2}$	$a_{1,3}$
$a_{2,0}$	$a_{2,1}$	$a_{2,2}$	$a_{2,3}$

The row-by-row arrangement will be stored in order of increasing address as follows:

$a_{0,0}$	$a_{0,1}$	$a_{0,2}$	$a_{0,3}$	$a_{1,0}$	$a_{1,1}$	$a_{1,2}$	$a_{1,3}$	$a_{2,0}$	$a_{2,1}$	$a_{2,2}$	$a_{2,3}$

$\uparrow$ Base address

The column-by-column arrangement will also be stored in order of increasing address, as follows:

$a_{0,0}$	$a_{1,0}$	$a_{2,0}$	$a_{0,1}$	$a_{1,1}$	$a_{2,1}$	$a_{0,2}$	$a_{1,2}$	$a_{2,2}$	$a_{0,3}$	$a_{1,3}$	$a_{2,3}$

$\uparrow$ Base address

6.5.3. *Registration*

We use the term registration or record (structure in *C* and record in *Ada*) for a set of consecutive data-fields united under a common symbolic name and arranged starting from a certain address. In general, these data are of different types, as opposed to tables, which are exclusively composed of data of the same type. The programmer places various fields in consecutive memory positions. The first byte or the first word of these fields is easily reached using indirect addressing with offset *[Rn+#imm8]*, where the *Rn* register points to the start of the registration, i.e. it contains the lowest address, and where *imm8* is positive, calculated in bytes. The first byte of the first field corresponds to zero offset. If we consider a registration with a variant part (typically a set of characters), we must reserve the memory space necessary for the largest variant. It is therefore interesting that the variant field is the last in the registration.

6.5.4. *Non-dimensional table, character string*

The size of a table cannot be known during the writing of a program or changed during execution. It is therefore more convenient to be able to create a dynamic memory allocation: the table is created during execution and the place that it occupies in memory is reserved (allocated) at that moment. This technique is directly possible if we use an operating system capable of allocating a given amount of memory.

In a more restricted software environment, where the programmer is the only master on board and must manage everything him- or herself, this becomes more difficult but not impossible. A common technique for doing this consists of temporarily using space (the time of the execution of the procedure) in the system stack; this storage zone will be lost when the program returns to procedure.

Outside the case of dynamic allocation, the variables are said to be static: they call a permanent table, the reservation is made in advance (*SPACE, FILL,* etc.) and the size of the memory space reserved is fixed. We must therefore reserve a place in memory that will allow us to receive the largest table we could possibly expect.

A second problem appears here. Since the table is of variable size, what size is it at the moment we are interested in? There are two methods of showing the size of a table:

– in the first, we create a structure where the first field contains the current size of the table;

– the second is the table itself.

In the second method, we mark the end of the table with an element that has an agreed special value. For example, it is quite usual for the NULL character (value = 0, not to be confused with the character '0', which has the value 0x30) to end a character string.

REMARK 6.10.– we must remember to reserve a memory place for the marker element at the end of the table, so for n elements using a table we need space for n+1 elements.

6.5.5. *Queue*

A queue is a FIFO (First In, First Out) data structure. The elements in the queue, which are generally all of the same type, are placed in contiguous positions in the memory. To manage the queue, we use the two registers, *Rt* and *Rq*, where *Rt* points to the head – the first element in the queue – and *Rq* to the free position that follows the last element of the queue. Removals are made at the head of the queue and additions at the end. For elements on 8, 16 or 32 bits, we use the post-displaced addressing mode to both add (*{Rq],±#<imm>*) and remove (*[Rt],±#<imm>*) elements.

The disadvantage of such a queue is that it only grows toward the increasing addresses as it is used. This means that we frequently produce a circular queue by limiting the maximum address that can be reached. Trying to go beyond this involves the return of the current address to the lowest expected value. The position of the queue then fluctuates between these two extreme addresses during execution.

When we add an element: if the queue pointer reaches the head pointer, the queue is full and cannot accept any further additions. If during a removal the head pointer reaches the queue pointer, the queue is empty and no further removals are possible (see Figure 6.1).

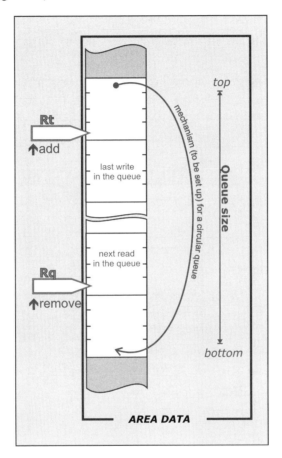

Figure 6.1. *A 32-bit queue that grows by increasing the addresses*

6.5.6. *Stack*

A stack is a LIFO (Last In, First Out) structure. The data are arranged consecutively in the memory during stacking. They are unstacked in the inverse order to their order of stacking: the last placed will be the first removed. A single *Rp* pointer is sufficient for managing a stack. We distinguish between two stack management modes:

– the direction of stack increase:

- ascending: successive writing is done to increasing addresses,

- descending: successive writing is done to decreasing addresses;

– management of stack pointer evolution:

- before writing and after reading: the stack pointer points to the last element written,

- before writing and after reading: the stack pointer points to the next free element.

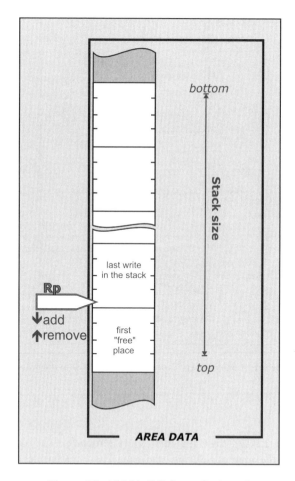

Figure 6.2. *A 32-bit (full descending) stack*

In the Cortex-M3 architecture, a LIFO stack mechanism exists in the hardware. It is managed by the stack pointer (*SP*, see section 2.2.2). This stack, called the system stack, is by default descending and with pre-decrementation in writing (also known as a *Full-Descending Stack*), see Figure 6.2.

Be careful not to unalign a stack intended to receive words (or half-words, respectively). The address contained in the register must be doubly (respectively singly) even, i.e. ending with two (respectively, one) zero! This is the reason that it is not recommended that you construct a mixed stack where you stack bytes, half-words and words indiscriminately.

Queues and stacks of which the elements are not bytes nor half-words nor words are the most delicate to manage. It is necessary to calculate analog shifts similar to those we have seen for tables. An often more advantageous technique consists of adding a level of indirection by establishing stacks or queues consisting of the addresses (references) of elements. The position and size of the elements are then of no real importance.

Chapter 7

Internal Modularity

The concept of a procedure, a sequence of instructions able to be called as a subroutine, has been presented in section 3.3.5. In this chapter, we will look at how to use this elementary syntactic construction to write correct and easy to use subroutines, by applying the principles of modular programming. We will see how to implement the passing of arguments to a subroutine and how to create local variables.

7.1. Detailing the concept of procedure

7.1.1. *Simple call*

A procedure is a set of instructions designed to provide a particular service, usually ending with the instruction *BX LR*. The procedure, which may be called by a *BL* (Branch and Link) instruction, is placed in the calling procedure. This instruction saves the return address (which we will denote `@ret` from now on) by using the link register (*LR*) to store the value of the instruction pointer (also called the *Program Counter*, *PC*) which contains the address of the instruction following the branch, then jumps to the first instruction of the procedure being called. At the end of the procedure's execution, the *BX LR* instruction restores the original *PC* value by loading the contents of the *LR* and execution resumes at the address following the *BL*. Example 7.1 illustrates this principle of a simple call to a procedure.

7.1.2. *Nested calls*

During a call, the return address is stored in a register. If the called procedure itself makes a call to a procedure, the call mechanism will automatically erase the current contents of the *LR* in order to be able to store the new return address. If nothing else is done, the return address of the first call level will be definitively lost and the procedure no longer has any way of returning to where it came from.

This problem is quite typical in ARM assembly language. Indeed, the vast majority of designers have directly integrated this possibility of nested calls into their choice of architecture. Thus the return address, rather than being stored in a register, is placed onto the system stack in accordance with its last in, first out (LIFO) evolution. During the return, if the system stack has been correctly managed during the procedure, the programmer will be able to recover the return address that is pointed at by the stack pointer (SP). Successive nesting of calls to procedures consequently leads to successive stacking on the system stack.

This being understood, it is sufficient to do the same thing manually in our procedures. Indeed, as in Example 6.13, by stacking (PUSH) the register LR from the entry in the procedure, the programmer causes the value of *LR* to be saved. At the moment of return, we recover this address by reading the stack (*POP*) and can then carry out the return of the procedure by using the *BX LR* instruction.

With this hardware architecture option, ARM provides the possibility of calling a procedure without using a read/write cycle on the system stack. This presupposes the absence of nested calls but allows time-saving in the case of a simple call.

EXAMPLE 7.1.– *Simple call to a procedure*

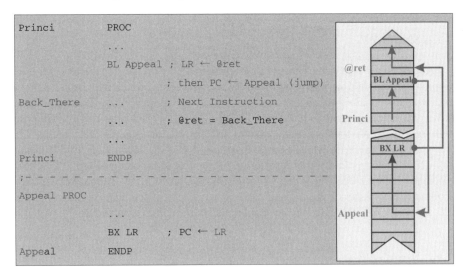

7.1.3. "Red wire" example

In this chapter, we will rely on a simple but sufficient example: a procedure whose role is to extract a maximum of two unsigned 32-bit integers. In all variations of the solutions we put forward for this example, the data used will be two variables stored at addresses named *ValOne* and *ValTwo*. The results are placed at the address *Maxi*.

Here is a first version of the procedure, titled *MaxVer1*. It directly accesses the data that it needs.

This version of encoding the proposed problem is deliberately "greedy" in terms of register use; a more economical solution could just use two registers. Would this gain anything in terms of processing time or code size? In terms of code size, no. In terms of processing time, saving of the registers is dependent on the number of registers put into the list (approximately two clock cycles per register for each *PUSH* and each *POP*. A gain in time can then be expected if we minimize the number of registers used (and so the number of registers to be saved) when applying a more economical solution.

EXAMPLE 7.2.– *Research into the maximum – complete initial version*

```
;******************************************************
; DATA SECTION
;******************************************************
       AREA MyData, DATA, ALIGN=2
;- - - - - - - - - - - - - - - - - - - - - - - - - -
ValOne   DCD 345
ValTwo   DCD 0xABF
Maxi     SPACE 4
;******************************************************
; CODE SECTION
;******************************************************
       AREA MyCode, CODE, readonly, ALIGN=2
;- - - - - - - - - - - - - - - - - - - - - - - - - -
; Main Procedure
;- - - - - - - - - - - - - - - - - - - - - - - - - -
main   PROC
       BL MaxVer1          ; Call to the procedure
       ENDP
```

```
;- - - - - - - - - - - - - - - - - - - - - - - - - - - - - - - - - - - - -
; Procedure that researches the maximum
; Arguments passed : none
; Global variables : ValOne, ValTwo, Maxi
; Used registers : R0, R1, R2, R4
;- - - - - - - - - - - - - - - - - - - - - - - - - - - - - - - - - -
MaxVer1        PROC
               PUSH {R0-R4}          ; Save the modified registers
               LDR R0,=ValOne        ; Load of the
               LDR R1,[R0]           ; first value
               LDR R3,=ValTwo        ; Load of the
               LDR R2,[R3]           ;     second value
               CMP R1,R2
               BHS Bon               ; If ValOne < ValTwo ...
Change         MOV R1,R2             ;    ... then exchange
good           LDR R4,= Maxi         ; Storage at Maxi
               STR R1,[R4]           ; of the result contained in R1
               POP {R0-R4}           ; Restore saved registers
               BX LR                 ; Return
Infinity       B Infinity            ; End of the program
               ENDP
```

REMARK 7.1.– In the examples presented, the registers used are systematically saved at the start of the procedure and restored at the end of it. This practice, as we have already mentioned (see section 6.3.2) allows the use of these procedures without asking too many questions. Put in a library, they can easily be reused without fear of side effects, i.e. changing the work environment of the processor by executing the procedure.

There are two exceptions to this rule:

– The first exception, as we will see later, concerns the registers used for passing arguments. In this case, the user must manage the contents of the registers in order to use the procedure, *thus saving them* becomes useless or even counter-productive.

– The second exception is an imperative need to get the memory space or central processing unit (CPU) time for the procedure.

In this case, everything is fine, but we should bear in mind that a program that crashes also loses a lot of time!

7.2. Procedure arguments

7.2.1. *Usefulness of arguments*

From the point of view of the calling program, the *MaxVer1* procedure changes the value of the result at the *Maxi* address by using the values recorded in *ValOne* and *ValTwo*. Written like this, such a procedure is hardly satisfying because it is necessary to give it data with specific names, which makes it impossible to reuse the procedure in another program, unless we always use the same names for the data.

Also, in modular programming, it is recommended that we avoid directly using global variables. This is made possible by the use of explicit call arguments. The subroutine then becomes easily reusable if it follows the conventional rules for passing arguments.

7.2.2. *Arguments by value and by reference*

Each argument can be passed by value or reference. If it is passed by value, a copy of the data is provided to the called by the calling procedure, so that its potential modification by the latter does not affect the original: the modification remains local to the subroutine called. When an argument is passed by reference, we provide the address to the subroutine that, by indirection, could possibly change the value of the data at that address.

No assembly language has instructions to call a subroutine incorporating the concept of argument, and the *BL* instruction for Cortex-M3 is no exception; it therefore raises the question of by which mechanisms it is possible to provide a procedure with the values or the relative addresses of the arguments. Essentially, there are two techniques, but both can be reduced to the same basic idea: arguments are positioned according to an agreed order in a predetermined region of the memory.

7.2.3. *Passing arguments by general registers*

General registers provide an initial easy, quick and effective method of passing arguments. The values of arguments or their addresses (references) are placed in the agreed registers and the procedure can be used immediately.

7.2.3.1. *Passing arguments by value*

In our example, we have three arguments to consider: the two pieces of data at entry, and the result at exit. Here is a first modification of the example (*MaxVer2*) where the two entry arguments are passed by value and the value of the result is returned. In the presentation of these examples, only the modified parts are rewritten; the declarations of sections, reservations, etc., are completely identical.

EXAMPLE 7.3.– *Research into the maximum: passing by register and by value*

```
                    . . .
;- - - - - - - - - - - - - - - - - - - - - - - - - - - - - - -
main    PROC
                LDR R0,=ValOne          ; Load of the
                LDR R1,[R0]             ;          first value
                LDR R3,=ValTwo          ; Load of the
                LDR R2,[R3]             ;          second value
                BL MaxVer2              ; Call to the procedure
                LDR R4,= Maxi           ; Writing of the result …
                STR R1,[R4]             ;          … contained in R1
Infinity        B Infinity              ; End of the program
                ENDP
;- - - - - - - - - - - - - - - - - - - - - - - - - - - - - - -
MaxVer2         PROC
                CMP R1,R2
                BHS Good                ; If ValOne < ValTwo ...
ExChange        MOV R1,R2               ;     ... ValTwo becomes the max
Good            BX LR                   ; Return
                ENDP
```

In this version, there is no *PUSH/POP* at all. In fact, the procedure only uses the registers for passing arguments, so saving them is useless.

Notice in this example the benefits of passing arguments: the (*MaxVer2*) procedure becomes able to carry out the maximum search for any pair of 32-bit integers, provided that they are placed in registers *R1* and *R2*. We could isolate the (*MaxVer2*) procedure in another module: the scope of data stored at addresses *VarOne* and *VarTwo* would then be limited to the calling program, which would correspond to reinforcement of the localization of these resources. This means that the data referred to by *VarOne*, *VarTwo* and *Maxi* belong only to the calling procedure, whereas in the previous example, they were shared by the caller and the called. If we analyze this example, we can see that the procedure provides the calling program with the value of the result via register *R1*. This procedure behaves like a function in a higher-level language, such as *ANSI C*, for which the prototyping would be:

> long int Max Ver2 (long int Arg1, long int Arg2);

and the use, with the three previously declared long integers would be:

> Maxi = MaxVer2 (VarOne, VarTwo);

Indeed, the assignment of the value of the result is carried out by the calling program, exactly as in the assembly language program.

Compilers generally use passing by register because it is simpler and more direct (and so quicker).

REMARK 7.2.– When we want to call a routine written in assembly language from a program developed in C, it is necessary to know the conventions of the passing of arguments that the compiler uses. For example, the ARM RealView compiler uses registers R0 to R3 to pass up to four entry arguments. The return is systematically carried out by register R0 (supplemented with R1 in the case of the return of a *double* coded on 8 bytes). If the passing of arguments by register is no longer possible, for example if there are more than four entry arguments, the compiler completes the process using passing by system stack.

7.2.3.2. *Passing arguments by reference*

Let us look at another possibility: this time the three arguments are provided by reference. By indirection, the (MaxVer3) procedure stores the results in its memory allocation.

EXAMPLE 7.4.– *Research into the maximum: passing by register and by reference*

```
        . . .
;- - - - - - - - - - - - - - - - - - - - - - - - - - - - - - -
main    PROC
        LDR R0,=ValOne    ; Passing of the @ of the first argument
        LDR R3,=ValTwo    ; Passing of the @ of the second argument
        LDR R4,= Maxi     ; Passing of the @ of the exit argument
        BL MaxVer3        ; Call to the procedure
Infinity B Infinity       ; End of the program
```

```
            ENDP
;- - - - - - - - - - - - - - - - - - - - - - - - - - - - - - -
MaxVer3     PROC
            PUSH {R1-R2}     ; Save the modified registers
            LDR R1,[R0]      ; Read the first argument
            LDR R2,[R3]      ; Read second argument
            CMP R1,R2
            BHS Good         ; If ValOne < ValTwo ...
ExChange    MOV R1,R2        ;       ... ValTwo becomes the max
Good        STR R1,[R4]      ; Store the result contained in R1
            POP {R1-R2}      ; Restore the saved registers
            BX LR            ; Return
            ENDP
```

It should be noted that the exit argument is passed on entry. This paradox is explained by the fact that we charge the procedure by storing the result. It is therefore necessary to provide this address (at entry). It is quite common for an argument passed by reference to be used at both entry and exit. The argument can take the received value at entry and assign a new value in return.

The analogy in C would give the prototyping:

Void MaxVer3 (long int *Arg2, long int *Arg3);

and the usage as:

MaxVer3 (&VarOne, &VarTwo, &Maxi);

7.2.4. Passing arguments by a stack

The number of registers being limited, new arguments risk erasing previous ones as calls for nested procedures. When we return to the calling procedure, there is the risk that this procedure will no longer hold all or part of its call arguments. It is therefore necessary to use the system stack to make the necessary saves. Starting from this statement, it becomes natural to directly use a LIFO (system stack or heap) structure to store the different component arguments of the procedure to be executed.

REMARK 7.3.– If the programmer is drawn to define a subroutine requiring more than 10 arguments (so there are more than 10 registers for passing arguments using just the by-register technique), it would be quite reasonable for him or her to consider restructuring the program or the data in order to develop a new organization based on simpler block-functions.

The problem really arises during nested calls (recursion, for example) where it is necessary to save the succession of passing arguments to descend through the different call levels. The problem of the loss of these arguments can be settled if we consider reserving a place in memory where the arguments could be placed instead of putting them in the registers.

The final idea is therefore to arrange the arguments directly in a stack: no more size problems (provided that we have correctly sized our stack, i.e. we have reserved enough memory space for its functioning) nor troubles with saving because the stack, naturally, grows as we push arguments.

The arguments of a procedure thus managed through a stack (i.e. placed on the stack before the call, used in the procedure, and then deleted upon return to the calling function) belong to the dynamic data category. This means that they are created and destroyed on demand during execution. Generally such data are made in a free memory zone, which is named the heap or user stack. Here, we arrange part of this heap into the form of a LIFO structure managed by a general register, *Rn*.

Three major steps therefore punctuate the evolution of this heap when it deals with passing arguments:

– creation: the calling program stacks the arguments before calling the procedure;

– use: access to arguments is carried out with the help of the indirect indexed addressing mode *[Rn + #offset]*;

– disappearance: this means removing the arguments when they are no longer of use. There are two options: either the calling procedure removes them, or the called procedure unstacks them. The following sections demonstrate the two options.

REMARK 7.4.– Just as the technique used for carrying the passing of arguments must be part of the documentation provided to use a procedure, so the creator of a procedure using the stack must also inform the future user of who should clear the stack of dumped arguments before the call. *A priori* this choice has no particular consequence, but it absolutely must be respected. Indeed, a stack drift cannot be seen on a unitary test but in the case of multiple calls this drift could lead to stack overflow, which can be catastrophic.

In the following examples, the heap corresponds to a pre-decrementation stack, but we could have chosen a post-incrementation stack – it makes no difference. We take *R11* to be the pointer register on the argument stack, and we assume that it has been suitably initialized to point to the initially empty stack. Example 7.5 shows how such a reservation can be made. In this example, the SP is initialized twice in order to show the two different, but equivalent, syntaxes. A single initialization is sufficient.

EXAMPLE 7.5.– *Reservation and initialization of a user stack*

```
Size_Stack      EQU 128
;- - - - - - - - - - - - - - - - - - - - - - - - - - - - - - -
        AREA MyData, DATA, ALIGN=2
;- - - - - - - - - - - - - - - - - - - - - - - - - - - - - - -
User_Stack      SPACE 4*size_Stack   ; Memory space reservation
Top_Stack                       ;            for the stack
;- - - - - - - - - - - - - - - - - - - - - - - - - - - - - - -
        AREA MyCode, CODE, readonly, ALIGN=2
;- - - - - - - - - - - - - - - - - - - - - - - - - - - - - - -

            . . .
            LDR R11, = Top_Pile     ; Direct initialization
            LDR R11, = User_Stack + Size_Stack * 4
                                    ; Equivalent syntax
            . . .
```

7.2.4.1. *Passing arguments by value: the caller unstacks*

In this fourth version, all arguments are passed by value, even return arguments. For this, a *hole* is made in the stack, meaning that the value 0 is stored before the call without this value being a utility in the entry of the procedure. The only aim of this storage is to reserve the necessary space to pass the return result, this zone being modified at the end of the procedure.

By convention in this version, the caller is in charge of clearing the stack. This corresponds to an incrementation of 12 bytes (three arguments of 4 bytes each) of the SP just before the return to the caller.

We should note that there is not, strictly speaking, deletion of the memory but simple freeing up of memory in raising the pointer. Thus, during the following use the values still present in the memory, cases will only at that moment be destroyed by overwriting.

EXAMPLE 7.6.– *Research into the maximum: passing by user stack and by value*

```
        ...
;- - - - - - - - - - - - - - - - - - - - - - - - - - - - - - - -
main    PROC                    ①

        LDR R0,=ValOne

        LDR R1,[R0]

        STR R1,[R11,#-4] !      ②      ; Stacking of argument 1

        LDR R0,=ValTwo

        LDR R2,[R0]

        STR R2,[R11,#-4] !      ③      ; Stacking of argument 1

        MOV R1,#0

        STR R1,[R11,#-4] !      ④      ; Hole for the return argument

        BL MaxVer4                     ; Call

        LDR R4,= Maxi                  ; Loading of Maxi address

        LDR R1,[R11]                   ; Loading of the result

        STR R1,[R4]                    ; Storage of the result

        ADD R11,#12             ⑥      ; Cleaning of the stack
Infinity B Infinity                    ; End of the program

        ENDP


MaxVer4 PROC

        PUSH {R1-R2}                   ; Save modified registers

        LDR R1,[R11, #8]        ⑤      ; Loading of the 1st argument

        LDR R2,[R11, #4]               ; Loading of the 2nd argument

        CMP R1,R2

        BHS Good                       ; If ValOne < ValTwo ...
ExChange MOV R1,R2                     ; ... ValTwo becomes the max
```

```
Good   STR R1,[R11]                ⑤         ; Storage of the result

       POP {R1-R2}                            ; Restore saved registers

       BX  LR                                 ; Return

       ENDP
```

In this listing, the circled numbers that appear have nothing to do with the syntax of the assembler. These are just markers to be compared with those shown in Figure 7.1. They indicate how the user SP evolves during the execution of the program. We can equate them with breakpoints that freeze the state of the processor at a given moment to observe the evolutions.

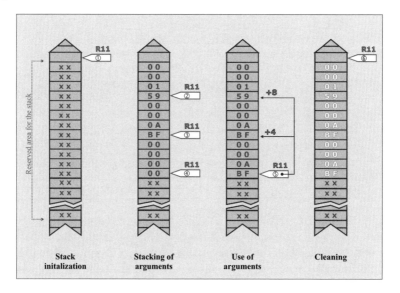

Figure 7.1. *Arguments passed by values on a user stack*

Note that the stack is subject to pre-decrementation, so we assume that it grows towards the bottom of the memory, i.e. that the current address of the stack decreases in the course of stacking. At each moment the pointer *R11* points to the address where the last writing was carried out.

In this program, the pair of instructions *MOV R1,#0* and *LDR R1,[R11,#-4]!* can be replaced by a simple *SUB R11 #-4*. There is good equivalence in global function, except that the value of the result is initially undetermined (it is not initialized by value 0), which in our case has absolutely no consequence. A final, less orthodox (but more optimal in terms of processing time) option would be to stack just two arguments at the call. The called program would then have to stack the third, once the calculations are made, in overwriting one of the two entry arguments.

7.2.4.2. *Passing arguments by reference: the called unstacks*

Here is another version where the three arguments are this time passed by reference, always by the stack. In this version it is the responsibility of the called to unstack. This version is a little harder to read, because it uses double indirections, post- and pre-offsets and multiple readings. Let us look at all of this in detail.

The calling program stores the three addresses corresponding to the three arguments of the procedure on the user stack. Compared to the previous example, little changes: there are always pre-decrementations of pointer *R11*. What happens in the procedure is a little more complex. The procedure first saves the five registers (*R1* to *R5*) used by the sequence. There is then a multiple reading (*LDM R11!,R3-R5*), which means:

> R3 ← [R11] so the address of Maxi
>
> R4 ← [R11+4] so the address of ValTwo
>
> R5 ← [R11+8] so the address of ValOne
>
> R11 ← R11+ 12 after displacement of the pointer

This is a four-in-one: there are operations in a single line of instructions. Do not be deceived, though – the execution requires four clock cycles because it requires four writings to memory. This is why the *Program Status Register x* (*xPSR*) uses *IC* Interruptible-Continuable)/*IT* (If Then) bits (see Figure 2.4) to keep track of the number of writings that have been completed. In the case of interruption, Cortex-M3 can complete the writing cycle upon return.

REMARK 7.5.– We have already noted the double oddity of the instruction set (see section 5.7.2). R11 acts like a pointer but does not need brackets and an exclamation point signifying, in this case, a post-displacement (and not a pre-displacement, as for a classic LDR). This can trip you up!

The reading of *ValOne* and *ValTwo* values and the writing of the result in *Maxi* is achieved by double pointing. As shown in Figure 7.2, *R11* is the first pointer that allows the initialization of the auxiliary pointers *R4* and *R5* to assign, with a second pointing, *R1* and *R2* on entry. It also allows the initialization of auxiliary pointer *R3* in order to write the result contained in *R1*. We would like to be able to use this double pointing in a general syntax:

```
LDR R1,[[R11]]              ; Horror!!!!
```

but this syntax does not exist. This is quite understandable because it signifies two different but simultaneous activations of the memory access bus.

EXAMPLE 7.7.–

```
        ...
;- - - - - - - - - - - - - - - - - - - - - - - - - - - - - - -
main    PROC
        LDR R0,=ValOne          ①
        STR R0,[R11,#-4]!       ②    ; Stacking @ of argument 1
        LDR R0,=ValTwo
        STR R0,[R11,#-4]!       ③    ; Stacking @ of argument 2
        LDR R0,= Maxi
        STR R0,[R11,#-4]!       ④    ; Stacking @ of the return argument
        BL MaxVer5                   ; Call
Infinity B Infinity                  ; End of the program
        ENDP
;- - - - - - - - - - - - - - - - - - - - - - - - - - - - - - -
MaxVer5 PROC                    ⑤    ; Save the modified registers
        PUSH {R1-R5}                 ; Save the modified registers
        LMD R11 !,{R3-R5}       ⑥    ; Multiple reading of the 3 @ arg.
                                     ;    and post incrementation
                                     ;   =>cleaning at the same time
        LDR R1,[R5]                  ; Loading of the 1st argument
        LDR R2,[R4]                  ; Loading of the 2nd argument
        CMP R1,R2
        BHS Good                     ; If ValOne < ValTwo ...
ExChange
        MOV R1,R2                    ; ... ValTwo becomes the max
Good    STR R1,[R3]                  ; Storage of the result
        POP {R1-R5}                  ; Restore saved registers
        BX LR                        ; Return
        ENDP
```

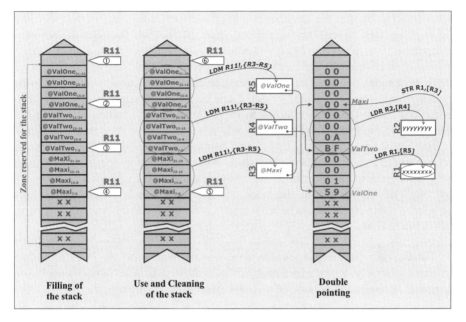

Figure 7.2. *Arguments passed by reference on a user stack*

7.2.5. Passing arguments by the system stack

This is the final variant that we will present (Example 7.8 and Figure 7.3) to illustrate the passing of arguments. Rather than passing arguments by a stack managed by a general register, we pass arguments by stacking them in the system stack. This is managed by the system *SP*. This is regularly used by compilers and implies that the system stack must be of sufficient size.

We must recognize that, in addition to the problem of maximum stack size, use of the system stack is quite delicate, even if the case of the ARM assembler is not the most critical[1]. The difficulties stem from the fact that the system stack is used for things other than the simple passing of arguments. This is particularly the case when saving temporary data (contents of the register, return address in the case of nested calls, etc.); consequently the SP fluctuates according to the *PUSH/POP* inserted into the procedure. We should therefore consider these fluctuations in order to reach the arguments.

---

1 Most assemblers store the return address on the system stack, rather than in a specific register, when they perform a procedure call. There is thus a mixture of arguments, return addresses and other saving registers, which complicates the management of this stack.

A safer option is to use an annex pointer: it is frozen at the entry of the procedure (after it is itself saved) at the current value of the SP. It therefore becomes independent of the previously mentioned fluctuations and enables easier management of argument recovery. In the following example, the *R9* register plays this role of annex pointer. The *SP* evolves (circled numbers) along with the different stackings/unstackings. It should be noted, and this point is extremely important, that at the call return the SP is returned to its initial point. The calling procedure has done the clearing (the calling program could just as well have done the same thing). A multiple reading choice (*LDM* (LoaD Multiple)) has also been made for the recovery of arguments on the system stack. As this instruction does not allow us to have a supplementary offset in its addressing modes, it was necessary to offset *R9* by four bytes at the top of the stack, so that the schedule pointer is correctly positioned at the arguments to be recovered. An alternative to this version is to carry out single readings (*LDR* (LoaD Register)) with supplementary offset.

Finally, note that it is not possible to recover arguments with the *POP* instruction or, more precisely, if we implement this as well it is then no longer possible to guarantee the non-modification of registers affected by the procedure.

EXAMPLE 7.8.– *Research into the maximum: passing by reference and by system stack*

```
            . . .
;- - - - - - - - - - - - - - - - - - - - - - - - - - - - -
main        PROC
            LDR R0,=ValOne
            PUSH R0                 ; Stacking of @ parameter 1
            LDR R0,=ValTwo
            PUSH R0                 ; Stacking @ parameter 2
            LDR R0,= Maxi
            PUSH R0                 ; Stacking of the return parameter
            BL MaxVer6              ; Call
Infinity    B Infinity             ; End of the program
            ENDP
;- - - - - - - - - - - - - - - - - - - - - - - - - - - - -
MaxVer6     PROC
            PUSH {R9}       ; Save modified register
            MOV R9,SP       ; Initialization of annex pointer
            ADD R9,#4       ; Offset on R9
            PUSH {R1-R5}    ; Save modified registers
```

```
                LDM R9,{R3-R5} ; Loading of the 3 @ arguments
                LDR R1,[R5]    ; Loading of the 1st argument
                LDR R2,[R4]    ; Loading of the 2nd argument
                CMP R1,R2
                BHS Good       ; If ValOne < ValTwo ...
ExChange        MOV R1,R2      ;    ... ValTwo becomes the max
Good            STR R1,[R3]    ; Storage of the result
                POP {R1-R5,R9} ; Restore saved registers
                SUB SP,#12     ; Cleaning of the system stack
                BX LR          ; Return
                ENDP
```

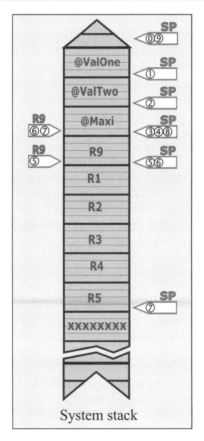

Figure 7.3. *System stack evolution (demonstrating the code in Example 7.8)*

7.2.6. *On the art of mixing*

All of the versions of passing arguments that have been presented in the previous sections can mix at will. This is both the strength and the flexibility of programming in assembly language, but it is also the difficulty. We can in fact, and for example, pass a first argument by value and by register, a second by reference and by system stack and recover the results of the procedure on a user stack. It is easy to understand that such a mixture risks causing terrible problems. Thus, unless you are obliged (by motivations that can appear obscure) to do so, it is best to avoid mixing.

7.3. Local data

To carry out its work, a subroutine may have to use its own data. These are the local data of the subroutine. The rule of localization invites us to place these data so that they are only visible and usable by the proprietary subroutine. The simplest way of doing this in assembly language is to use the general registers to contain the local variables. It works perfectly in simple cases, especially if the local data are not too numerous. Unfortunately, the number of registers is limited. What is more, this method is not usable in the case of calls to nested subroutines or for a recursive function without needing several saves. We could consider planning the creation of these local data in a specific data section, but this leads to a "waste" of memory because it is only used during the execution of the procedure. A more satisfactory solution would be to superimpose all of these sections by specifying them as being *COMMON*, that is specifying them as attributes in the declaration of the section: *AREA Mydata DATA align=2, COMMON*, so that they share the same portion of memory. We can, however, apply the same criticism to this method of superimposition as for the case of arguments arranged in a fixed space: the launch of a subroutine can lead to a partial or total loss of local data from the calling program. We therefore prefer to create the data in a dynamic manner at the beginning of the execution of the procedure. Here are two options, both using the heap:

– in addition to the stack for the arguments, we use a second stack for the local variables;

– during execution we place them on the same stack as the arguments.

REMARK 7.6.– Local variables dynamically created on a stack can equally be created on a user stack (a heap) or on the system stack. As in the case of passing arguments, the use of the system stack is more delicate, and therefore dangerous. As such, if there are no imperatives linked to memory use, it is always preferable and safer to use the user stack itself.

We will illustrate the use of a user stack, upon which both the procedure arguments and local variables will be arranged. We assume that the user stack is duly created and initialized, with *R11* as the SP register.

7.3.1. *Simple reservation of local data*

Let us first look at a first method where the local variables are simply reserved in the user stack by the calling program. The procedure considered in Example 7.9 and Figure 7.6 starts by resetting the local variables, the body of the procedure having not been developed. We assume that the procedure receives two 32-bit arguments, denoted *Arg1* and *Arg2*, which are stored on the same user stack during the call.

REMARK 7.7.– It is not necessary to consider that the local variables are initialized at zero. In fact, they occupy a memory space that can be used many times, and the freeing up of memory is only done by offsetting pointers aimed at the memory zones concerned. The values are therefore neither erased nor saved.

The different steps in the management of the user stack for the management of local variables are:

– *Creation*: let us take the case of four local variables: one of 32 bits, one of 16 bits, and two of 8 bits. On top of the arguments, we reserve them a place (4+2+1+1 bytes) by creating a *hole* in the stack, thanks to this instruction placed at the start of the procedure: *SUB R11,#8*.

– *Use*: we distribute these 8 bytes at will between the various local variables. In Example 7.9, the datum *Local32* (32 bits) is reached by *[R11,#4]*, the datum *Local16* (16 bits) by *[R11,#2]*, *Byte1* (8 bits) by *[R11,#1]* and *Byte2* (8 bits) by *[R11]*. Note that these symbols are not defined *a priori*.

– *Removal*: this is carried out by an offset towards the top of the stack that is used to fill the hole. We can use this passing, as is done in this example, to also remove the two arguments passed at the call, which in our case corresponds to the instruction *ADD R11,#16*.

EXAMPLE 7.9.– *Erasing of local variables*

```
Erase_Local    PROC
               PUSH {R1,R2,R10}      ; Save modified registers
               MOV R10,R11           ; Assignment of annex pointer
               SUB R11,#8            ; "Hole" for the 4 local variables
               MOV R2,#0             ; for erasing
               STR R2,[R11,#4]       ; Erase Local32
```

```
STRH R2,[R11,#2]        ; Erase Local16

STRB R2,[R11,#1]        ; Erase Byte2

STRB R2,[R11]           ; Erase Byte1

LDR R1,[R10,#4]         ; Loading of 1st parameters

LDR R2,[R10]            ; Loading of 2nd parameter

......                  ; Body of

......                  ;        the procedure

ADD R11,#16             ; removing of local

                        ; variables (8) and arguments (8)

POP {R1,R2,R10}         ; Restore saved registers

BX LR                   ; Return

ENDP
```

An annex pointer (*R10*) was initialized (after the save) to access the arguments. This choice is not compulsory; it simply allows us to have separate pointers for accessing arguments and local variables, which can be more useful and above all more readable. However, the call arguments remain accessible from *R11+8*. Figure 7.6 corresponds to the configuration of the user stack, once reservation has been made for the local variables and annex pointer *R10* has been initialized (after the *SUB R11,#8* instruction).

Let us take the example of the calculation (by the *Max_Four* procedure) of the maximum of a table of four unsigned integers. These numbers will be named *N1*, *N2*, *N3* and *N4* in the procedure. *Max_Four* will receive these four arguments that are passed by value from the user stack. It carries out its calculation by calling the *MaxVer4* function three times, as defined in Example 7.6. All of its arguments are also stacked by value. The procedure returns the result by value via the *R4* register.

Here are the expressions of this calculation:

M1 = Maximum (N1,N2)

M2 = Maximum (N3,N4)

Result = Maximum (M1,M2)

We place *M1* and *M2* in local variables and apply the rule "whoever stacks, unstacks!"

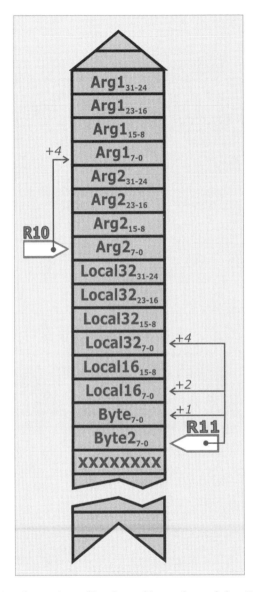

Figure 7.4. *Relative place of local variables on the stack (see Example 7.9)*

Let us start with the few call lines that simply use post-incrementation for reading different values of *Table* (pointed to by *R0*) and pre-decrementation for writing to the stack (pointed to by *R11*).

EXAMPLE 7.10.– *Call to the Max_Four procedure*

```
                    . . .
;- - - - - - - - - - - - - - - - - - - - - - - - - - - - - - - - - - -
main            PROC
                    . . .
                LDR R11,=Top_stack
                LDR R0,=Table
                LDR R1,[R0],#4
                STR R1,[R11,#-4]!       ; Stack Table[0] (N1)
                LDR R1,[R0],#4
                STR R1,[R11,#-4]!       ; Stack Table[1] (N2)
                LDR R1,[R0],#4
                STR R1,[R11,#-4]!       ; Stack Tableau[2] (N3)
                LDR R1,[R0]
                STR R1,[R11,#-4]!       ; Stack Table[3] (N4)
                BL Max_Four
                ADD R11,#16            ; Whoever stacks unstacks
                LDR R0,=ResuMax
                STR R4,[R0]           ; The result is in R4
Infinity        B Infinity            ; End of program
                ENDP
```

Let us now look at the procedure itself. This listing is accompanied by circled numbers that, with the help of Figure 7.5, allow us to visualize the state of the user stack just after the execution of the marked instruction.

EXAMPLE 7.11.– *Body of the Max_Four procedure*

```
Max_Four        PROC
                PUSH {LR}              ; Nested call
                PUSH {R1,R2,R10}       ; Save modified register
                MOV R10,R11            ; Initialization of argument pointer
                SUB R11,#8        ⓪    ; Hole to create 2 local variables
                LDR R1,[R10,#12]       ; Load N1
                STR R1,[R11,#-4]!
                LDR R1,[R10,#8]        ; Load N2
```

```
STR R1,[R11,#-4]!
MOV R1,#0
STR R1,[R11,#-4]!  ①  ; Hole on the stack for the return
BL MaxV4
LDR R1,[R11]
STR R1,[R11,#16]        ; Assignment of M1
ADD R11,#12        ②  ; Whoever stacks unstacks
LDR R1,[R10,#4]        ; Load N3
STR R1,[R11,#-4]!
LDR R1,[R10]           ; Load N4
STR R1,[R11,#-4]!
MOV R1,#0
STR R1,[R11,#-4]!  ③  ; Hole on the stack for the return
BL MaxV4
LDR R1,[R11]
STR R1,[R11,#12]       ; Assignment of M2
ADD R11,#12        ④  ; Whoever stacks unstacks


LDR R1,[R11,#4]       ; Assignment of M1
STR R1,[R11,#-4]!
LDR R1,[R11,#4]       ; Assignment of M2
STR R1,[R11,#-4]!
MOV R1,#0
STR R1,[R11,#-4]!      ; Hole on the stack for the return
BL MaxV4           ⑤
LDR R4,[R11]          ; Assignment of final result
                      ; (retour via R4)
ADD R11,#12          ; Whoever stacks unstacks


ADD R11,#8           ; Free space relative to local variables
POP {R1,R2,R10}      ; Restore modified registers
POP {LR}             ; Restore relative to nested call
BX LR                ; Return


ENDP
```

We recognize that there are simple, faster and more precise ways of calculating an average of four numbers. This example aims to give a condensed illustration of several points covered previously (passing of arguments, stack, complex addressing mode, local variables, etc.).

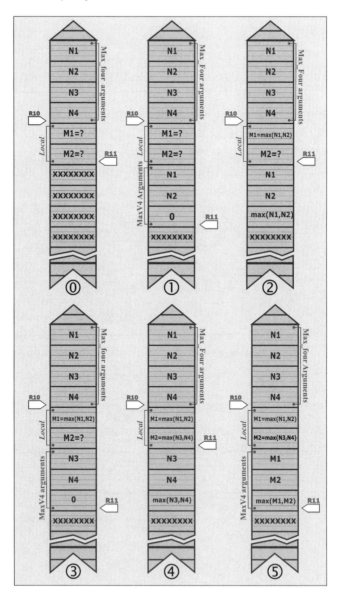

Figure 7.5. *Max_Four: evolution of the user stack*

7.3.2. *Using a chained list*

7.3.2.1. *Fixed point on the stack*

Example 7.11 showed how delicately the previously proposed method needs to be used. It is clear that the current position of *R11* must be perfectly mastered: any error in stack alignment is fatal to the execution of the program. As each time we add elements to this stack and then remove them, the relative position of the arguments and local variables is modified, we realize that the re-reading of a program will be difficult, the modifications laborious, and the errors formidable.

A preferable method consists of sacrificing a register – let us say *R9* – so that it marks a fixed point, a kind of anchor, on the stack. It is this technique that was used to separate access to arguments from access to local variables. Thus frozen, all offsets will be calculated from this fixed point, such that SP *R11* continues to live its independent life yo-yoing along the stack. The position of stacked elements is also separated from *R11*. Once again, all the work returns to the called procedure in a similar way to what was done with the management of register *R10* for parameter access.

Applying to the example of resetting local variables, the lines of code become:

EXAMPLE 7.12.– *Resetting local variables: version with annex pointer*

```
Erase2_Local   PROC
        PUSH {R1,R2,R9, R10}   ; Save modified registers
        MOV R10,R11            ; Annex pointer (arguments)
        MOV R9,R11             ; Annex pointer (local variables)
        SUB R11,#8             ; Hole to create the 4 local variables
        MOV R2,#0              ; For erasing
        STR R2,[R9,#-4]        ; Reset Local32
        STRH R2,[R9,#-6]       ; Reset Local16
        STRB R2,[R9,#-7]       ; Reset Byte2
        STRB R2,[R9,#-8]       ; Rest Byte1
        LDR R1,[R10,#4]        ; Loading of 1st parameter
        LDR R2,[R10]          ; Loading of 2nd parameter
        ......                 ; Body of
        ......                 ;        the procedure
        ADD R11,#16            ; Removing of local
                               ; variables (8) and arguments (8)
        POP {R1,R2,R9,R10}     ; Restore modified registers
        BX LR                  ; Return
        ENDP
```

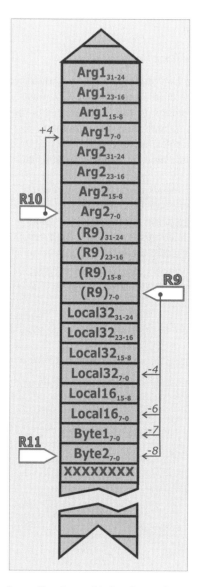

Figure 7.6. *Relative place of local variable locales on the stack (see Example 7.12)*

7.3.2.2. *Chaining*

We have generalized the previous method to all called procedures, but used the same register *R9* as the stack annex pointer. Let us therefore take the case of a *proc1* procedure calling a *proc2* procedure, which calls a *proc3* procedure.

Let us place ourselves at the deepest call level (see Figure 7.7), and so at the start of *proc3*. *R9* points to its save, which indicates the position of *R9* at the start of the call to *proc2*, which itself indicates the position of *R9* at the start of the call to *proc1*. *R9* therefore manages a chained list, which allows us, without altering the value contained in *R9*, to recover any local variable or argument of *proc1* and *proc2* by starting at *proc3*.

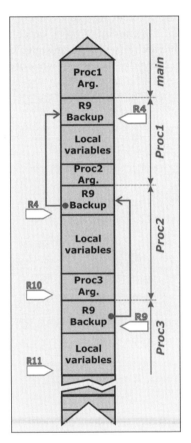

Figure 7.7. *Local variables: state of the user stack*

It is sufficient for this to be able to recover the previous values of *R9*, without loading its current value; for example, see the following:

EXAMPLE 7.13.– *Nested call and chained local variables*

LDR R4,[R9]	; R4 backup R9 for proc2
LDR R5,[R4]	; R5 backup R9 for proc1

Figure 7.7 shows how the different arguments nest on the user stack. If we wish, this allows us to implement a hierarchy of local variables, as allowed in Ada for example. Indeed, such a hierarchy is very interesting for writing a compiler, but little used because it is very heavy for the current work of a programmer in assembly language on a μcontroller.

Chapter 8

Managing Exceptions

Understanding of exception mechanisms is an essential step when it comes to computer hardware. The core of a μcontroller is responsible for the execution of algorithms, task management and calculations necessary for the project, but all of this organization would be useless if it was not accompanied by the possibility of interfacing (in the electronic sense) with the physical process that it has to manage. As was explained in Chapter 1, it is the responsibility of the μcontroller designer (and not the Advanced RISC Machine or ARM) to develop these peripherals. These can be thought of as micromachines that are independent of the core and perform specific tasks (counting time, converting an analog signal into its numerical equivalent, periodically generating a square signal, etc.). Their preferred means of communication is the *interrupt*. By this specific mechanism, the micromachine signals to Cortex-M3, asynchronously with the current code execution, that it has finished its task and that Cortex-M3should therefore respond accordingly.

A similar mechanism is engaged when, during the running of a code sequence, a "serious" event occurs and its processing requires a particular regime. As an example, let us take the case of an attempt to read the contents of a memory address that, for some reason, fails. This type of event is strictly specific to the functioning of the core and is usually launched synchronously with an instruction. It is then possible to speak of software *traps*.

Finally, another type of communication can arise, which concerns the launch of a reset or a Non-Maskable Interrupt (*NMI*). These two events are generally transmitted by specific external pins of the processor and can be thought of as "emergency stops".

Interrupts, *traps*, *Reset* and *NMI* come under the generic term exceptions. The technique used to respond to these different cases of "exception" is similar and is the topic of this chapter. The *Nested Vectored Interrupt Controller* (NVIC) receives orders and manages all exceptions, so in this chapter, we will detail many of this unit's registers.

8.1. What happens during *Reset*?

Before describing these mechanisms and what consequences they imply at a programming level in greater detail, let us look at the case of *Reset*. This is the most serious and most inescapable event (or exception, to be more precise) that can happen to any *μ*processor. A system *Reset* can have different origins. In the case of Cortex-M3, these can be:

– exterior, meaning that a circuit particular pin that must, by default, be at a high logic level has passed to a low level;

– launched by a *watchdog*[1];

– launched by software by setting the *SYSRESETREQ* bit of the *Application Interrupt and Reset Control Register* (AIRCR) in the *NVIC* to 1.

Reset also corresponds to a "cold start", or power-up of the circuit. If it corresponds to setting the *Reset* pin of the circuit to a lower level (known as a soft reset, corresponding in practice to the user pressing a button wired to this pin), it generally does not bode well for the progress of the application running on the processor.

During a *Reset* phase, the processor starts by reinitializing all registers. In the documentation, we find the value taken by each register following a *Reset*. This initialization puts the processor in privileged *Thread* mode. Then Cortex-M3 reads the contents of address 0x00000000 (the lowest memory mapping address) to assign it to register *R13*. Once this has been done, it initializes the stack pointer. This first assignment is imperative because an exception can occur at any time and because the treatment of this exception, as we will see later, requires access to the system stack. The processor must therefore be in a position to process an exception and consequently must have a valid stack pointer. The memory address recorded in these 4 bytes must correspond to the top of a memory zone with read/write access. In a third stage, Cortex-M3 reads the contents of the next word, namely the contents of addresses 0x00000004 to 0x00000007. This word will be used in the initialization of

---

1 The watchdogs are bits that must (when these units are engaged) be periodically set to 1. This mechanism allows the μcontroller to ensure that the running program is not blocked in an infinite loop, among other things.

the instruction pointer (*R15*). It must therefore correspond to an address in the CODE zone where the startup routine that allows correct initialization of the whole processor, depending on the characteristics of the application, is stored.

This mechanism brings to light the concept of the *Interrupt Vector Table* (IVT) or *Interrupt Descriptor Table* (IDT), see Figure 8.2). This table, in addition to the initial value of the stack pointer, must contain the addresses of all interrupt handlers (also known as an interrupt service routine [ISR]) for possible exceptions. The assembler (or the compiler in the case of higher-level languages) will therefore be tasked with creating this so that when an exception occurs, the current processing is correctly diverted to the associated ISR. Example 8.1 shows how it starts to create this table. All of the initial values (*Reset_Handler, NMI_Handler*, etc.) correspond to procedures that the linker will be capable of locating to correctly complete the table.

EXAMPLE 8.1.– *Initialization of an IVT*

```
            AREA RESET, DATA, READONLY

            EXPORT Vectors

Vectors     DCD initial_sp          ; @ of the top of the memory space

                                    ;          reserved for the stack

            DCD Reset_Handler       ; @ of subroutine Reset_Handler

            DCD NMI_Handler         ; @ of subroutine NMI_Handler

            DCD HardFault_Handler   ; @ subroutine HardFault_Handler

            DCD MemManage_Handler   ; @ subroutine MemManage_Handler

            DCD BusFault_Handler    ; @ of subroutine BusFault_Handler

            . . .                        . . .
```

Each exception has an entry in the table that is located by its position. Thus, the memory address where the address of the processing routine for exception number "position" is stored corresponds to:

$$@_{Input\_Treat} = @_{Base} + position * 4$$

where $@_{Base}$ is fixed in the CODE zone at *0x00000000*. We should note that with this configuration it is not possible to dynamically redefine the IVT (i.e. during a program) because it is created and set during the creation of the executable. Dynamic management of the table can be useful for enabling the processor to react to the evolution of its environment. This option of relocating the *IVT* is possible. In order to do this, it is necessary to provide a memory zone of $4*(N + 1)$ bytes, where N is the maximum number of exceptions making up the table. This new memory zone should be created in *DATA* memory if dynamic management is desired, but it is also possible to carry out a simple static reallocation by placing it in the *CODE* zone. In the *VECTTBL* register of the *NVIC* (see Figure 8.1, it is then possible to specify a relative address (with respect to the base of the *SRAM* [Static Random-Access Memory] or *CODE* zone according to the choice fixed by the *TBLBASE* bit) for this new table. This manipulation calls for a lot of caution, particularly regarding the alignment of addresses in this zone. It must also be guaranteed that the switching does not put the processor in an ambiguous situation by perfectly initializing this new *IVT* before reassigning the register.

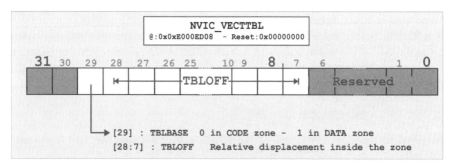

Figure 8.1. *Register for displacement of the Interrupt Vector Table (NVIC_VECTTBL)*

EXAMPLE 8.2.– *Example of the Reset handler*

```
Reset_Handler PROC
              EXPORT Reset_Handler [WEAK]
              IMPORT __main
              LDR R0, =main
              BX R0
              ENDP
```

When processing a *Reset,* the typical example presented in Example 8.2 is that which we may find by using ARM's own development suite, Keil Microcontroller Development Kit (MDK)-ARM. During the launch of *Reset*, the processor will jump to the address of the procedure *__main* (with two underscore symbols – be aware of this!), which has been created elsewhere in the project (hence the use of an *IMPORT*). This procedure does not generally exist in the project, but it is automatically included by using the *MicroLib* library (assembly option). This procedure provides, among other things, the code that initializes all variables in the project (which corresponds to the use of directives *DCB, DCW*, etc.) and ends with a jump to the *main* procedure (without the underscores) which is, by convention, the entry point of your project. It is quite possible to do this without *MicroLib*, by using another procedure (see, for example, the use of a GNU compiler/assembler in Appendix D) or by developing one that is especially dedicated to a specific configuration, but the work is relatively sizeable and often delicate.

8.2. Possible exceptions

Reset and *NMI* can both be thought of as requests for special exceptions. They are also unavoidable, to the extent that their appearance is impossible to inhibit and their priority level gives them precedence above all other possible sources. The other possible exceptions can be displayed in an IVT, see Figure 8.2. Indeed, for each exception it is necessary to provide the corresponding processing routine and consequently to store its address in the table.. These aforementioned routines do not need to be provided because we can rely on the fact that the exceptions will not occur. A such hypothesis is completely controllable at the level of interrupts but it presents a particularly risky challenge when it comes to traps

Example 8.3 of *NMI* processing shows that it is simplest to provide for the processing of an exception (but not the most effective in the case of an embedded application), since it amounts to an infinite loop (*B.* corresponds to a jump to its own address). We might imagine that this would be sufficient at this phase of development, but it would certainly be necessary to provide something more robust for an autonomous application. It should be noted that the exportation of *NMI_Handler* is of the *WEAK* type. This is therefore the essential minimum created and provided by the development environment. In this way the developer could design a more specific and robust processing of this exception elsewhere in the project that would be substituted for this first version, and the address of which would ultimately fill the IVT.

EXAMPLE 8.3.– *Example of a NMI handler*

```
NMI_Handler  PROC
             EXPORT NMI_Handler [WEAK]
             B .
             ENDP
```

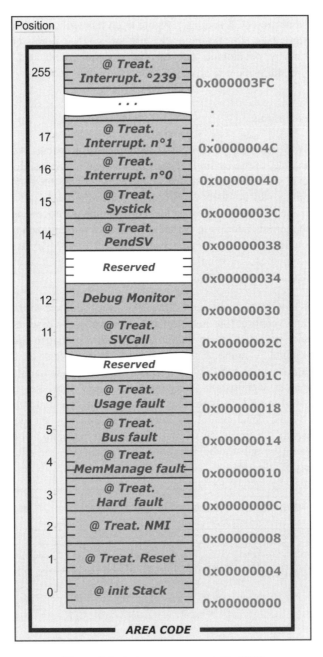

Figure 8.2. *An interrupt vector table (TVI)*

8.2.1. *Traps*

Entries three to 15 of the *IVT* make up the set of software traps. The first for correspond to faults. These are serious events for which the processor cannot correctly finish an instruction. On the occasion that these faults arise, ARM has provided the means by which to trace the origins of these faults through a "triple" register:

– MMFSR (Memory Manage Fault Status Register);

– BFSR (Bus Fault Status Register);

– UFSR (Usage Fault Status Register).

This is a triple register in the sense that these three names correspond to 2 bytes and a half-word of a *NVIC* memory word placed at 0x*E000ED*28 (see Figure 8.4). Reading the *MMFSR* word will therefore give all three registers, but reading 1 byte at this same address only gives the contents of the first byte. The *MMSFR* is therefore part of the register. A user encountering a "fault" problem could, by reading the contents of these registers, track down the cause of these faults. Only the contents of *UFSR* will be explained (see section 8.2.1.4) as they correspond globally to issues that cover software rather than hardware, and to which a developer could respond.

8.2.1.1. *Hard fault: a serious hardware fault*

A *hard fault* trap could also be called a *double fault*. This trap is triggered if a *usage fault, bus fault* or *memory management fault* arises but its processing does not work (the *TVI* is badly initialized, for example). It can also correspond to a *bus fault* during the reading of the *TVI*. This trap is therefore very serious because it corresponds to the processor being incapable of responding to a problem requiring a specific treatment. As we will see later, it is placed just after *Reset* and the *NMI* in the order of priority and, like the previous two exceptions, its priority level cannot be modified.

8.2.1.2. *Memory management fault*

This trap, as its name indicates, corresponds to a memory management problem and can only arise with the (optional) existence of the memory protection unit . As this unit is not covered in this book, the associated trap will not be developed any further. This fault, like the next two, can be inhibited through the *System Handler Control and State Register* (SHCSR) of the *NVIC*, see Figure 8.3. This is the case elsewhere after a *Reset*, since the different *enable* bits are all set to 0. Indeed, the 16-bit weight of this register allows us to authorize (or block) the transmission of this fault to Cortex-M3 and therefore to authorize (or prevent) its specific treatment.

However, we cannot solve the problem by inhibiting it. Similarly the 0 (or 13)-bits weight allow us to find out, as we will see later in the chapter, whether the specific treatment of the exception is active (or pending). As these last two bits have write access, it is possible to artificially trigger exceptions by setting these bits to 1. It is recommended that act cautiously in doing this, however, insofar as the save context is not always guaranteed.

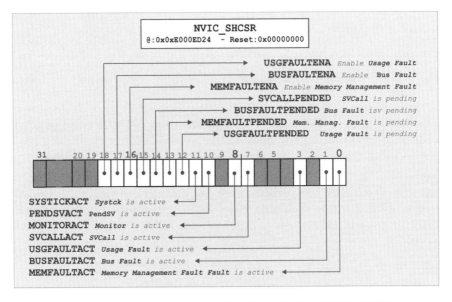

Figure 8.3. *System Handler Control and State Register (NVIC_SHCSR)*

8.2.1.3. Bus fault

With this trap, problems that are potentially present in the development phase begin to appear. This corresponds to it being impossible for the processor to retrieve an instruction (*prefetch abort*) or carry out reading/writing of a datum (*data abort*). The typical case in which Cortex-M3 falls into this trap is that of bad pointer management (and so indirect addressing), where the virtually pointed address (the contents of the indirection register) does not correspond to a valid data address. Another common problem is the bad use of a peripheral that, for example, tries to retrieve a word so that it can only provide one byte. In certain cases, the *BFAR* (*Bus Fault Address Register*) preserves the memory address that produced the fault. Bit 17 of the *SHCSR* register allows us to validate or invalidate this trap and bits 14 and 1 allow us to determine its activity state (active or pending).

8.2.1.4. *Usage fault*

This last fault, of which a report on what triggers it is the subject of the 16-bit *UFSR*, is a fault that, as opposed to a *bus fault*, is more concerned with software than hardware problems. It can therefore occur in the deployment phase (not only in the development phase) so it is important to provide treatment for it and to see how it can be caused:

– division by zero: in the case of floating point numbers, it is possible to de-normalize the result to return a value corresponding to infinity. In integer arithmetic, such an operation poses an unsolvable problem. So, the processor indicates this fault and switches the weight 9 bit (*DIVBYZERO*) of *UFSR* to 1;

– unalignment: as we have seen, it is possible to access unaligned data. This option comes with limitations, however, and when we violate these constraints the trap is triggered and bit 8 (*UNALIGNED*) is activated. It is also activated if unaligned access is prohibited and such access is attempted;

– access to a coprocessor: the Cortex-M3 set has several instructions for a potential coprocessor. If no such unit is present, the response is a *usage fault* and bit 3 (NOCP) switches to 1. By finding this bit, the treatment routine can be written to offer an emulation of this coprocessor (which allows us to augment the portability of the code to different types of processors);

– impossible return: here this means an attempt to load the program counter (*PC*) pointer with an illegal value during the return from an exception. The details of possible values are given in section 8.4. Bit 2 (*INVPC*) switches to 1;

– invalid state: the T bit of the *EPSR* (Execution Program Status Register) allows us to distinguish, in the general ARM architectures, the switch from *ARM* mode to *Thumb* mode. As Cortex-M3 only supports *Thumb* mode, any attempt to switch to *ARM* mode is sanctioned by this fault, with bit 1 (INVSTATE) being activated. This problem can happen accidentally by forcing the value of *PC* with an even value (so the least significant bit (LSB) is at 0), during a jump or procedure return (*BX LR*) for example. Indeed, in coding jump instructions (see section 5.6) when the LSB is at 0, the processor as well as the branch must switch to *ARM* mode, which is impossible for Cortex-M3;

– undefined instruction: the last case that provokes this fault is when bit 0 (UNDEFINSTR) is set to 1. In this case, the *PC* points to an instruction that is not decodable by the core. The most common case is a jump to an address that is valid, but does not contain the correct code (a *Literal Pool*, for example).

A *usage fault* can be deactivated. To do this, we set bit 18 of the *SHCSR* to 0. Bits 12 and 3 of this register allow knowledge of the activity state (active or pending).

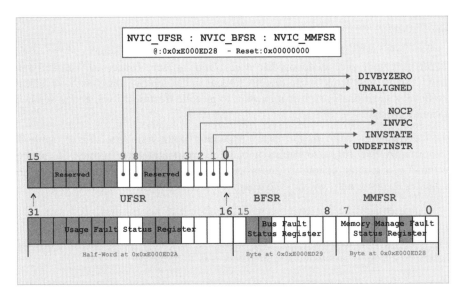

Figure 8.4. *Multiple Fault Status Registers (NVIC_MMFSR/NVIC_BFSR/NVIC_UFSR)*

8.2.1.5. *The SVCall trap*

This is typically a function put in place when designing an operating system, or more modestly a software micro-kernel, allowing faster and more systematic deployment of various applications. A typical operation is the use of a serial. We want the user to be able to transfer data via this medium but we do not want him or her to be able modify the different configuration registers and so have access at a hardware level. The kernel designer could therefore provide the services associated with this function (sending/receiving a character) and allow use via a *SVC* (SerVice Call) request to the kernel. This division between low-level services and applications ensures coherence and security[2].

This trap is therefore called at a software level by the instruction *SCV n*, where $n<255$ is a value (that is immediately coded) that represents a specific kernel service. This service calling mechanism is the same for all exceptions. It would therefore be necessary to refer to the documentation of this hypothetical kernel to find out about the different services and how to use them. It is interesting, however, to dwell on what the handler of this exception can do to recover the value *n*. In fact, the instruction encodes the value *n* using immediate addressing, so this value is not in a register but in the code itself. The only method by which we can recover its

2 By developing this service, it is possible to build the two "pillar" functions of the STDIO.h library (in C language).

memory encoding is by recovering the seventh datum on the system stack (see section 8.4 for context saving). This then poses the problem of knowing which stack (*Main Stack Pointer* [*MSP*] or Stack Pointer Process [PSP]) we need to work with, and so knowing which mode the processor was in when the exception was triggered. This information is contained in the value *EXC_RETURN* stored in the link register (*LR*) during context saving. With this principle established, we can break down Example 58 into three steps:

– choosing the stack point according to the *LR* test;

– recovering the storage address of the instruction that caused the exception from the stack (first indirection);

– recovering the code itself (second indirection).

EXAMPLE 8.4.– *Typical beginning of a SVCall handler*

```
SVC_Handler   PROC
              AND R0,LR,#0X000F    ; Mask on the 4 lsb
              CMP R0, #0x0001      ; Call from Handler Mode
              BEQ StackMSP
              CMP R0, #0x0009      ; Call from Thread Mode
                                   ;           with privileged
              BEQ StackMSP
              CMP R0, #0x000D      ; Call from Thread Mode
                                   ;           without privileged
              BNE Exit             ; Exec_Return is unidentifiable…
                                   ; …strange!
StackPSP      MRS R0,PSP           ; …Wwe use PSP
              B Search_Ser
StackMSP      MRS R0,MSP           ; …We use MSP
Search_Ser    LDR R1,[R0,#6*4]     ; PC pointer is the 7th save
              LDRB R7,[R1, #-2]    ; Immediate value is the second byte

              . . . .              ; R7 contains the passed value n
Exit          BX LR                ; Return
              ENDP
```

The *SVC* instruction is in fact coded on two bytes. For example, *SVC 3* is encoded as the half-word *DF*03. The first byte (0x*DF*) is the *SVC* opcode, and the second byte is the immediate value. Once this base is put in place, all that remains is to write the call-to routines corresponding to different kernel services with reference to a jump table or an *If...ElseIf...ElseIf...* based on the value contained in *R7*.

This trap cannot be masked insofar as it is called purely at the software level; it is completely synchronous and predictable. Bits 15 and 7 of the *SHCSR* allow us to determine its activity state (active or pending).

8.2.1.6. *The monitor*

To perform all of the developments and tests of a given application, Cortex-M3 offers a hardware structure called *debug*. The development unit has the option of freezing the core (*Halt* mode) and so taking complete control of the running of the code and all of the exceptions (apart from *Reset* and the *NMI*) that can occur. It is not always possible or desirable, however, to completely freeze the processor. For example, it is sometimes desirable to preserve the activity of certain tasks, such as the acceptance of higher level exceptions while patching the rest of the code to monitor it, in order to ensure at least a minimum of security.

The second *debug* method, and the one that corresponds to this specific trap, can be of great use. The different events that require a switch to *debug* mode will then trigger exception 12. The writing of an adequate handler (commonly called a monitor) allows us to correctly treat the different debugging requests. Bit 8 of the *SHCSR* tells us whether a *debug* exception monitor is active. The activation/deactivation of *debug* mode is possible and is managed at the level of the configuration registers of dedicated units.

8.2.1.7. *The PENDSV service*

This service has a similar function to the *SVC* service. It allows us, with the writing of the corresponding handler, to send a request to a higher software level. This second option exists because *SVC* cannot respond in all cases, to the extent that it is only triggered by the execution of a specific instruction. It is impossible to call this instruction in the treatment routine of an exception that is at a higher priority level. Such a case would cause a *hard fault*. This system call therefore does not correspond to a specific instruction.

The technique used consists of software switching the exception to pending (hence its name) by activating bit 28 of the *ICSR* (*Interrupt Control State Register*), see Figure 8.5. Indeed, in this register, different exceptions (*SysTick*, *PendSV* and *NMI*) can have their pended status changed. It should be noted that, for security reasons, the switch into pended mode and the exit from pended mode are done through two different bits for *PendSV* and *SysTick*. The simultaneous activation of both bits is ineffective. The switch to one of the *PENDSVCLR* (or *PENDSTCLR*) bits also erases the *PENDSVSET* (or *PENDSTSET*).

8.2.1.8. *The internal SysTick timer*

It is the responsibility of the μcontroller designer to supply peripherals, and in particular those necessary for the measurement and management of time. ARM has chosen to equip Cortex-M3 with a timer called *SysTick*. This choice allows us to augment the portability of the code between different μcontrollers, especially at the level of a real-time kernel. Indeed, such a high-level layer cannot get along without a scheduler, which itself relies on a timer to regulate its task dispatching policy. The programming of this timer is the subject of Appendix B.

When the timer overflows, exception 15 – if it has been validated – is triggered, and bit 11 of the *SHCSR* register is switched to 1 when the exception becomes active. As was mentioned in the previous section, it is possible to cause this trap to be set to pended though the *PENDSTSET* bit of the *ICSR* of the *NVIC*. Conversely, it is possible to end the pended mode of this exception with the *PENDSTCLR* bit of the same register.

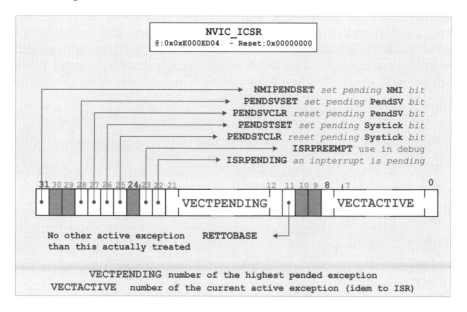

Figure 8.5. *Interrupt Control State Register (NVIC_ICSR)*

8.2.2. *Interrupts*

The next 239 entries of the *IVT* depend on the μcontroller and the choices that the circuit designer makes. The interrupt number is also variable depending on the complexity and "wealth" of the chosen circuit. As an example, since it has been brought up in Chapter 1, STM32F103RB uses 67 interrupt vectors for its internal needs at the peripheral level. These 67 vectors occupy the addresses 0x00000040 to 0x0000014C of the *IVT*. It is therefore necessary to refer to the specific documentation of each μcontroller to know and understand the usefulness of all these interrupts.

There are mechanisms that are common to all designs, however: interferences with the *NVIC*. Indeed as this unit receives and manages all of the exceptions, it is normal to find within it registers that just act on the behavior of peripherals, or at least the behavior in the triggering of interrupts. First, there are the *NVIC_ISER[x]* (*Interrupt Set-Enable Registers*), which validate the transmission of these interrupts and in a symmetrical manner. Then there are the *NVIC_ICER[x]* (*Interrupt Clear-Enable Registers*), which invalidate the transmission. It should be noted that, as was seen for putting the *PendSV* and *SysTick* traps into pended, validation and invalidation occur through distinct bits in separate registers being set to 1, when a binary state would have been sufficient to transcribe this duality. In each case the resetting of bits will have no effect and, like a toggle, switching a *SET* (or *CLEAR*) bit to 1 will reset the *CLEAR* (or *SET*) bit of the dual register. The 8 *ISERs* occupy the addresses 0xE000E100 to 0xE000E11C and each of the 32 bits corresponds to an interrupt, as shown in Figure 8.6. A similar complete distribution for the *ICERs* between addresses 0xE000E180 and 0xE000E19C corresponds to the invalidation bits.

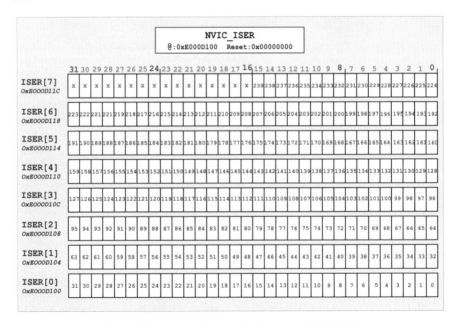

Figure 8.6. *Interrupt Set-Enable Register (NVIC_ISER)*

Two other groups of registers, with the same characteristics as *ISERs* and *ICERs*, allow us to change the pended status of an interrupt. This involves the 8 *NVIC_ISPER[x]* (*Interruption Set-Pending Registers*) switching to pended mode (thereby forcing one of these bits at 1 to trigger through the handler of the corresponding interrupt) and the eight *NVIC_ICPER[x]* (*Interrupt Clear-Pending Registers*) to cancel the pended mode (and so cancelling a interrupt request). These two groups of registers occupy addresses 0xE000E200 to 0xE000E21c (for *ISPER*) and 0x*E000E280* to 0x*E000E29C* (for *ICPER*).

Finally, with the same principle of bit distribution, we can use the *NVIC_IASR[x]* (*Interrupt Active Status Registers*), which have read only access to know whether the corresponding exception is active (bit at 1) or not (bit at 0). These registers occupy the addresses 0x*E000E*300 to 0x*E000E*31*C*.

8.3. Priority management

Events that are susceptible to producing an exception usually occur in an asynchronous, and therefore unpredictable, manner. It is admittedly always possible to trigger these mechanisms by executing code; this is naturally the case for *SVC*. It is also the case for all interrupts, through the *ISPERs*, but this possibility remains rather atypical. It is therefore necessary to consider several exceptions occurring simultaneously, either in exactly the same clock cycle or some clock cycles after, but close enough that the processing of the first exception is not completed before the next begins.

ARM has taken this multiple management into account and it is the responsibility of the *NVIC* to receive and organize the different requests into a hierarchy. For this purpose, each exception has a *priority level*. This level is a value for which the associated priority will be higher when the value is lower. *Reset, NMI* and *Hard fault* have their priorities fixed at -3, -2 and -1 respectively. All other exceptions have priority levels that can be configured with a positive number coded on 8 bits. The *NVIC_SHPR[x]* (*System Handler Priority Registers*, see Figure 8.7) contain the configurable levels for traps and the *NVIC_IPR[x]* (*Interrupt Priority level Registers*, see Figure 8.8) contain the programmable levels for interrupts. Thus configured, it appears that *Reset* always has priority over *NMI*, which itself has priority over *hard fault*, and that is unchangeable.

On the other hand, it is the responsibility of the developer to define the order of all remaining exceptions, all of these levels initially being equal to 0 after a *Reset*.

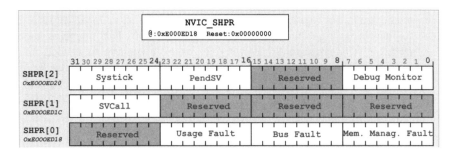

Figure 8.7. *System Handler Priority Registers (NVIC_SHPR)*

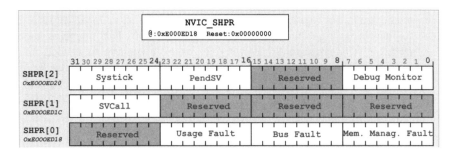

Figure 8.8. *Interrupt Priority Registers (NVIC_IPR)*

8.3.1. *Priority levels and sublevels*

Figures 8.7 and 8.8 show that priority levels are encoded on one byte. In theory, there are therefore 256 different priority levels. Sadly it is not so simple in practice. ARM provides two subtleties:

– a designer may want fewer levels, coded not only on the base 8 bits but on only 3, 4… or 7 bits. This choice, which cannot be reconfigured by the user, is managed so that only the most significant bits (MSBs) of the level are significant. So on 3 bits the 8 possible levels are 0x00, 0x20, 0x40…, 0xE0. On 4 bits, the 16 levels would be 0x00, 0x10, 0x20…, 0xF0. One of the (small) programming problems concerns the calculation of the value to be positioned in the register to code a given priority level. A left-hand shift of the number of bits necessary for the encoding is sufficient to carry out this translation. Example 8.5 shows the few lines of programming in the case of encoding levels on five bits in the processing routine associated with *SysTick*;

– the existence of sublevels: in the *NVIC_AIRCR,* the 3-bit field *PRIGROUP* (weight 8 to weight 10) allows us to split the 8 bits of the level into two in order to separate the priority levels and sublevels. This separation – and it is here that things get a little more complicated – is not relative to the number of bits chosen by the designer to grade their priority levels; it can simply intervene with the non-significant bit and consequently can be without effect.

Figures 8.9 to 8.14 illustrate all of the combined options resulting from these two subtleties. The bits marked *x* give the priority level encoding and those marked with a *y* concern the encoding of sublevels. In each figure, the value to be given to the 3-bit *PRIO-GROUP* field in order to define the desired level/sublevel separation is indicated. It should be noted that in order to write in the *AIRCR*, it is essential (for hardware security) that the 16 MSB (*VECTKEY*) of the written value contains exactly 0x*FA*05, otherwise the writing will not be carried out. The significance of the other bits of the register is given in Figure 8.15, however they are not *a priori* directly useful in a common programming.

EXAMPLE 8.5.– *Priority level setting for the SysTick Handler*

```
;- - - - - - - - - - - - - - - - - - - - - - - - - - - - - - - - - -
; Setting of the priority level
; for the SysTick Handler
;- - - - - - - - - - - - - - - - - - - - - - - - - - - - - - - - - -
    LDRB R0,=0xE000ED23    ; Address of the SHPR register
    MOV R1,#9              ; 5 bytes of encoding we chose a level 9 (on 32) here
    LSL R1,#3              ;      => (8-5) left shift to assign MSB
    STRB R1,[R0]          ; Register assignment and so priority setting
```

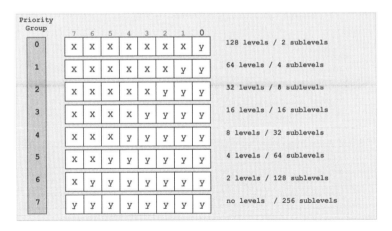

Figure 8.9. *Management of the priorities on 8 bits*

Priority Group	7	6	5	4	3	2	1	0	
0	x	x	x	x	x	x	x	0	128 levels / no sublevels
1	x	x	x	x	x	x	y	0	64 levels / 2 sublevels
2	x	x	x	x	x	y	y	0	32 levels / 4 sublevels
3	x	x	x	x	y	y	y	0	16 levels / 8 sublevels
4	x	x	x	y	y	y	y	0	8 levels / 16 sublevels
5	x	x	y	y	y	y	y	0	4 levels / 32 sublevels
6	x	y	y	y	y	y	y	0	2 levels / 64 sublevels
7	y	y	y	y	y	y	y	0	no levels / 128 sublevels

Figure 8.10. *Management of the priorities on 7 bits*

Priority Group	7	6	5	4	3	2	1	0	
0	x	x	x	x	x	x	0	0	64 levels / no sublevels
1	x	x	x	x	x	x	0	0	64 levels / no sublevels
2	x	x	x	x	x	y	0	0	32 levels / 2 sublevels
3	x	x	x	x	y	y	0	0	16 levels / 4 sublevels
4	x	x	x	y	y	y	0	0	8 levels / 8 sublevels
5	x	x	y	y	y	y	0	0	4 levels / 16 sublevels
6	x	y	y	y	y	y	0	0	2 levels / 32 sublevels
7	y	y	y	y	y	y	0	0	no levels / 64 sublevels

Figure 8.11. *Management of the priorities on 6 bits*

Priority Group	7	6	5	4	3	2	1	0	
0	x	x	x	x	x	0	0	0	32 levels / no sublevels
1	x	x	x	x	x	0	0	0	32 levels / no sublevels
2	x	x	x	x	x	0	0	0	32 levels / no sublevels
3	x	x	x	x	y	0	0	0	16 levels / 2 sublevels
4	x	x	x	y	y	0	0	0	8 levels / 4 sublevels
5	x	x	y	y	y	0	0	0	4 levels / 8 sublevels
6	x	y	y	y	y	0	0	0	2 levels / 16 sublevels
7	y	y	y	y	y	0	0	0	no levels / 32 sublevels

Figure 8.12. *Management of the priorities on 5 bits*

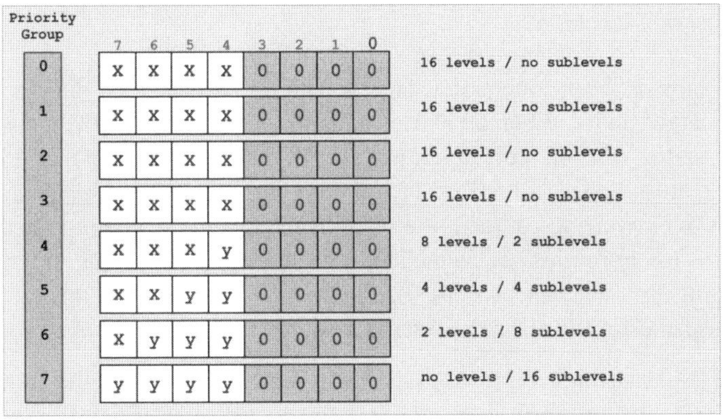

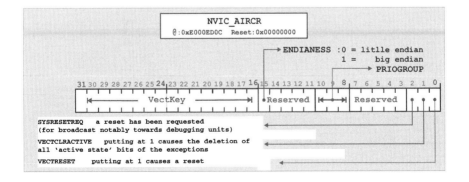

Figure 8.13. *Management of the priorities on 4 bits*

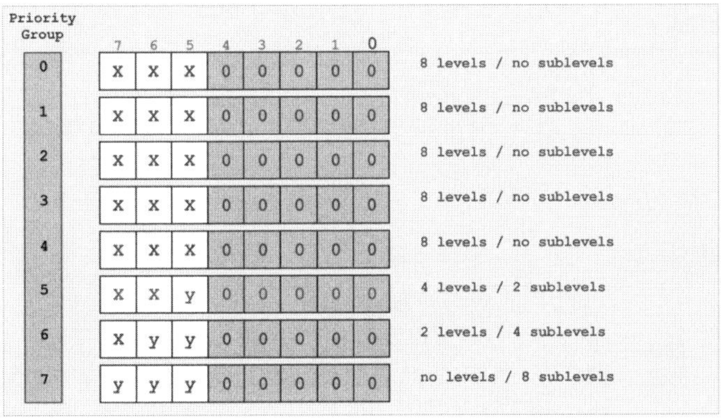

Figure 8.14. *Management of the priorities on 3 bits*

Figure 8.15. *Register of management of Reset and priority sub-levels (NVIC_AIRCR)*

8.3.2. *The nested mechanism*

As has already been touched on, an exception can have two different statuses: *active* or *pended* status. When an exception is triggered, it is automatically switched to pended status; the bit corresponding to the SHCR (for traps) or ISPER (for interrupts) then switches to 1. In a standard case, i.e. if it is the only pended bit (or if its priority level overrides others), the NVIC switches the interrupt to active status, the process of re-routing is launched, and the pended status is erased (the corresponding bit switches back to 0). Figure 8.16 lays out the timetable for this standard case and for the different cases considered below:

– Case no. 1: a higher priority exception (A) arises during the processing of exception (B): the processing of (B) is interrupted but (B) remains active. The processing of (A) is launched and when that is finished (exception return) the processing of (B) restarts where it left off.

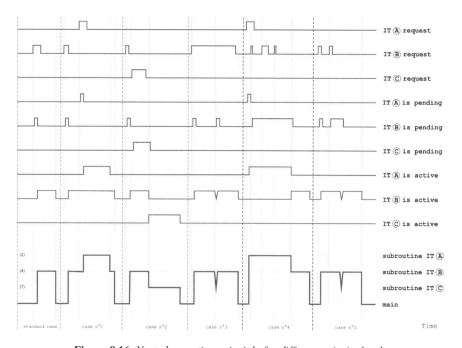

Figure 8.16. *Nested exception principle for different priority levels*

– Case no. 2: a lower priority exception (C) arises during the processing of exception (B): (C) retains pending status, and will switch to active and be processed when the processing of (B) is finished, unless an exception with a higher priority level than (C) appears in the meantime.

– Case no. 3: at the end of interrupt (B)'s processing, the request is always on[3]. The pending status is switched to true immediately after the return from the interrupt and if no other exception has appeared in the meantime, the active status and a new execution of the treatment routine will be validated. We call this a re-entrant interrupt.

– Case no. 4: a request (or several requests) for interrupt (B) occurs when the status of this interrupt is already pended (a higher priority interrupt, (A), is being processed). Nothing else happens. (B) stays pended and (A) stays active. There is no accumulation or stacking of requests for the same source.

– Case no. 5: a request for interrupt (B) occurs when the status of this interrupt is active. Its pended status (which was reset during the switch to active status) switches back to 1. At the end of processing, the interrupt directly switches back to active. We also call this a re-entrant interrupt.

– Case no. 6: if two interrupt requests of the same priority level, (B) and (B'), come simultaneously, or if both have pended status and at the end of the current processing their priority level overrides others, it is the priority sublevel that determines which of the two will switch to active status. If they also have the same priority sublevel, it is their order number that separates them, with the smallest overriding. So if the *SysTick* (number 15) is at the same level and sublevel as a *Usage fault* (number 6) and both are able to switch to active, the *usage fault* will have priority (6 against 15), and so will be processed first.

8.4. Entry and return in exception processing

The *NVIC* registers undergo a certain number of modifications during the running of an exception, but this is not the only activity governed by the processor because it must execute a processing routine.

8.4.1. *Re-routing*

When the exception switches to active status, Cortex-M3 carries out a series of operations in order to allow the execution of the specific handler. Part of the re-routing sequence has already been described: that which consists of recovering the address where the routine is stored in the IVT. Once recovered, this address will modify the *PC* instruction pointer and the routine will be executed. There are other operations, however, that are performed before this asynchronous jump:

---

3 It should be noted that the interrupt request bit is not automatically reset when the interruption is launched. It is the responsibility of the associated handler to perform this reset.

– eight registers are stored on the stack (*MSP* if the processor is in *Handler* mode and, in theory, *PSP* if it is in *Thread* mode: however, it is possible for *Thread* mode to use the *MSP* stack). These registers are, in order of stacking, *PC, PSR, R0, R1, R2, R3, R12* and *LR*. The stack is originally in the state shown in Figure 8.17 when starting the processing routine;

– the processor, if it has not already, switches into *Handler* mode. The stack must be *MSP* during exception processing;

– the *LR* is initialized with a return code (*EXC_RETURN*) that will allow it to correctly return from the exception. Indeed in this processor, in the opposite way to many other types of architecture, there is no exception return instruction. This return is triggered when the *PC* instruction pointer is loaded with a known value of return code. This return code allows us to inform the processor of the mode in which it must return (*Thread* or *Handler*) and so which system stack to use (*MSP* or *PSP*). The three unique values allowed are those in Table 8.1; any other code will cause a *usage fault* (the *INVPC* bit of *UFSR* being switched to 1).

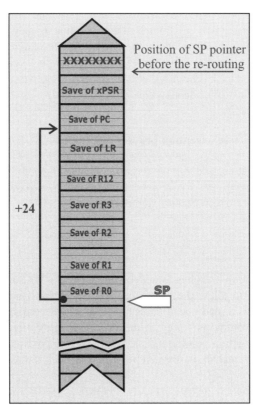

Figure 8.17. *State of the system stack after an exception re-routing*

REMARK 8.1.– It is interesting to note that register R0 to R3 are those systematically used by the C compiler (ARM RealView). The saving of register R12 is most surprising and could surely be used to carry out the passing of one argument to interrupts.

Value	Kind of return
0xFFFFFFF1	Return to Handler mode – the stack is MSP
0xFFFFFFF9	Return to Thread mode – the stack is MSP
0xFFFFFFFD	Return to Thread mode – the stack is PSP

Table 8.1. *Exception return code stored in the LR*

8.4.2. *Return*

The return from exception is, from an instruction point of view, very similar to that which we could write to cause a return to a classic routine. It consists of transferring the contents of *LR* to the *PC* pointer. This transfer is usually carried out by Branch and eXchange (*BX*) *LR*. As in the case of nested calls (see section 7.1.2), the *LR* can be altered during the processing of the routine exception (e.g. it could call to some routine or other inside the exception procedure). It is therefore essential to save *LR* at the start of the procedure, in order to restore it just before transferring it to the instruction pointer in order to trigger the return. This restoration/transfer can be carried out by a single instruction: *POP PC*. Finally, let us note that the loading instruction *LDR PC, ???* can also carry out this exception return, knowing that the *???* must correspond to something (an immediate value, a register, etc.) containing one of the three permitted values. When *PC* receives this value of *EXC_RETURN*, it knows in which stack the eight registers have been saved. It is then in position to carry out the restoration. In the course of restoration, it then re-modifies the *PC* instruction pointer with its value before the re-routing, allowing the processor to resume the normal course of executions from the place where they were stopped.

8.4.3. *"Tail-chaining" and "late-arriving"*

In a standard functional cycle, the latency time between *NVIC* receiving the interrupt request and the start of the first instruction of the interrupt processing routine is 12 clock cycles. It can also produce situations where two exceptions follow each other, in which case the restore/save sequence may run differently in order to optimize this latency time.

In the case of *tail-chaining*, as in case no. 3 (see Figure 8.16) it involves an exception (C) that must switch to active at the end of the previous exception (B). In this case it is pointless to perform the restoration at the end of (B) and to then immediately perform the save in order to launch (C), since there was no register modification between the two points. This double sequence is therefore skipped. At the return time of (B), the processor switches directly to the processing of (C) and restoration only takes place at the return of (C). In this case, the switch from (B) to (C) takes only 6 of the 12 cycles necessary without this "trick".

The case of *late-arriving* involves a higher priority exception (A), which occurs when the re-routing sequence of a lower level exception (B) has already started. This could correspond to case no. 1 by advancing the rising edge of the *IT* request (A) so that it takes place just after *IT* (B) switches to the active state. Here also the latency time can be optimized by not performing a double save; i.e. by not launching a save sequence after (A), since the save point is the same as (B). (A) will be substituted for (B) in the re-routing and (B) will be switched to pended. At the end of (A), unless other higher priority exceptions have arisen, a *tail-chaining* mechanism will be implemented in order to resume the re-routing of (B).

8.4.4. *Other useful registers for the NVIC*

As we have seen in the course of this chapter, the *NVIC* module is the true conductor for the organization of an exception handler into a hierarchy. To complete our account of its potential, there are some registers left to explain.

BasePri, *PriMask* and *FaultMask* are three core registers; therefore they do not occupy a memory address. They are not part of the *NVIC*, but their role is nevertheless directly linked to exception management. They are described as special in the documentation because they are not directly accessible. In order to access them, the code must use the special instructions *MRS* (Move from Register to Special) for reading and *MSR* (Move to Special Register) for writing, see Chapter 5. These two instructions require privileges in order to be executed.

The registers *PriMask* and *FaultMask* each have only one significant bit at 0. Thus when reading, the 31 MSB are always at 0 and, symmetrically, writing to these bits will have no effect. These two registers, as their name suggests, allow us to mask exceptions. When the LSB is at 1 in *FaultMask*, no exceptions, apart from the *NMI* exception, will switch to active state and, if a request intervenes, will stay in pended state. As soon as the bit is reset, pended exceptions will switch to an active state following the order of their respective priority. *PriMask* is identical to *FaultMask*, with the difference that in addition to *NMI* it also allows the launching of the third exception with a non-configurable priority level, namely a *hard fault*.

Prohibiting all (or nearly all) possible exceptions can be useful in "catastrophic" situations for which a real-time kernel will switch the processor to a "quasi-degraded" mode to hopefully provide solutions to these situations.

BasePri is similar. This involves a register of which the eight LSBs can be significant. In effect, they contain a mask at the minimal priority level of exceptions that could switch to active state. All exceptions with a lower priority level would remain pended. Setting this register to 0x00 is equivalent to the absence of the mask. Two small pitfalls should be avoided for adjusting *BasePri*. First, it must be remembered that the priority scale is the reverse of normal numbering (level 3 is lower than level 2). Then, as could be done for adjusting priorities in associated registers (see Example 8.5), we must not forget to carry out the $8 - n$ shifts on the left of the desired value if the processor only codes priority levels on n bits.

The *NVIC_STIR* (*Software Trigger Interrupt Register*) is the last register of *NVIC* that we will consider here. This register (@ 0x*E*000*EF*00) is an alternative to using the *NVIC_ISPER* register, since in writing a value in the LSB (*INTID*) this amounts to switching interrupt *INTID* into pending status. In an application to emulate the triggering of an interrupt with software, this second route will undoubtedly be faster and more practical to implement.

Chapter 9

From Listing to Executable: External Modularity

In the context of native development, the computer system on which an applied project is developed is exactly the same as the one that will execute the project. When we write a program for a μcontroller, this is never the case: indeed, there is no program under Cortex-M3 that allows us to develop another executive for Cortex-M3. The programmer is in a *cross-development* situation where the writing and generation of an executable is done on a host computer system and the execution is transported to the given target hardware. There may be a subtlety in this basic schema, however, which is the use of an emulator that allows us to develop a project without a real target. This emulator is a program that works on the host system and simulates the functioning of the μcontroller cycle-by-cycle, instruction by instruction. Although there are excellent emulators that are able to very accurately replicate the internal functioning of a processor, it is not unusual to find differences when executing on a real processor and the final validation phase cannot be carried out without testing on a real target.

In the course of the cross-development phase, between writing the code in one (or several) "listing" file(s) and the execution of this code on a given processor, there are different stages (and therefore different tools), each of which is necessary for the proper realization of the whole. These are:

– the *assembler*, which interprets a source listing to create an object file;

– the *linker*, which puts together the different objects of the project and parts of the library to make the executable file;

– a *loader*, which transfers the executable in the memory to the card (or to the emulator, if there is one);

– a *symbolic debugger,* which at a minimum allows the starting and stopping of the execution on the target but also, as the name suggests, looks for possible errors in the application created.

Figure 9.1 shows how the different tools can be connected to each other.

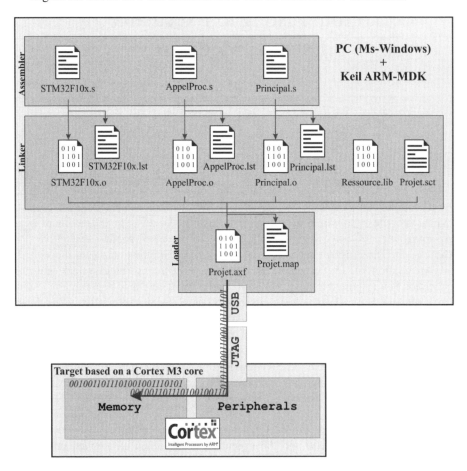

Figure 9.1. *Synoptic of the ARM toolchain*

For Cortex-M3-based μcontrollers, there are many toolchains that can work under Windows or Linux. Consulting the *Development Tools – Software* pages on ARM's website gives us an idea of the palette of options and the difficulties that can occur, before having written even a line, in choosing the best tool for your needs and practices.

This chapter, like the other parts of this book and especially Chapter 3 on assembly directives, uses the *Keil-ARM-MDK* (*Microcontroller Development Kit*) [KEI] chain, which is ARM's own tool[1]. Some elements of the GNU (GNU's not UNIX) chain are given in Appendix D. This chapter is only interested in the basic principles of the different tools implemented in a cross-development chain, so transposition to another product can be done without much difficulty.

REMARK 9.1.– In the course of this chapter, the explanations will be limited to those that are useful for understanding how the development chain proceeds to construct a **simple executable**. This implies that the code is absolute and cannot be relocated. Advanced concepts such as dynamic linkers, for example, will not be addressed.

Let us now return to the concept of modularity presented in Chapter 7, by examining what happens when the modules making up a program are spread over several files (external modularity).

9.1. External modularity

9.1.1. *Generic example*

In order to most clearly expose the different points addressed later in this chapter, we will use a simple example. The project whose general architecture appears in Figure 9.1 is made up of five files:

– *STM32F10x.s* is a file supplied by the Keil development environment. It contains, among others, a reservation and initialization of the system stack, a declaration of different interrupt vectors and the minimum routines (limited to a single infinite loop) for the most critical exceptions handlers;

– a *resource.lib* library containing a number of input/output routines, dependent on hardware and inaccessible to the developer in source format;

– a *Project.sct* memory description file;

– two "source" files, written in assembly language: *Principal.s* (see Example 9.1) and *CallProc.s* (see Example 9.2).

This entire project is of restricted algorithmic interest. The use of global variables and code optimization could be discussed in detail but as it is, it allows us

---

1 Since the 2005 repurchase of Keil by ARM.

to illustrate the aim of this chapter as simply as possible. This project consists of calculating the weighted average of two numbers like so:

$$Resu = \frac{(Val_1 * Coef(1)) + (Val_2 * Coef(2))}{(Coef(1) + Coef(2))}$$

The two half-words *Val1* and *Val2* are read by a resource library routine and are declared, as *Resu*, which stores the result in a Data section of the principal module *Principal.s*. *Coef* is the byte table of the two elements declared in a Data section of the *CallProc.s* module.

EXAMPLE 9.1.– *Listing of the Principal.s module*

```
;/****************************************************************/
              THUMB
;/****************************************************************/
; IMPORT/EXPORT
;/****************************************************************/
              IMPORT ||LibRequestarmlib|| [CODE,WEAK]
              IMPORT Ave_Weight
              IMPORT ReadData
              EXPORT main
              EXPORT Val1
              EXPORT Val2
              EXPORT Resu
;/****************************************************************/
; DATA SECTION
;/****************************************************************/
              AREA mydata, data, readwrite
Val1   SPACE 2
Val2   SPACE 2
Resu   DCW 0
;/****************************************************************/
; CODE SECTION
;/****************************************************************/

              AREA mycode, code, readonly
```

```
main            PROC
                LDR R0,= Val1
                BL ReadData            ; Read first data (Val1)
                LDR R0,= Val2
                BL ReadData            ; Read second data (Val2)
                BL CallProc
Infinity        B Infinity             ; End of program
                ENDP


                END                    ; End of module
```

EXAMPLE 9.2.– *Listing of the CallProc.s module*

```
;/***************************************************************/
; IMPORT/EXPORT
;/***************************************************************/
                EXPORT Ave_Weight
                IMPORT Val1
                IMPORT Val2
                IMPORT Resu
;/***************************************************************/
                AREA mydata, data
Coef            DCB 8,12               ; Fixed coefficients
;/***************************************************************/
                AREA mycode, code
Ave_Weight      PROC
                LDR R0, =Val1
                LDRH R4,[R0]
Weighting       LDR R0, =Coef
                LDRB R2,[R0]
                MUL R4,R2              ; Weighting of Val1
                LDR R0, =Val2
                LDRH R5,[R0]
                LDR R0, =Coef
                LDRB R3,[R0, #1]
                MUL R5,R3              ; Weighting of Val2
Sum
```

```
            ADD R4,R5
            ADD R2,R3
Average
            UDIV R4,R2              ; Calculation of the average
            LDR R0, =Resu
            STRH R4,[R0]           ; Storage of the result
            BX LR
            ENDP
            END                    ; End of Module
```

9.1.2. *Assembly by pieces*

Our example is made up of three "source" files, which we also call modules. This could be confusing, but the use of this term predates modular programming, and has not completely fallen into disuse. In the following, when we say module it means separated file (external module) and not procedure, which defines internal modularity as discussed in Chapter 8. The declarations and instructions of a program can therefore be split at will into several files, so long as the syntax is respected. In particular, any section of code or data will be closed with the end of the module or by the opening of a new module. Similarly, any open procedure will be closed (*ENDP* directive) in a module. The assembler is capable of individually translating each module into machine language, which we call assembly by pieces. The linker will later group the resulting object modules into a coherent whole in the form of a single file called an executable (or more precisely loadable for execution).

9.1.3. *Advantages of assembly by pieces*

Separate assembly presents some interesting advantages[2]:

– Individual trial: each module that is accompanied by a trial module can be tested individually. If each module tried separately works, we can hope that the final version that reunites all of the modules will also work. Conversely, if a module does not work the project as a whole cannot correctly respond to all specifications.

– localization of the consequences of a modification: the modification of a module only affects the re-assembly of this module followed by the call to the linker;

– recovery of a module: we can reuse a module in another program;

---

2 These various remarks are also true for a compiler.

– reation of libraries: we can create libraries of utility functions (input–output, floating point or complex calculations, trigonometric functions, hyperbolics, ellipticals, transcendents, and others);

– distribution and copyright: we can distribute libraries of procedures and data in the form of object modules without supplying the source program.

9.1.4. *External symbols*

What are the actual consequences if our program is written in pieces? To answer this question, it is necessary to analyze the relationships between the modules of the program in order to understand the necessity of the directives presented later.

Generally, a module can contain code and data, which are placed in one or more sections, as are the symbols (section names, procedure names and labels). In our project, each of the *Principal.s* and *CallProc.s* files contain a code section and a data section.

The instructions that the module contains can refer not only to data or procedures located in the same module, but also to data or procedures[3] defined in another module. In a higher-level language, we talk about importing data or procedures. The *Principal.s* module calls (and therefore imports) the *Ave_Weight* procedure from the *CallProc.s* module and the *ReadData* from the library *resource.lib* procedure. Symmetrically, the *CallProc.s* file uses the *Val1, Val2* and *Resu* variables declared in the *Principal.s* module. Such references are therefore called external module references.

In all cases, the assembler, when carrying out the translation of a particular module, does not know the contents of other modules. It is consequently unable to attribute a numerical value to the symbol (an address or datum) concerned in the code-word representing the instruction.

When it reads the listing, the assembler will draw up a list of symbols, which it divides into three categories:

– absolute symbols: these are the symbols whose associated value is fully defined in the listing. Typically, these are constants (directive *EQU*). When the assembler encounters this symbol, it can resolve it without ambiguity and determine the code-word to be stored in memory;

– relocatable symbols: these are symbols belonging to the current module but whose numerical value cannot be determined. They are variables, initialized or

_____

3 This is the same for branch instructions.

otherwise, that are declared in a data section of the module, and the labels or procedure names of a code section. In all cases the symbols correspond to addresses. At program construction level, the assembler can only give them a relative value. This allows the assembler to locate them in the section where they were declared;

– external symbols: these are symbols that do not belong to the module and to which the assembler is unable to give any value. When we use such an external reference in a module, it is necessary to indicate to the assembler that the symbol concerned is defined in another module. In the absence of this indication, the assembler will consider it to be an undefined symbol and will produce an error message. This directive is the *IMPORT* directive.

The assembly phase of *CallProc.S* locates the symbols presented in Example 9.3.

Even if it does not appear clearly, a certain number of pieces of information are associated with this table: the membership of a particular section and the places where the symbols are used. We will note that if it is impossible to attribute a value, the assembler will give the value 0 to an external symbol. It should also be noted that the three symbols *Weighting*, *Sum* and *Average* have no algorithmic use insofar as they are labels that are not used in the instructions; they only play the role of comments. However, the assembler finds and situates them like other symbols, but it also records this characteristic of non-use. Subsequently if the data are still not used, they will not be stored in the symbol table unless explicitly requested by marking them as such with the *KEEP* directive (see section 3.5.2).

EXAMPLE 9.3.– *Symbol list located in the CallProc.s module*

```
Relocatable symbols
              Coef 00000000
              Ave_Weight 00000000
              Average 0000001C
              Weighting 0000000E
              Sum 00000018
External symbols
              Resu 00000000
              Val1 00000000
              Val2 00000000
```

9.1.5. *IMPORT and EXPORT directives*

Seen from the outside world, each module by default behaves like a black box, with its own resources and symbols. *A priori* its symbols are not accessible by other modules. This prevents any outside world interference inside the module. However, we must consider the case of a module containing certain symbols to be used by one or more other modules. These symbols, called exportables, must be explicitly marked as such because, by default, symbols defined in a module are private, meaning that they are only visible in that module. The scope of exportable symbols (equivalent to visibility in assembly language) is global, unlike private symbols whose scope is only local. Thus, any symbol can only be private or exportable (global).

There are two dual directives for setting these visibility properties. The position of these directives in the module is free, but the convention is to place them at the head because they symbolize interface with the outside world.

The first, *EXPORT*, allows us to inform the assembler and the linker that the symbol defined could be merged with a identical symbol used in another module. The existence of this directive shows that the visibility of a given symbol is limited by default to the module itself. In other words, when naming a new symbol it is not necessary to worry about its possible existence in another module. The syntax is as follows:

EXPORT symbol [WEAK,type]

The option *WEAK* specifies whether the symbol is defined elsewhere (in the current module or in any other module); this definition will be prioritized for exportation. This option is used for the declaration of symbols associated with exception vectors (see Example C.1 in Appendix C). It is therefore possible for the developer to rewrite an exception handler: its name needs to be correctly recognized in order to modify the interrupt vector table without conflicting with the routine written by default.

The *type* option allows us to specify, if needed, whether the symbols must be treated as a datum (*type* will then be *DATA*) or as code (*type* will then be *CODE*). By default, the assembler chooses the *type* that seems best adapted by simply copying the *type* of the section in which it is declared.

IMPORT can be substituted for *EXTERN*; these two directives are almost entirely equivalent. With the *EXTERN* directive, a symbol will only be included in the symbol table if it is used in the module. As a result if, for example, the symbol

VarForgot is declared in a project and is not used in the code of the current module, the directive *IMPORT VarForgot* will generate a linker error, since it will be still be included in the list and is consequently searched for by the linker. Conversely, directive *EXTERNE VarForgot* will do nothing and the linker will therefore not worry about not finding it.

The *IMPORT* directive performs the opposite function of the preceding directive: it enables the assembler to know whether such a qualified symbol comes from an external module. If this is the case, it can accept the symbol's use in the module's code.

IMPORT symbol [WEAK,type]

The *type* option has the same meaning as it does in the *EXPORT* directive.

In the absence of the *WEAK* option on a symbol, if the linker cannot recognize the symbol (i.e. if the symbol does not exist elsewhere in the project), it will cause a fatal error in the construction of the project. Conversely, if the symbol is marked as *WEAK* during its importation, the linker will always be able to resolve the symbol by giving it a default value, if any. If the symbol is a destination (*B symbol*, for example) its default value will be the address of the next instruction. The jump will then be equivalent to *NOP* (No Operation). In other cases, the default value will be 0. Poorly controlled use of *WEAK* in the importations of a variable can be dangerous.

As an example, let us imagine forgetting the exportations of *Resu* in the *Principal.s* file and the confirmation of this same symbol by *WEAK* in *CallProc.s*. This would result in a project that was correctly constructed, but the result would be stored at the memory address 0x0000000! We must then hope that a *Reset* will not occur afterwards, since the stack address would no longer be valid (see section 8.1). Like the *EXTERN* directive for *IMPORT*, the *EXPORT* directive can be substituted (with no subtlety of use in this case) by the *GLOBAL* directive.

9.2. The role of the assembler

The principal role of the assembler is to translate the contents of the source module written in assembly language into machine language code-words (which we should remember are coded on 16 or 32 bits). It is not capable of carrying out a complete work, however, because it lacks a series of data: it does not know the value of external symbols, nor the address where each section defined in the source will be placed. Nevertheless, it is capable of carrying out its job. We will see how it proceeds and how it prepares the work for the linker, which will finish the formation of the program.

9.2.1. *Files produced by the assembler*

The assembler principally produces two files (see Figure 9.1): the binary object file (*.obj*), which will be used by the linker, and a listing file (*.lst*) for use by the developer who wants to see the result of the assembler's work[4]. Example 9.3 was a small part of a "*.lst*" listing file. Example 9.4 shows another extract, which more focused on the translation of different sections of the *Principal.s* source file.

EXAMPLE 9.4.– *Extract of the Principal.lst file*

```
10 00000000        ;************************************************
11 00000000        ; IMPORT/EXPORT
12 00000000        ;************************************************
13 00000000
14 00000000        IMPORT ||LibRequestarmlib|| [CODE, WEAK]
15 00000000
16 00000000        IMPORT Ave_Weight
17 00000000        IMPORT ReadData
18 00000000
19 00000000        EXPORT main
20 00000000        EXPORT Val1 [CODE]
21 00000000        EXPORT Val2
22 00000000        EXPORT Resu
23 00000000
24 00000000        ;************************************************
25 00000000        ; DATA SECTION
26 00000000        ;************************************************
27 00000000
28 00000000                   AREA myData, data, readwrite
29 00000000
30 00000000 00 00  Val1 SPACE 2
31 00000002 00 00  Val2 SPACE 2
```

---

4 Long ago in computer science, before toolchain existed, it was through reading this file that the developer could know the errors that were detected by the assembler and where they were located.

```
32 00000004 10 00      Resu DCW 0x10

33 00000006

34 00000006            ;**************************************************

35 00000006            ; CODE SECTION

36 00000006            ;**************************************************

37 00000006                      AREA mycode, code, readonly

38 00000000

39 00000000            main    PROC

40 00000000

41 00000000 4804                 LDR R0,= Val1

42 00000002 F7FF                  FFFE BL ReadData

43 00000006 4804                 LDR R0,= Val2

44 00000008 F7FF                  FFFE BL ReadData

45 0000000C

46 0000000C F7FF FFFE             BL Ave_Weight

47 00000010

48 00000010

49 00000010 E7FE      Infinity B Infinity ; End of program

50 00000012

51 00000012                       ENDP

52 00000012

53 00000012                       END          ; End of module
            0000
            0000 0000
            0000 0000
```

When the assembler has completed its work, the fruit – which will be used later by the linker – is an *object* file code in *ELF* (*Executable and Linking Format*). This format was originally created by and for UNIX. The encoding is binary (and so not directly viewable using a classic text editor) and contains assembled code that may have been compiled previously (objects, executables and function libraries).

Encoding in ELF is unique but its content will be significantly different depending on whether it is an input file to a linker or whether it is an executable file for an operating system. Let us consider the first case. The ELF file begins with a header followed by a set of sections. Parts of the ELF sections that we find in this file correspond to sections declared in the assembler source. These sections are completed from other sections that contain information allowing further pursuit of the construction of the executable image of the project. We can cite containing the symbol table (see section 9.2.3) or those dedicated to relocation tables (see section 9.4) as examples of sections. Finally, other sections are optional, such as those that group the necessary data for the functioning of a debugger (see section 9.4).

REMARK 9.2.– There are specific programs for reading files coded in ELF in order to retrieve and view information related to its content. In the ARM development chain, this tool corresponds to the executable FROMELF program.

9.2.2. *Placement counters*

The assembler carries out all of its work in a relative manner. For each module it numbers each line, as you can see in the first column of Example 9.4. This first search is not very complicated, since it just consists of locating the *ASCII* character *carriage return* in the processed listing. It should be noted, however, that empty lines are also located, an important detail for a development system that must indicate the line where an error is located or for development when the listing is put in parallel with disassembled code. For each section – whether it is code or data – the assembler also uses a placement counter (the second column of the *lst* file) whose initial value is 00000000. The departure address of each section is therefore provisionally set at 0. In the case of a code section, insofar as it carries out its translation, the assembler increases the value of the placement counter by 2 or 4, depending on the size of the instruction. The placement counter therefore indicates the relative position of each instruction. It works in the same way for each data section, the incrementation of its internal counter depending on the size of the variable.

For each new section, the placement counter restarts at 000000. If a section is closed but opens a second time in the same source file, the placement counter is not reset to 0 but continues from the last previous value, which *de facto* means the concatenation of two half sections.

9.2.3. *First pass: symbol table*

Classically an assembler works in two passes. In the first pass, it scans all of the text to raise all of the symbols and establish a symbol table. We have already shown how this table was presented in Example 9.3, however there is another important element to be added: the *Literal Pool* zones. In fact, when an assembler scans all of the instructions making up the code, it locates the addresses (always in a relative manner) of the section being analyzed where it will be possible to store the immediate values that must be coded on 32 bits in these specific zones (see section 4.2.2.3). The assembler therefore provides the necessary reservations by inserting lines in the places thus determined. These lines, to the extent that they will receive as-yet-unresolved data (relocatable symbols), are filled with 0s in the first pass. In Example 9.4 there are two instructions to load the *R0* register with the addresses of *Val1* (line 41) and *Val2* (line 43). These two instructions will be coded as reading the program counter (*PC*) with relative indirection towards the *Literal Pool* zone, a 10-byte zone initialized at 0 that we can see just after line 52. In the present case, two padding bytes have been added to those that are effectively necessary to align the *Literal Pool* zone with a doubly even address.

To evaluate the labels that locate the instructions, in the course of the first pass the assembler examines the operands of instructions and deduces the length of the code-word by translating the instruction. This allows us to calculate the value (which is always relative) of the placement of the next instruction: the value of the label is that of the current placement counter. This value is not definitive, since the section begins at 0. The real value of the label will only be known after memory placement (relocation) by the linker: labels are therefore necessarily relocatable.

9.2.4. Second pass: translation

During the second pass, the assembler carries out the translation using the values of the symbol table.

For external symbols, it uses a value that can only be provisional, since at best it will only know to follow the work of the linker.

In the specific case shown below involving the loading of an immediate value via a *Literal Pool* zone, the encoding of the instruction is exact and definitive. Indeed, the assembler determines the zone where the immediate value, coded on 32 bits, will be stored. Access to the datum will be relative to the value of the *PC*. Thus, in the listing we can see that the instruction *LDR R0, =Val1* is coded as 4804. In observing the encoding principle of the *LDR* instruction (see Example 9.2), the most significant bit (48) is also the opcode of the instruction followed by the 3 bits 000 to code *R0*. The immediate value *imm8* here is 0x04, so the offset to reach the *Literal Pool* is therefore 4*4 = 16 bytes. This relative value then allows us to refer to an indirection access by *[PC,#16]*. It should be noted on the listing, however, that the relative placement of the *Literal Pool* is at 0x00000012, and so has a differential of 18 bytes. There is therefore a difference of two bytes caused by the existence of a pipeline, implying that the value of *PC* at the time of the actual execution of the instruction will be different to the value of that where the instruction is stored.

For references to internal labels, the assembler uses the value of the label given by its symbol table. In some cases, as in the case of jumps for example, encoding relative to the operand is possible. Thus the translation is direct. For references to external labels, the encoding is never directly possible to the extent that the label is unresolved. The assembler will therefore introduce a partially false operand code that will belong to the linker, in order to give the correct value. In our example, the jump to the *ReadData* (line 42) procedure is coded as 0x*F7FFFFFE*. The first seven bits also correspond to the opcode of the *BL* (Branch with Link) instruction (11110) but the remaining 23 bits do not allow the decoding of a valid subroutine address in this state. In this case we are dealing with a coded instruction that must be "relocated" by the linker.

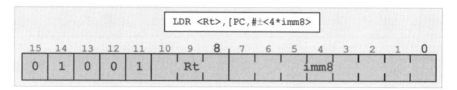

Figure 9.2. *Thumb encoding of an LDR instruction*

9.2.5. *Relocation table*

Finally we obtain a partially erroneous code. It is erroneous in the sense that any absolute reference to a label or any use of external symbols leads to false code-words. As it will be corrected by the linker, it is necessary for the assembler to provide the linker with useful information. The assembler communicates this information with a relocation table where the list of instructions to be corrected is indicated, as are the rules to apply to make the corrections. We will not go into how these relocation tables work, partly because complete information on their functioning is unavailable but partly because the developer does not have direct access and consequently it is impossible to modify its contents. It is still interesting, however, at least for curiosity's sake, to look at the contents of one of these tables: Example 9.5 gives the third ELF section of the *Principal.o* file. This section corresponds to the relocation table of the *CODE* section *mycode* of the corresponding source file.

We can see that for this small section of code the linker will have five relocations to carry out. Each of these relocations is marked by its offset (second column). Relocation may come completely from outside (*Ref* indicated in the last column) or in a relative manner with respect to another section of the current module (the name of the section where the relative datum will be situated appears in the last column).

EXAMPLE 9.5.– *Extract from an ELF file: the relocation table*

```
** Section #3 '.relmycode' (SHT_REL)
                Size : 40 bytes (alignment 4)
                Symbol table #6 '.symtab'
                5 relocations applied to section #2 'mycode'
```

#	Offset	Relocation Type	Wrt	Symbol	Defined in
0	0x00000008	10 R_ARM_THM_CALL	12	ReadData	Ref
1	0x00000008	10 R_ARM_THM_CALL	12	ReadData	Ref
2	0x0000000C	10 R_ARM_THM_CALL	13	Ave_Weight	Ref
3	0x00000014	2 R_ARM_ABS32	8	Val1	#1 'mydata'
4	0x000000018	2 R_ARM_ABS32	9	Val2	#1 'mydata'

9.3. The role of the linker

The linker completes the creation of a program by bringing together the various modules into a single file called an executable.

9.3.1. *Functioning principle*

When we call the linker (also called the *link editor*), we give it a list of modules to bring together that contain each of a number of input sections. The linker is also informed of the memory layout of the target on which the program will be executed. This layout is coded in the *Project.sct* file. The work to be done is relatively simple: the different input sections are grouped in order to give them addresses compatible with the memory layout.

In our example, by invalidating the options that allow the inclusion of debugging information, the *CallProc.o* file contains 16 different sections, and the *Principal.o* file contains 11 of them. We then indicate that there is 128 KB of read-only memory (ROM) from address 0x08000000 and 20 KB of random access memory (RAM) from address 0x20000000.

REMARK 9.3.– The memory layout used here is that of a STM32103RB, which is the μcontroller of the target for this project. The absence of memory for the lowest addresses should be noted, as this is contrary to the imposed localization of the interrupt vector table (see Example 8.1). This contradiction is only apparent because STMicro has chosen to insert an alias between the [0x00000000–0x07FFFFFF] zone and another zone as a function of the state of two pins after a reset. The principle of this maneuver is to be able to find the reset vector (and so the reset code) in internal Flash, in system memory or in internal static RAM. Here the target zone of the alias is [0x08000000–0x10000000], which corresponds to the internal Flash memory. In this project, the lower addresses are present, even if they are virtual.

Let us remember that Cortex-M3 architecture is of the Harvard type, so there is a complete separation of the code and data zones (see Figure 1.5). The linker must therefore assign the code sections with addresses present in the [0x00000000–0x1FFFFFFF] zone and the data sections with addresses present in the [0x20000000–0x2FFFFFFF] zone.

Each input section received by the linker has a type and attributes. The three main types are:

– a *RO* (*Read Only*) zone, which is a ROM or Flash zone whose typical content is code. It is common (in the GNU world, for example) to see the abbreviation *.text* for this type of section;

– a *RW* (*Read/Write*) zone, which is a RAM zone whose typical contents are initialized data. The usual synonym for this is *.data*;

– a *ZI* (*Zero Initialized*) zone. This is also a read/write zone that will contain uninitialized data. By default *ZI* zones are set to 0. This type of section is also called *.bss*.

In addition to this typing, there is a whole series of attributes which, in the case of those found at the head of *ELF* files, allow the recording of different information that may be needed by the linker, loading or even symbolic debugging.

In a first simplistic (but not completely false) vision, the work of the linker therefore consists of retrieving the list and the size of the set of code and data sections, bringing them together and distributing them in corresponding memory zones. It concatenates the different pieces by properly merging the symbol tables: it is sufficient to correct the values of the labels of successively added modules by progressively incrementing the size of the sections. Finally, the linker changes the initial address of each section by determining its definitive address. Once more, it carries out the correction of instructions using the relocation tables. This simplistic vision is not enough: in fact the product of the linker cannot properly be called an executable file. It produces an image of an executable that will be "seen" differently at the loading level or at the execution level itself.

9.3.2. *The products of the linker*

9.3.2.1. *The MAP file*

One of the files produced is a file reporting the chosen memory mapping (*Project.map*). As with *.lst* files, it has no use in the rest of the process (loading, execution and symbolic debugging) but it is rich in information for the curious programmer. This file contains the list of all symbols encountered during the creation of the executable with the numerical values they have been associated with, their size, their section of origin, etc. An extract of this table is given in Example 9.6. We can tell from this extract that a number of symbols appear in the table that were not specifically used in the listings. Let us not forget that, more or less explicitly, the assembler uses libraries. *Resources.lib* is a library that is explicitly included in the project. The ARM-Keil development suite also includes the *MicroLib* library, whose role is to supply, for example, initialization routines. All of these inclusions bring their share of symbols that we then find in the *.map* file. We can also verify that the section addresses or code labels have been resolved and that their addresses are now found at an address in the *CODE* mapping zone. The *Ave_Weight* procedure, which in the relocation table given for this section in Example 9.5 has a value of 0x0000000C, and is now settled at the physical address 0x0800017D.

EXAMPLE 9.6.– *Extract of the Principal.map report linker file*

Symbol Name	Value	Type	Size	Object(Section)
RESET	0x08000000	Section	236	stm32f10x.o(RESET)
.ARM.Collect$000000	0x080000ec	Section	0	entry.o(.ARM.Collect$000000)
.ARM.Collect$000001	0x080000ec	Section	4	entry2.o(.ARM.Collect$000001)
.ARM.Collect$000004	0x080000f0	Section	4	entry5.o(.ARM.Collect$000004)
.ARM.Collect$000007	0x080000f4	Section	8	entry7.o(.ARM.Collect$000007)
.ARM.Collect$002712	0x080000fc	Section	4	entry2.o(.ARM.Collect$002712)
__lit__000000	0x080000fc	Data	4	entry2.o(.ARM.Collect$002712)
.text	0x08000100	Section	28	stm32f10x.o(.text)
.text	0x0800011c	Section	36	init.o(.text)
i.__scatterload_cp	0x08000140	Section	14	handlers.o(i.__scatterload_cp)
i.__scatterload_nul	0x0800014e	Section	2	handlers.o(i.__scatterload_nul
i.__scatterload_zi	0x08000150	Section	14	handlers.o(i.__scatterload_zi)
Mycode	0x08000160	Section	28	test.o(mycode)
Mycode	0x0800017c	Section	56	callproc.o(mycode)
Mydata	0x20000000	Section	12	test.o(mydata)
Mydata	0x2000000c	Section	2	callproc.o(mydata)
Coef	0x2000000c	Data	2	callproc.o(mydata)
STACK	0x20000010	Section	512	stm32f10x.o(STACK)

Main	0x08000161	ThumbCode	18	test.o(mycode)
Ave_Weight	0x0800017d	ThumbCode	38	callproc.o(mycode)
ReadData	0x080001a3	ThumbCode	2	callproc.o(mycode)
Val1	0x20000000	Data	2	test.o(mydata)
Val2	0x20000002	Data	2	test.o(mydata)
Resu	0x20000004	Data	8	test.o(mydata)
__initial_sp	0x20000210	Data	0	stm32f10x.o(STACK)

9.3.2.2. *The executable file image*

The file used later is the image of an executable. It is not an executable file, insofar as it must be transferred into the processor memory before being able to begin its execution. In order to make this transfer possible and effective, the ARM-Keil development range once again uses an *ELF* to code and store the results of this work.

Before detailing the composition of this file, let us first observe the information returned by the toolchain. This concerns the relative size of the different sections that will make up the executable. For the project presented in this chapter, here is the report:

Program Size: Code = 200 RO-data = 268 RW-data = 12 ZI-data = 516

– the *code* zone takes 200 bytes. *A priori*, there is nothing to say about this. Our two "source" files contain only 22 lines of instructions (six for *Principal.s* and 16 for *CallProc.s*). This generates between 44 (encoding only in Thumb) and 88 (encoding only in Thumb2) bytes of code, but the project is not limited to that. The code is also made up of other files (*STM32F10x.s* and *Resource.lib*) and the *MicroLib*;

– the *RW-data* zone takes 12 bytes. The listings show only four declarations of variables, accounting for 10 bytes (two for *Coef*, two for *Val1*, two for *Val2* and four for *Resu*). The two extra bytes are false bytes that are added because the initialization sequence works with word transfers (and so four bytes): 12 bytes corresponding to three writes. However, they are reserved by the linker to avoid initialization causing undesired modification of memory zones;

– the *ZI-data* takes 516 bytes: in our project, these uninitialized data are related to the system stack. This is created in the *STM32F10x.s* file (see Appendix C), which has a size of 512 bytes. The extra four bytes are due to alignment. In the declaration options of the section that hosts the stack, we find the option *Align = 3*. This implies that the reservation address of the stack must start at a triply even address (ending in three bits at 0). If we look at the memory mapping in Figure 9.6, the last stored variable is *Coef* at the address 0x2000000C. The first free triply even address is therefore the address 0x20000010; this corresponds to the address of the system stack (*STACK*). The three "lost" bytes are, however, counted in the total number of bytes in the *ZI-data* zone;

– there remains one zone of data placed in ROM: *RO-data*. This type of zone does not appear clearly in the list of input sections. After all, logically it seems quite paradoxical to declare variables to have RO access. These zones do not correspond to *Literal Pool* zones (see section 4.2.2.3), which, although they are immediate value zones are an integral part of the code and are accounted for as such. In fact, this *RO-data* corresponds to the 59 entries in the interrupt vector table (236 bytes). To make up the final 268 bytes, it adds 12 bytes that make up a table called *Region$$Table$$*. in the ARM context. This table works as we shall describe a little later to (re)initialize the *RW-data* or to reset the *ZI-data* just after a reset.

This dissection shows us, at the level of execution, that a simple program is made up of four distinct memory elements. The principal work of the linker is therefore to impose a memory mapping for these different regions (see Figure 9.3) according to the declared memory of the target.

The resulting file is therefore a set of sections (now called output sections) that are grouped into completely determined memory zones. The *ELF* file contains these files, which in the case described for the input sections have attributes and properties. The first of these sections is has the attribute *ER_IROM1, ER*, meaning *Execution Region*. This regions contains the interrupt vector tables, all of the code and the *Region$$Table$$* table. The next section is the *RW-data* containing all of the initialized data, then the section describing the *ZI-data.* These sections will allow the development system to produce data that will be concretely loaded into memory. These data are presented as a list of memory addresses followed by the content with which they must be assigned. The role of the loader is to carry out this writing. These addresses are, however, only code zones (and so correspond to values frozen during execution). By definition, this excludes *RW-data* and *ZI-data*. The image of the executable is made up of *code*, *RO-data* and a copy of *RW-data* placed just after the *Region$$Table$$* table. There is therefore a conveyance of *RW-data* to a permanent memory zone, which leaves the possibility of reinitializing all program variables after each reset.

Let us return and complete what happens following a *Reset* (see section 8.1). The processor, once initialized, executes the routine presented in Appendix C. This procedure ends with a jump to the __main label. This label is the entry point of a routine that will implement the initialization of *RW-data* and (by resetting corresponding memory addresses) the creation of *ZI-data*. This information is read in the *Region$$Table$$* table, which contains the start addresses of variables and those of their copy in permanent memory as the number of words to be copied. It also contains the addresses of uninitialized zones (which will be erased by being reset) and the number of words that they contain. This table is an essential element for the *MicroLib* library and also for the embedded application as it allows the target to be restarted in completely determined conditions.

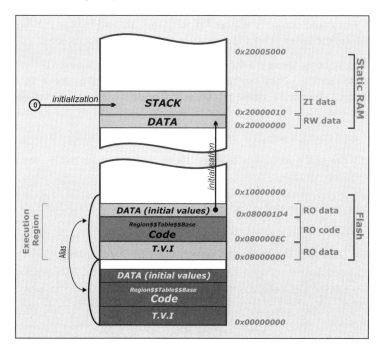

Figure 9.3. *Mapping of the different regions of a project*

REMARK 9.4.– The principal program, as for C, must contain a main procedure that corresponds to the entry point of the user program. This label is declared PUBLIC in order to be visible to the outside initialization sequence. The bootstrap procedure ends with a call to the reference__main, which is the entry point of the *MicroLib* library. Once its work has been carried out, this library calls the user procedure by a branch of the main label.

9.3.2.3. *The "Scatter_loading" file*

As we have just seen, the linker needs a description of memory distribution in order to know where to allocate the different sections that will make up its executable. In the chain tool Keil μVision, there is an interface that allows us to enter the addresses where different blocks of memory are located. By default, once given the μcontroller of the target, the memory addresses equipping the chip (*on chip memory*) are filled. If there are other memory devices present on the target, it is necessary to supply their specifications, including the memory mapping. Nevertheless, the linker does not directly use the interface data but the *Scatter_loading* file that is automatically generated by the interface. This file is a text file that describes the memory distribution formally and with its own syntax. An advanced user could perfectly edit and modify this file and bypass the interface to directly inform the linker. This file is divided into three distinct regions:

– loading regions: these are the memory zones where code and *RO-data* will be transferred to memory. They can be multiple, although as in the case of the example for a simple executable, a single region is sufficient to hold all of the data to be transferred;

– execution regions: these are the regions where the code will be stored;

– read/write (*RW*) accessible regions: these are the regions where the program variables will be stored.

For the presented example, the *Scatter_loading* file can reassemble the lines in Example 9.7.

EXAMPLE 9.7.– *Example of a memory description file: a simple case*

```
LR_IROM1 0x08000000 0x00020000 { ;  ①

                ER_IROM1 0x08000000 0x00020000 { ;  ②

                    .ANY (+RO) ;  ③

                }

                RW_IRAM1 0x20000000 0x00005000 { ;  ④

                    .ANY (+RW +ZI) ;  ⑤

                }

}
```

Let us decipher these few lines:

– line ① delimits the loading region: the linker must generate an *ELF* file so that the list of addresses where the charger will make the transfers will be included between 0x08000000 and 0x08020000. This region encompasses (the presence of the characters { and } encapsulates the declaration) all of the regions corresponding to different entities of the executable image;

– line ② indicates where address's internal *ROM* memory is in the execution region. In our case it involves the internal Flash of STM32, which corresponds to 128 KB starting from address 0x08000000. It should be noted that this corresponds exactly to the loading region addresses, and it is absolutely normal because the code will be written in its definitive placement;

– line ③ specifies to the linker that all *RO* input sections must be placed in this execution region;

– line ④ delimits the *RW* accessible region. It recognizes the 20 KB of *static RAM* available inside the STM32 from address 0x20000000;

– line ⑤ allows us to indicate to the linker that it should place all initialized (*RW*) or uninitialized (*ZI*) variables in this region.

For each execution region included in the loading region, it is possible to specify which parts of the code and data should be included. This only makes sense when there are several loading zones and we have specified the distribution between the different zones. Classically, each of these regions will correspond to different memory zones. Indeed, for a consequent embedded application, on a real target, it is in fact common to have memory devices that just complete memory that already exists inside the μcontroller.

As an example, let us imagine running the example on a different target using two ROM zones (16 KB from address 0x00000000 and 4 KB from address 0x00500000) as well as two RAM zones (4 KB from address 0x20000000 and 1 KB from address 0x20030000). The *Scatter_loading* file would correspond to Example 9.8.

EXAMPLE 9.8.– *A memory description file: a case with multiple load regions*

```
CHARGE_ROM_1 0x00000000 0x00004000 {
            EXEC_ROM_1 0x00000000 0x00004000 {
                   principal.o (+RO)
                   .ANY (+RO)
            }
            Ext_RAM 0x20000000 0x00001000 {
                   principal.o (+RW,+ZI)
                   .ANY (+ZI)
               }
   }
   CHARGE_ROM_2   0x00500000 0x00001000 {
            EXEC_ROM_2 0x00500000 0x00001000 {
                           AppleProc.o (+RO)
            }
```

```
             SRAM 0x20030000 0x00000400 {

                             AppleProc.o (+RW,+ZI)

                             .ANY (+RW)

             }

   }
```

This second memory distribution is not particularly realistic but it allows us to see how it is possible to impose on the linker a distribution of the different modules on the four memory zones. The *RO* code and data of the *principal.o* module will have to be assigned at the first execution region that includes the *ROM EXEC_ROM_1* and the *Ext_RAM*. The second loading region (*LOAD_ROM_2*) will receive all sections of the *CallProc.o* module. It is also specified that the remaining *RO* data will be allocated to the *EXEC_ROM_1* region, that uninitialized data will be in the *Ext_RAM* region and that the rest of the initialized data will be placed in the *SRAM* region.

REMARK 9.5.– In a μcontroller, the memory is of a reduced size. During execution it is therefore often useful to have the option of reusing memory zones containing data when they become useless for the rest of the execution (outdated data). This practice is called overlay. Assembly language offers the option of superimposing various data sections in the same memory interval by using the COMMON direction (see section 3.5.1).

In the case of development with the free GNU tools, the protocol used is different. The linker uses a file to retrieve the information on the memory distribution of the target as well as the rules of attribution and arbitration of this memory for the different entities in the program. The formalism, not described here, is of the *Linker Descriptor* type whose standard extension is *.ld*. When we use this type of tool (see, for example, [COD]), it is possible to download example files whose modification is possible if the reader has understood the principles presented here.

9.4. The loader and the debugging unit

In a computer, we have enough resources to build a program intended to run on the same machine, or any similar machine equipped with the same processor and the same operating system; we call this *native development*. This is not the case in a μcontroller. It also requires another computer – the host – to build the software developed for the target μcontroller: this is called *cross development*. Once the software is created, it can be placed in ROM (by breaking down an *erasable programmable read-only memory* [EPROM]), which we implant on the card containing the μcontroller, but this approach is very inconvenient in the software-testing phase. We prefer to send it from the host to the μcontroller via a specialized connection so that the host places the image of the executable itself in Flash memory or RAM. This is no longer a load, but a *download*.

The "loader" program is responsible for properly copying the various sections of the program placed in the file containing the executable image to memory and then, if appropriate, launching the execution. This utility is included in most cross-development suites (such as toolchain).

The current generation of tools largely uses the *JTAG* (*Joint Test Action Group*) port standard to download programs directly to Flash memory. *JTAG* is a synchronous series bus standard. The *JTAG* debug adapter uses this protocol to communicate with the processor core. On a standard computer this bus is not present; the adapter will then communicate on the *PC* side with a classic connection (typically a Universal Serial Bus [USB]).

The development program or *debugger* is particularly useful for searching for errors in a program. The program being reviewed runs under the control of the debugger program. For this, the debugger obeys commands that the user has given it inline. This can launch the execution of the program in continuous mode or step-by-step mode: in the latter case, only a single instruction of the program is executed and the debugger takes back control. The user can place a *breakpoint* on an instruction of the program being reviewed before launching the execution of the program: this will interrupt the execution just before this instruction. At each stop in the program, the debugger provides the current contents of all registers of the processor, and the user can then find out the current state of the program; he/she can also look at the contents of the system stack or any other memory region. Thus he/she can know the current value of a datum for which he/she knows the address (thanks to the symbol table given by the linker), or for which he/she gives the name if the debugger is symbolic. At each time the program is stopped, the debugger also allows us to change the value contained in any register, or to change any variable or memory position, before resuming the execution.

Note that to do its job, a symbolic debugger must at least have the symbol table. In fact, all debuggers need a range of information that must be included in the executable file. For this, the programmer must indicate (by invoking the assembler and linker with specific options) that they must include the information necessary for development under the debugger.

As was presented in Chapter 1 on Cortex architecture (see section 1.2.1.2), there are several hardware units whose roles consist mainly of returning information to a host system without having any effect on the running of the program being executed. This can typically be achieved with the *Trace Macrocell* units that can, in real-time and without causing any alteration of the processor, analyze and transmit data on the behavior and performance of the target thus observed. This approach, known as non-intrusive in ARM documentation, is particularly interesting for system surveillance, or in the case of dysfunction that is particularly difficult to localize or explain.

In a classic development cycle, the first development steps require a much more intrusive approach, such as placing a breakpoint at a specified code address to stop the sequence during execution, analyzing the state of the processor at that precise moment, and then possibly resuming the execution step-by-step.

Cortex-M3 architecture offers two versions of these intrusive techniques:

– the first technique involves freezing the processor core at the software level. Cortex-M3 then switches to an internal state call *Debug State*, in which it is possible to specify the step-by-step running of the program being executed, among other things. The development system, via the *JTAG* port, acts (by *RW*) directly on the registers of the debugging units and allows control from outside the program that is running;

– the second, less intrusive approach consists of using a *Debug Monitor*, which is a software application embedded in Cortex-M3 that is triggered by an exception (see section 8.2.1.6). The exception then takes control of the running of the sequence executed by the processor and communicates with the development unit.

As the objectives of this book do not include a deep and thorough understanding of all aspects of Cortex-M3, we will not further explain the methods and internal architectures involved in debugging. It is nevertheless true that "lower-level" programming cannot be done without these development tools, if only because the programmer has no other way of observing what happens in the target.

APPENDICES

Appendix A

Instruction Set – Alphabetical List

The list of instructions given below is not exhaustive and is limited to common and classic instructions. Each instruction is given with the different formulations possible for operands.

A

ADC{S}<c> {<Rd>,} <Rn>, #<const>	Rd ← Rn + const
ADC{S}<c> {<Rd>,} <Rn>, <Rm> {,<shift>}	Rd ← Rn +shift(Rm)
ADD{S}<c> {<Rd>,} <Rn>,#<const>	Rd ← Rn + const
ADD{S}<c> {<Rd>,} <Rn>, <Rm> {,<shift>}	Rd ← Rn + shift(Rm)
ADD{S}<c> {<Rd>,} SP, #<const>	Rd ← SP + const
ADD{S}<c> {<Rd>,} SP, <Rm>{,<shift>}	Rd ← SP + shift(Rm)
ADR<c> <Rd>, <label>	Rd ← label address
AND{S}<c> {<Rd>,} <Rn>, #<const>	Rd ← Rn AND const
AND{S}<c> {<Rd>,} <Rn>, <Rm> {,<shift>}	Rn ← Rn AND shift(Rm)
ASR{S}<c> <Rd>, <Rm>, #<im5>	Rd ← Rm $>>_{im5}$
ASR{S}<c> <Rd>, <Rn>, <Rm>	Rd ← Rn $>>_{Rm}$

B

B<c> <label>	PC ← label
BFC<c> <Rd>, #<lsb>, #<Nb>	Rd[lsb+Nb-1 : lsb] ← 0
BFI<c> <Rd>,<Rn>, #<lsb>, #<Nb>	Rd[lsb+Nb-1 : lsb] ← Rn[Nb : 0]
BIC{S}<c> {<Rd>,} <Rn>, #<const>	Rd ← Rn AND NOT(const)
BIC{S}<c> {<Rd>,} <Rn>, <Rm> {,<shift>}	Rd ← Rn AND NOT(shift(Rm))
BL<c> <label>	LR ← return @ PC ← label
BLX<c> <Rm>	LR ← return @ PC ← Rm
BX<c> <Rm>	PC ← R

C

CBNZ<c> <Rm> <label>	PC ← label if (Rm ≠ 0)
CBZ<c> <Rm> <label>	PC ← label if (Rm = 0)
CLZ<c> <Rd>, <Rm>	Rd ← CLZ(Rn)
CMN<c> <Rn>, #<const>	Flags ← test(Rn + const)
CMN<c> <Rn>, <Rm>{,<shift>}	Flags ← test(Rn + shift(Rm))
CMP<c> <Rn>, #<const>	Flags ← test(Rn – const)
CMP<c> <Rn>, <Rm>{,<shift>}	Flags ← test(Rn – shift(Rm))

E

EOR{S}<c> {<Rd>,} <Rn>, #<const>	Rd ← Rn XOR const
EOR{S}<c> {<Rd>,} <Rn>, <Rm> {,<shift>}	Rd ← Rn XOR shift(Rm)

I

IT{x{y{z}}} <firstcond>	Fixes the execution of the next instruction block

L

LDM<c> <Rk>,{R$_i$-R$_j$ }	R$_k$← M$_{32}$ (Rn + 4(k − i)) with $k = i...j$
LDM<c> <Rk> !,{R$_i$ -R$_j$ }	R$_k$← M$_{32}$ (Rn + 4(k − i)) with $k = i...j$ then Rn ← Rn + 4 * $(j − i)$
LDMDB<c> <Rk>,{R$_i$-R$_j$ }	R$_k$ ← M$_{32}$ (Rn - 4(k − i + 1)) with $k = i...j$
LDMDB<c> <Rk> !,{R$_i$-R$_j$ }	R$_k$ ← M$_{32}$ (Rn - 4(k − i + 1)) with $k = i...j$ then Rn ← Rn - 4 *$(j − i)$
LDR<c> <Rt>, [<Rn> {, #±<imm>}]	Rt ←M$_{32}$ (Rn ± imm)
LDR<c> <Rt>, [<Rn>, #±<imm>] !	Rn ← Rn + imm then Rt← M$_{32}$ (Rn)
LDR<c> <Rt>, [<Rn>], #±<imm>	Rt←M$_{32}$ (Rn) then Rn ← Rn + imm
LDR<c> <Rt>, <label>	Rt ← label
LDR<c> <Rt>, [PC, #±<imm>]	Rt ←M$_{32}$ (Pc ± imm)
LDR<c> <Rt>, [<Rn>, <Rm>{,LSL,#<shift>}]	Rt ←M$_{32}$ (Rn + shift(Rm))
LDRD<c> <Rt>, <Rt2>, <literal>	Rt← M$_{32}$ (literal) Rt2← M$_{32}$ (literal + 4)
LDRD<c> <Rt>, <Rt2>, [PC, #±<imm>]	Rt← M$_{32}$ (PC + imm) Rt2 ←M$_{32}$ (PC + imm + 4)
LDRD<c> <Rt>,<Rt2>,[<Rn>{,#±<imm>}]	Rt ← M$_{32}$ (Rn + imm) Rt2← M$_{32}$ (Rn + imm + 4)
LDRD<c> <Rt>,<Rt2>,[<Rn>,#±<imm>] !	Rn ← Rn + imm then Rt← M$_{32}$ (Rn + imm) and Rt2← M$_{32}$ (Rn + imm + 4)

LDRD\<c\> \<Rt\>,\<Rt2\>,[\<Rn\>],#±\<imm\>	$Rt \leftarrow M_{32}(Rn + imm)$ $Rt2 \leftarrow M_{32}(Rn + imm + 4)$ then $Rn \leftarrow Rn + imm$
LSL{S}\<c\> \<Rd\>, \<Rm\>, #\<im5\>	$Rd \leftarrow Rm << im5$
LSL{S}\<c\> \<Rd\>, \<Rn\>, \<Rm\>	$Rd \leftarrow Rn << Rm$
LSR{S}\<c\> \<Rd\>, \<Rm\>, #\<im5\>	$Rd \leftarrow Rm >> im5$
LSR{S}\<c\> \<Rd\>, \<Rn\>, \<Rm\>	$Rd \leftarrow Rn >> Rm$

M

MOV{S}\<c\> \<Rd\>, #\<const\>	$Rd \leftarrow const$
MOV{S}\<c\> \<Rd\>, \<Rm\>	$Rd \leftarrow Rm$
MOVT\<c\> \<Rd\>, #\<imm16\>	$Rd[16:31] \leftarrow imm16$
MSR\<c\> \<Rn\>,\<spec_reg\>	$Rn \leftarrow spec\_reg$
MSR\<c\> \<spec_reg\>,\<Rn\>	$spec\_reg \leftarrow Rn$
MUL{S}\<c\> {\<Rd\>,} \<Rn\>, \<Rm\>	$Rd \leftarrow Rn * Rm$
MVN{S}\<c\> \<Rd\>, #\<const\>	$Rd \leftarrow NOT(const)$
MVN{S}\<c\> \<Rd\>, \<Rm\> {, \<shift\>}	$Rd \leftarrow NOT(shift(Rn))$

N

NOP\<c\>	do nothing
NEG\<c\> {\<Rd\>,} \<Rm\>	$Rd \leftarrow -Rm$

O

ORN{S}\<c\> {\<Rd\>,} \<Rn\>, #\<const\>	$Rd \leftarrow Rm$ OR NOT(const)
ORN{S}\<c\> {\<Rd\>,} \<Rn\>, \<Rm\> {,\<shift\>}	$Rd \leftarrow Rm$ OR NOT(shift(Rm))
ORR{S}\<c\> {\<Rd\>,} \<Rn\>, #\<const\>	$Rd \leftarrow Rm$ OR const
ORR{S}\<c\> {\<Rd\>,} \<Rn\>, \<Rm\> {,\<shift\>}	$Rd \leftarrow Rm$ OR shift(Rm)

P

POP\<c> {R$_i$-R$_j$}	R$_k$ ←M$_{32}$ (SP + 4*(k−i)) with k=i...j then SP← SP + 4 * (j − i)
PUSH\<c> {R$_i$-R$_j$}	M$_{32}$(SP − 4*(k−i+1))←R$_k$ with k=i...j then SP← SP − 4 *(j − i)

R

RBIT\<c> \<Rd>, \<Rm>	Rd[31-k] ← Rm[k] with k = 0... 31
REV\<c> \<Rd>, \<Rm>	Rd[31 : 24] ← Rm[7 : 0] Rd[23 : 16] ← Rm[15 : 8] Rd[15 : 8] ← Rm[23 : 16] Rd[7 : 0] ← Rm[31 : 24]
REV16\<c> \<Rd>, \<Rm>	Rd[31 : 24] ← Rm[23 : 16] Rd[23 : 16] ← Rm[31 : 24] Rd[15 : 8] ← Rm[7 : 0] Rd[7 : 0] ← Rm[15 : 8]
REVSH\<c> \<Rd>, \<Rm>	Rd[31 : 8] ← Signed promotion (Rm[7 : 0]) Rd[7 : 0] ← Rm[15 : 8]
ROR{S}\<c> \<Rd>, \<Rm>, #\<im5>	Rd ← rotation(Rm, im5 bits)
ROR{S}\<c> \<Rd>, \<Rn>, \<Rm>	Rd ← rotation(Rn, Rm bits)
ROR{S}\<c> \<Rd>, \<Rn>, \<Rm>	Rd ← rotation([Rn,C], Rm bits)

S

SBFX\<c> \<Rd>, \<Rn>, #\<lsb>, #\<Nb>	Rd[Nb-1 : 0] ← Rn[lsb + Nb−1 : lsb]
SMLAL\<c> \<Rd$_{lsb}$ >, \<Rd$_{PF}$ >, \<Rn>, \<Rm>	[Rd$_{msb}$:Rd$_{lsb}$] ← Rn * Rm + [Rd$_{msb}$:Rd$_{lsb}$]
SMULL\<c> \<Rd$_{lsb}$ >, \<Rd$_{PF}$ >, \<Rn>, \<Rm>	[Rd$_{msb}$:Rd$_{lsb}$] ← Rn * Rm

SSAT\<c> \<Rd>,#\<im5>,\<Rn>{,\<shift>}	if (Rn < 0) Rd ←
	min(-2$^{(im5-1)}$,shift(Rn))
	if (Rn >0) Rd ←
	max(2$^{(im5-1)}$ − 1,shift(Rn))

STR<c> <Rt>, [<Rn>, <Rm> {, LSL #<shift>}]	M_{32} (Rn +s hift(Rm))← Rt
STR<c> <Rt>, [<Rn> {,#±<imm>}]	M_{32} (Rn ± imm)←Rt
STR<c> <Rt>, [<Rn>, #±<imm>] !	Rn ← Rn + imm then M_{32} (Rn) ← Rt
STR<c> <Rt>, [<Rn>], #±<imm>	M_{32} (Rn) ← Rt then Rn ← Rn + imm
STM<c> <Rn>,{R_i-R_j }	M_{32} (Rn + 4(k − i)) ← R_k with $k = i...j$
STM<c> <Rn> !,{R_i-R_j }	M_{32} (Rn + 4(k − i)) ← Rk with k = i...j then Rn← Rn + 4 $(j − i)$
STMDB<c> <Rn>,{R_i-R_j }	M_{32} (Rn − 4(k − i + 1))←R_k with $k = i...j$
STMDB<c> <Rn> !,{R_i -R_j }	M_{32} (Rn − 4(k − i + 1))← R_k with $k = i...j$ then Rn← Rn - 4 $(j − i)$
STRD<c> <Rt>,<Rt2>,[<Rn>{,#±<imm>}]	M_{32} (Rn + imm) ← Rt M_{32} (Rn + imm + 4) ← Rt2
STRD<c> <Rt>,<Rt2>,[<Rn>,#±<imm>] !	Rn ← Rn + imm then M_{32}(Rn + imm) ← Rt and M_{32} (Rn + imm + 4) ← Rt2
STRD<c> <Rt>,<Rt2>,[<Rn>],#±<imm>	M_{32} (Rn + imm) ← Rt M_{32} (Rn + imm + 4) ← Rt2 then Rn ← Rn + imm
SUB{S}<c> {<Rd>} ,<Rn>,#<const>	Rd ← Rn − const
SUB{S}<c> {<Rd>} ,<Rn>, <Rm> {,<shift>}	Rd ← Rn − shift(Rm)
SUB{S}<c> {<Rd>} ,SP,#<const>	Rd ← SP − const
SUB{S}<c> {<Rd>} ,SP,<Rm> {,<shift>}	Rd ← SP − shift(Rm)
SBFX<c> <Rd>, <Rn>, #<pf>, #<Nb>	Rd[Nb-1 : 0]← Rn[pf+Nb-1 : pf] Rd[31 : Nb] ← Rd [lsb + Nb − 1]
SXTB<c> <Rd>, <Rm> {, <rotation>}	Rd ← rotation$_{32}$ (Rn)[7 : 0] Rd[31 : 8] ← Rd[7]
SXTH<c> <Rd>, <Rm> {, <rotation>}	Rd ← rotation$_{32}$ (Rn)[15 : 0] Rd[31 : 8] ← Rd[15]

T

TEQ<c> <Rn>, #<const>	Flags ← test(Rn XOR const)
TEQ<c> <Rn>, <Rm>{,<shift>}	Flags ← test(Rn XOR shift(Rm))
TST<c> <Rn>, #<const>	Flags ← test(Rn AND const)
TST<c> <Rn>, <Rm>{,<shift>}	Flags ← test(Rn AND shift(Rm))
TBB<c> [<Rn>, <Rm>] TBH<c> [<Rn>, <Rm>, LSL #1]	Pc ← PC + Rn[Rm] PC + Rn[Rm]

U

UBFX<c> <Rd>, <Rn>, #<lsb>, #<Nb>	$Rd[Nb\text{-}1:0] \leftarrow$ $Rn[lsb + Nb - 1 : lsb]$ $Rd[31 : Nb] \leftarrow 0$
UDIV<c> {<Rd>,} <Rn>, <Rm>	$Rd \leftarrow Rn \div Rm$
UMLAL<c> <Rd$_{lsb}$>, <Rd$_{PF}$>, <Rn>, <Rm>	$[Rd_{msb} \quad : Rd_{lsb}] \leftarrow Rn * Rm$ $+ [Rd_{msb} : Rd_{lsb}]$
UMUL<c> <Rd$_{lsb}$>, <Rd$_{PF}$>, <Rn>, <Rm> USAT<c> <Rd>,#<im5>,<Rn>{,<shift>}	$[Rd_{msb} \quad : Rd_{lsb}] \leftarrow Rn * Rm$ $Rd \leftarrow$ $\max(2^{(im5-1)} - 1 , shift(Rn))$
UXTB<c> <Rd>, <Rm> {, <rotation>}	$Rd \leftarrow rotation_{32}(Rn)[7:0]$ $Rd[31:8] \leftarrow 0$
UXTH<c> <Rd>, <Rm> {, <rotation>}	$Rd \leftarrow rotation_{32}((Rn)[15:0]$ $Rd[31:8] \leftarrow 0$

Appendix B

The *SysTick* Timer

B.1. Counters and timers in general

Counters and timers are two entities that we must encounter in a μcontroller. They both do exactly the same thing. Indeed they correspond to registers that count up or down and have rising or descending fronts, or both. The difference between the two names is that, in the case of timers, the front sequence that supplies the unit is periodic and has a known period (which is often adjustable). This implies that the value contained within the register corresponds to a time measurement, hence its name.

The main event that occurs in the process of incrementation (or decrementation, respectively) is the overflow (or underflow) of the capacity of the register. Many things can intervene in this event but the main two programmable actions on overflow (underflow) are sending an interrupt request and reloading a given value in the counting register, causing a sample call to a specific routine. This functionality is necessary for the development of a real-time kernel whose main role is sharing central processing unit (*CPU*) time between different tasks running on the processor. The motivation for the Advanced RISC Machine's (ARM's) choice to provide a timer inside the core was to be free from the specificities of the μcontrollers (and so to be free from the choice of developers) so that a real-time kernel base could be developed for all of the circuits based on Cortex-M3. On its website, ARM lists the partners proposing such a real-time kernels (*Real-Time Operating Systems*) – there are over 20, and the list is subject to frequent change.

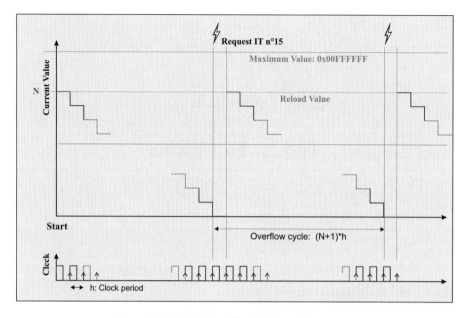

Figure B.1. *Principle of SysTick Timer functioning*

B.2. *SysTick*

The *SysTick* timer is a 24-bit decrementation timer. Unlike the complex timer units that we can find in a μcontroller, it has no functioning modes other than a 24-bit decrementation. Its overall operation is summarized in Figure B.1.

The *SysTick* unit is made up of four registers, which will be described in a moment. Three of these registers are classic: one to manage the state and configuration, one to contain the current countdown value, and one for the reloading value. The fourth is more particular and shows the reason for having this unit. It is a matter of a register containing the value-standard giving a reloading value in order to give a 10-millisecond interrupt periodicity.

One subtlety is in how to avoid mistakes in the programming of this timer. The interrupt request takes place when the current value switches from 1 to 0, but reloading only takes place at the next rising edge of the clock. This obviously means that in the case of periodic functioning (which is *a priori* the classic functioning) the interrupt call has a periodicity of $N + 1$ clock cycles, with N being the value stored in the reload register. In the example presented (Example B.1), this reload value is first calculated as the ratio (integer division) between the frequency of the internal clock (*Freq_Quartz*) and the request frequency (*Freq_Request*). This ratio is then decremented by one to take into account the interval between interrupt and reload. Finally, note that in such a calculation the request frequency does not necessarily match up to the real frequency of functioning. In fact, as this calculation rests on an integer division, there is no guarantee that the remainder from this division will be zero. Another, more atypical, function is possible and involves modification of the load value every time the handler is activated. By definition, it is no longer a periodic function but an alarm clock function reprogrammed each time, we assume being calculated to correspond with N cycles of the clock. As direct "by hand" reload by assignment of the current value is not possible, we can carry out this reprogramming by affecting the reload value, but with N instead of $N-1$. In fact, we could consider that the starting of the timer corresponds to the next interruption and as the activation will take place as the current value switches from 1 to 0, it is normal to start with the calculated value.

B.3. The *SysTick* registers

B.3.1. *The Current Value register*

When *SysTick* is active, the value of this register decreases with each rising front of the clock. As this timer is coded in 24 bits, the eight most significant bits in this register are always at 0. It is possible to get read access to find out the current value. However write access, if permitted, is limited: whatever value you want to write, such access would result in deletion of the contents. It is therefore not possible to write a value to this register – you can only erase one.

B.3.2. *The Control and Status register*

This register (see Figure B.2) has only four significant bits:

– *COUNTFLAG:* switches to 1 if the counting register (*Current Value*) has switched to 0. It is reset either when the processor reads the register containing this bit (*Control and Status*), or when the processor writes a value in the *Current Value* register. This bit allows the use of the timer without using interrupts, simply by scanning the state of this bit. Obviously this is not as effective as the interrupt because the scan uses CPU time. What is more, the detection is not concurrent with the event, so the precision of time measurement is not assured.

– *CLKSOURCE:* there are two clock sources that supply the timer. The first, which is standard and corresponds to the bit being set to 1, consists of using the internal clock of Cortex-M3. It is, however, possible (with the bit set to 0) to specify an external clock. This clock is only external to Cortex-M3 and not the μcontroller that integrates it and must be a fraction (at least 2.5 times smaller) of the internal frequency, simply because a higher frequency would be incompatible with the update of register values. It is necessary to consult the documentation of the circuit used to find out the frequency of these two clocks.

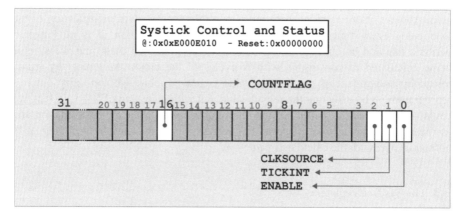

Figure B.2. *SysTick control and status register*

– *TICKINT*: when this is set to 1, it enables the launch of the *SYSTICK* exception (fifteenth entry in the table of interrupt vectors) when the decrementation of the timer gives 0.

– *ENABLE*: this is the bit that starts (bit at 1)/stops (bit at 0) the timer. As soon as this bit is activated, each rising front of the chosen clock causes the decrementation of the *Current Value* register. At the moment when it is switched to 1, the *Current Value* register is loaded with the value contained in the *Reload* register.

B.3.3. *The Reload register*

This register, insofar as it serves as a reset value for the *Current Value* register, can only receive a value between 1 and 0x00*FFFFFF*. It is possible to give it a value of 0, but this would inhibit the functioning of *SysTick*. After a *Reset,* the value of this register is unpredictable.

B.3.4. *The Calibration Value register*

A sampling time of 10 milliseconds seems to be a reference value, according to ARM, for calibrating the rate of a real-time kernel. This *Calibration Value* register (see Figure B.3) with read-only access allows us to find out the reload value to give in order to get this sampling value without having to dissect the μcontroller documentation. The main datum, *TENMS* (10 milliseconds) (the 24 least significant bits) is therefore a value set by the circuit designer. If we later want another sampling period, proportional to 10 ms, we just need to read this register, add 1 to get the number of cycles corresponding to these 10 ms, apply the necessary proportionality ratio (multiplication or division), subtract 1 and modify the reload value with this value.

Two bits complete this information:

– the 31-weight bit indicates that there is no external clock signal;

– the 30-weight bit indicates that the 10ms value is not exact because of the clock frequency value. The precision of a sampling based on *TENMS* is therefore not guaranteed.

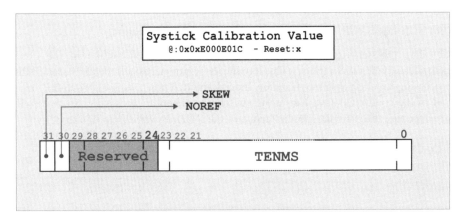

Figure B.3. *SysTick register calibration*

B.4. Example of *SysTick* programming

In this example, three generic procedures have been written. The first two (*Start_SysTick* and *Stop_SysTick*) allow us to start/stop the timer. The third (*SysStickSetPeriod*) is called by *Start_SysTick* to calculate the reload value needed to operate the *SysTick* periodicity at a chosen value (*Freq_Request*). We assume that the *SysTick* clock has a frequency of 8 MHz.

While configuring *SysTick*, the interrupt validation is set at 1. This (assuming that the priority levels are coherent and the interrupt vector table is correctly initialized) implies that the corresponding interrupt handler (*SysTick_Handler*) of this exception would be automatically called. During this processing, a global variable (*Time_Val*) is decremented, allowing the main program to start the timer until the variable is cancelled.

Some comments about this listing:

– The register addresses as well as the values of the two frequencies (that of the clock and that which we want) are "hard" coded, i.e. coded by constants, and consequently correspond to immediate addressing.

– The launch number (*Time_Val*) is contained in a half-word. In the example, the initial value given to the variable is used directly. This is also the case for the *Stop_SysTick* function.

– The start function, in addition to calculating the reload function, sets bits at 1 that make it possible to choose the internal clock in order to validate interrupts and to start the timer itself. These three settings to 1 are done separately by three logical "OR"s. A single "OR" is sufficient to do this in a single operation.

– The registers used by the procedures are not saved, unlike in the other examples given in this book. This operation is not necessary in the case of the processing function *SysTick_Handler*. Indeed, the two registers used (*R0* and *R1*) are part of the contextual save list during switching exception processing. So there will never be side effects linked to the launch of the *SysTick_Handler* in this case.

EXAMPLE B.1.– *SysTick programming library*

```
;*****************************************************************
; DATA SECTION
;*****************************************************************
        AREA MyData, DATA, ALIGN=0
;*****************************************************************
Freq_Quartz   EQU 8000000
Freq_Request  EQU 100
SysTick_CTRL  EQU 0xe000e010
SysTick_LOAD  EQU 0xe000e014
SysTick_VAL   EQU 0xe000e018
SysTick_CALIB EQU 0xe000e01C
Time_Val      DCW 123
;*****************************************************************
; PROGRAM SECTION
;*****************************************************************
        AREA MyCode, CODE, readonly, ALIGN=2
```

```
;******************************************************************

;- - - - - - - - - - - - - - - - - - - - - - - - - - - - - - - -
SystickSetPeriod PROC
              LDR R1,=Freq_Quartz    ; Read clock frequency
              SDIV R2,R1,R0          ; Calculation of number N of
                                     ;    cycles for desired  freq.
              SUBS R2,R2,#1          ; Modification of value N - 1
              LDR R3,=Systick_LOAD   ;    of reload register
              STR R2,[R3]
              BX LR
              ENDP
;- - - - - - - - - - - - - - - - - - - - - - - - - - - - - - - -
Start_SysTick  PROC
              PUSH LR
              LDR R0,=Freq_Request   ; Load value of requested period
              LDR R1,=SysTick_VAL
              STR R0,[R1]
              BL SystickSetPeriod    ; Initialization of reload
              LDR R0,=Systick_CTRL
              LDR R1,[R0]
              ORR R1,R1,#4           ; Choice of clock
              ORR R1,R1,#2           ; Authorization of interrupt
              ORR R1,R1,#1           ; Timer launch
              STR R1,[R0]
              POP PC
              ENDP
;- - - - - - - - - - - - - - - - - - - - - - - - - - - - - - - -
Stop_Systick   PROC
              LDR R0,=Systick_CTRL
              LDR R1,[R0]
              BIC R1,R1,#2           ; Deactivates systick interrupt
              BIC R1,R1,#1           ; Stops the timer
              STR R1,[R0]
              BX LR
              ENDP
;- - - - - - - - - - - - - - - - - - - - - - - - - - - - - - - -
```

```
SysTick_Handler PROC
            EXPORT SysTick_Handler
            LDR R0,= Time_Val        ; Loading of global variable
            LDRH R1,[R0]
            SUB R1,#1                ; Decrementation
            STRH R1,[R0]             ;       and storage
            BX LR
            ENDP
```

EXAMPLE B.2.– *Use of the library*

```
;*************************************************************
; PROGRAM SECTION
;*************************************************************
            AREA MyCode, CODE, readonly, ALIGN=2
;*************************************************************
main        PROC
            LDR R5,=Time_Val
            BL Start_Systick
Unfinished  LDRH R0,[R5]
            CMP R0,#0
            BNE Unfinished
            BL Stop_Systick
Infinite        B Infinite           ; End of program
            ENDP
```

Appendix C

Example of a "Bootstrap" File

This appendix contains the code and some explanation of the *STM3210x.s* file used in the generic project presented earlier (see Chapter 9). This file is a bootstrap file, meaning that it allows us to carry out a minimal initialization of the μcontroller (here a STMicroelectronics *STM32F103RB*). This file was made and provided by Keil with their μVision development suite. Its inclusion (or that of a different or modified version) in a project is necessary to allow the development of a complete project. As this file defines the specific interrupt vectors of the μcontroller for which it was written, it is obvious that if it was written for a different processor a certain number of lines would be different, removed or added. However, the general structure would stay the same.

C.1. The listing

EXAMPLE C.1.– *A bootstrap file: the STM32F10x.s file*

```
;/****************************************************************/
;/* STM32F10x.s : Startup file for ST STM32F10x device series */
;/****************************************************************/
;/* < "Use Configuration Wizard in Context Menu" > */
;/* This file is part of the uVision/ARM development tools. */
;/* Copyright (c) 2005-2007 Keil Software. All rights reserved. */
;/* This software may only be used under the terms of a valid,
current, */
;/* end user licence from KEIL for a compatible version of KEIL
```

```
software */
/* development tools. Nothing else gives you the right to use
this software. */
;/****************************************************************/
;/****************************************************************/
;// <h> Stack Configuration
;// <o> Stack Size (in Bytes) <0x0-0xFFFFFFFF :8>
;// </h>
;/****************************************************************/
Stack_Size      EQU 0x00000200
AREA STACK,     NOINIT, READWRITE, ALIGN=3
Stack_Mem       SPACE Stack_Size
__initial_sp


;/****************************************************************/
;// <h> Heap Configuration
;// <o> Heap Size (in Bytes) <0x0-0xFFFFFFFF :8>
;// </h>
;/****************************************************************/
Heap_Size       EQU 0x00000000
                AREA HEAP, NOINIT, READWRITE, ALIGN=3
__heap_base
Heap_Mem        SPACE Heap_Size __heap_limit
                PRESERVE8
                THUMB


;/****************************************************************/
; Vector Table Mapped to Address 0 at Reset
                AREA RESET, DATA, READONLY
                EXPORT __Vectors
__Vectors       DCD __initial_sp            ; Top of Stack
                DCD Reset_Handler           ; Reset Handler
                DCD NMI_Handler             ; NMI Handler
                DCD HardFault_Handler       ; Hard Fault Handler
                DCD MemManage_Handler       ; MPU Fault Handler
                DCD BusFault_Handler        ; Bus Fault Handler
                DCD UsageFault_Handler      ; Usage Fault Handler
```

```
                DCD 0                            ; Reserved
                DCD 0                            ; Reserved
                DCD 0                            ; Reserved
                DCD 0                            ; Reserved
                DCD SVC_Handler                  ; SVCall Handler
                DCD DebugMon_Handler             ; Debug Monitor Handler
                DCD 0                            ; Reserved
                DCD PendSV_Handler               ; PendSV Handler
                DCD SysTick_Handler              ; SysTick Handler


; External Interrupts
                DCD WWDG_IRQHandler              ; Window Watchdog
                DCD PVD_IRQHandler               ; PVD through EXTI Line
detect
                DCD TAMPER_IRQHandler            ; Tamper
                DCD RTC_IRQHandler               ; RTC
                DCD FLASH_IRQHandler             ; Flash
                DCD RCC_IRQHandler               ; RCC
                DCD EXTI0_IRQHandler             ; EXTI Line 0
                DCD EXTI1_IRQHandler             ; EXTI Line 1
                DCD EXTI2_IRQHandler             ; EXTI Line 2
                DCD EXTI3_IRQHandler             ; EXTI Line 3
                DCD EXTI4_IRQHandler             ; EXTI Line 4
                DCD DMAChannel1_IRQHandler       ; DMA Channel 1
                DCD DMAChannel2_IRQHandler       ; DMA Channel 2
                DCD DMAChannel3_IRQHandler       ; DMA Channel 3
                DCD DMAChannel4_IRQHandler       ; DMA Channel 4
                DCD DMAChannel5_IRQHandler       ; DMA Channel 5
                DCD DMAChannel6_IRQHandler       ; DMA Channel 6
                DCD DMAChannel7_IRQHandler       ; DMA Channel 7
                DCD ADC_IRQHandler               ; ADC
                DCD USB_HP_CAN_TX_IRQHandler     ; USB High Priority
                DCD USB_LP_CAN_RX0_IRQHandler    ; USB Low Priority
                DCD CAN_RX1_IRQHandler           ; CAN RX1
                DCD CAN_SCE_IRQHandler           ; CAN SCE
                DCD EXTI9_5_IRQHandler           ; EXTI Line 9..5
                DCD TIM1_BRK_IRQHandler          ; TIM1 Break
```

```
            DCD TIM1_UP_IRQHandler            ; TIM1 Update
            DCD TIM1_TRG_COM_IRQHandler       ; TIM1 Trigger
            DCD TIM1_CC_IRQHandler            ; TIM1 Capture Compare
            DCD TIM2_IRQHandler               ; TIM2
            DCD TIM3_IRQHandler               ; TIM3
            DCD TIM4_IRQHandler               ; TIM4
            DCD I2C1_EV_IRQHandler            ; I2C1 Event
            DCD I2C1_ER_IRQHandler            ; I2C1 Error
            DCD I2C2_EV_IRQHandler            ; I2C2 Event
            DCD I2C2_ER_IRQHandler            ; I2C2 Error
            DCD SPI1_IRQHandler               ; SPI1
            DCD SPI2_IRQHandler               ; SPI2
            DCD USART1_IRQHandler             ; USART1
            DCD USART2_IRQHandler             ; USART2
            DCD USART3_IRQHandler             ; USART3
            DCD EXTI15_10_IRQHandler          ; EXTI Line 15..10
            DCD RTCAlarm_IRQHandler           ; RTC Alarm
            DCD USBWakeUp_IRQHandler          ; USB Wakeup


;/****************************************************************/
            AREA |.text|, CODE, READONLY
Reset_Handler   PROC
            EXPORT Reset_Handler   [WEAK]
            IMPORT __main
            LDR R0, =__main
            BX R0
            ENDP


; Dummy Exception Handlers (infinite loops which can be modified)
NMI_Handler     PROC
            EXPORT NMI_Handler     [WEAK]
            B .
            ENDP
HardFault_Handler
            PROC
            EXPORT HardFault_Handler       [WEAK]
            B .
```

```
                ENDP
MemManage_Handler
                PROC
                EXPORT MemManage_Handler        [WEAK]
                B .
                ENDP
BusFault_Handler
                PROC
                EXPORT BusFault_Handler         [WEAK]
                B .
                ENDP
UsageFault_Handler
                PROC
                EXPORT UsageFault_Handler       [WEAK]
                B .
                ENDP
SVC_Handler     PROC
                EXPORT SVC_Handler      [WEAK]
                B .
                ENDP
DebugMon_Handler
                PROC
                EXPORT DebugMon_Handler [WEAK]
                B .
                ENDP
PendSV_Handler PROC
                EXPORT PendSV_Handler  [WEAK]
                B .
                ENDP
SysTick_Handler
                PROC
                EXPORT SysTick_Handler [WEAK]
                B .
                ENDP


Default_Handler PROC
```

```
EXPORT WWDG_IRQHandler              [WEAK]
EXPORT PVD_IRQHandler               [WEAK]
EXPORT TAMPER_IRQHandler            [WEAK]
EXPORT RTC_IRQHandler               [WEAK]
EXPORT FLASH_IRQHandler             [WEAK]
EXPORT RCC_IRQHandler               [WEAK]
EXPORT EXTI0_IRQHandler             [WEAK]
EXPORT EXTI1_IRQHandler             [WEAK]
EXPORT EXTI2_IRQHandler             [WEAK]
EXPORT EXTI3_IRQHandler             [WEAK]
EXPORT EXTI4_IRQHandler             [WEAK]
EXPORT DMAChannel1_IRQHandler       [WEAK]
EXPORT DMAChannel2_IRQHandler       [WEAK]
EXPORT DMAChannel3_IRQHandler       [WEAK]
EXPORT DMAChannel4_IRQHandler       [WEAK]
EXPORT DMAChannel5_IRQHandler       [WEAK]
EXPORT DMAChannel6_IRQHandler       [WEAK]
EXPORT DMAChannel7_IRQHandler       [WEAK]
EXPORT ADC_IRQHandler               [WEAK]
EXPORT USB_HP_CAN_TX_IRQHandler [WEAK]
EXPORT USB_LP_CAN_RX0_IRQHandler [WEAK]
EXPORT CAN_RX1_IRQHandler           [WEAK]
EXPORT CAN_SCE_IRQHandler           [WEAK]
EXPORT EXTI9_5_IRQHandler           [WEAK]
EXPORT TIM1_BRK_IRQHandler          [WEAK]
EXPORT TIM1_UP_IRQHandler           [WEAK]
EXPORT TIM1_TRG_COM_IRQHandler [WEAK]
EXPORT TIM1_CC_IRQHandler           [WEAK]
EXPORT TIM2_IRQHandler              [WEAK]
EXPORT TIM3_IRQHandler              [WEAK]
EXPORT TIM4_IRQHandler              [WEAK]
EXPORT I2C1_EV_IRQHandler           [WEAK]
EXPORT I2C1_ER_IRQHandler           [WEAK]
EXPORT I2C2_EV_IRQHandler           [WEAK]
EXPORT I2C2_ER_IRQHandler           [WEAK]
EXPORT SPI1_IRQHandler              [WEAK]
EXPORT SPI2_IRQHandler              [WEAK]
```

```
        EXPORT USART1_IRQHandler        [WEAK]
        EXPORT USART2_IRQHandler        [WEAK]
        EXPORT USART3_IRQHandler        [WEAK]
        EXPORT EXTI15_10_IRQHandler     [WEAK]
        EXPORT RTCAlarm_IRQHandler      [WEAK]
        EXPORT USBWakeUp_IRQHandler     [WEAK]
WWDG_IRQHandler

PVD_IRQHandler

TAMPER_IRQHandler

RTC_IRQHandler

FLASH_IRQHandler

RCC_IRQHandler

EXTI0_IRQHandler

EXTI1_IRQHandler

EXTI2_IRQHandler

EXTI3_IRQHandler

EXTI4_IRQHandler

DMAChannel1_IRQHandler

DMAChannel2_IRQHandler

DMAChannel3_IRQHandler

DMAChannel4_IRQHandler

DMAChannel5_IRQHandler

DMAChannel6_IRQHandler

DMAChannel7_IRQHandler

ADC_IRQHandler

USB_HP_CAN_TX_IRQHandler

USB_LP_CAN_RX0_IRQHandler

CAN_RX1_IRQHandler

CAN_SCE_IRQHandler

EXTI9_5_IRQHandler

TIM1_BRK_IRQHandler

TIM1_UP_IRQHandler

TIM1_TRG_COM_IRQHandler

TIM1_CC_IRQHandler

TIM2_IRQHandler

TIM3_IRQHandler

TIM4_IRQHandler
```

```
I2C1_EV_IRQHandler
I2C1_ER_IRQHandler
I2C2_EV_IRQHandler
I2C2_ER_IRQHandler
SPI1_IRQHandler
SPI2_IRQHandler
USART1_IRQHandler
USART2_IRQHandler
USART3_IRQHandler
EXTI15_10_IRQHandler
RTCAlarm_IRQHandler
USBWakeUp_IRQHandler


                B .
                ENDP


; User Initial Stack Heap


                IF :DEF :__MICROLIB          ;- - - - - - - - -
                EXPORT __initial_sp
                EXPORT __heap_basev
                EXPORT __heap_limit


                ELSE                         ;- - - - - - - - -
                IMPORT __use_two_region_memory
                EXPORT __user_initial_stackheap
__user_initial_stackheap LDR R0, = Heap_Mem
                LDR R1, =(Stack_Mem + Stack_Size)
                LDR R2, = (Heap_Mem + Heap_Size)
                LDR R3, = Stack_Mem
                BX LR


                ENDIF                        ;- - - - - - - - -
                END
```

C.2. Important points

This listing requires some explanation, even if its blind use causes no major problems:

– In this version, the system stack (*Stack_Mem*) is 512 bytes in dimension. The top of the stack is marked with *__initial_stack*, which is the first address following the reserved zone as the system stack is pre-decrementation.

– A heap (*Heap_Mem*) is reserved in the same way as the reservation for the system stack. This reservation is for the use of the C compiler (standard library). It is interesting to note, however, that in this case the reservation is completely fictitious since the size (*Heap_Size*) reserved is zero. It is only there to avoid causing resolution errors during link editing.

– The interrupt vector table corresponds to a set of words initialized with the addresses of exception processing routines that exist lower in the module. It starts by storing the highest address of the previously declared stack. The STM32 used in this project is built around 43 interrupt vectors.

– The interrupt handler set is limited to a single *B.*, or infinite loop. This module is therefore only a simple skeleton for the development of more adapted routines. These routines are really wells: if an exception is launched and nothing but the skeleton has been developed, it is impossible to escape other than by *Reset*.

– The external exceptions (which correspond to interrupts) are all grouped in the same routine. This routine has some 43 different names. All of these names are *WEAK* (another statement will be given priority over them) and exported to be visible from other modules.

– The *Reset* handler is the only one that contains a little code. It simply calls the *__main* routine, which is the entry point to the *MicroLib* library. This same routine will end it by a jump to the label *main*, which is the entry point of the project. The *MicroLib* source is not directly accessible; but by opening a disassembly window in debug mode, it is possible to view its content.

– At the end of the listing are lines that allow the export of the addresses of the stack and heap, in particular for the *MicroLib* library if it is included in the project. Otherwise (*ELSE* alternative), it is assumed that the standard library is used, in which case the *__user_initial_stackheap* procedure is necessary for its correct running and for where it exports to. This procedure fills the *R0* to *R3* registers with the addresses of reservation delimitations from the stack and the heap.

Appendix D

The GNU Assembler

The set of examples presented in this work are written for the ARM-MDK (Microcontroller Development Kit). Another compiler/assembler/link editor trio, however, is currently used to construct such projects. This is the compilation chain GNU[1]-GCC (GNU Compiler Connection), which as its name suggests comes from the world of free and cooperative software. This appendix is based specifically on the Sourcery G++ Lite tools for ARM EABI (Embedded-Application Binary Interface). This precision is important insofar as, although the tools are designed to be generic, they still have specificities and peculiarities that make them somewhat more difficult to understand and use. As an example to illustrate this, take the official documentation for the Sourcery G++ assembler. This documentation is 328 pages long, and 202 pages (Chapter 9) are dedicated to the characteristics unique to each processor. Despite the peculiarities, it is interesting to draw on the common points between the different GNU compilers/assemblers/link editors in order to be able to develop programs with different tools and/or processors.

The ARM-MDK and GNU-GCC projects are not cross-compatible, which might seem surprising since the processor and thus the instruction set are very similar. The two major differences are found in the syntax used for the directives (for the assembler) and in the way of describing the memory (for the link editor). We should note that the use of the GNU GCC tool is still possible in the Keil μVision environment, which is interesting as this environment is completely functional in its free trial version and so it is possible to use the μcontroller emulator that it offers.

---

1 GNU is a Unix-like computer operating system and corresponds to the recursive acronym "GNU is Not Unix"

In the first part of this appendix, we will list the main directives necessary to develop a project, for instance that which was presented in Chapter 3. In section D.2 we will give an example of a program written with these syntax rules that aims to make up for the absence of the MicroLib library. We will not develop the aspects tied to the linker, and especially the memory description file, here due to the complexity of their construction. The Sourcery G++ suite for ARM EABI is supplied with the typical files (*generic.ld* for example) from which it is possible to start.

D.1. GNU directive

In the GNU world, the set of instructions that we want to give to the compiler or assembly (directives) will be introduced by a keyword prefixed by a "." (dot). The vast majority of directives that we have explored (see Chapter 3) have their direct equivalents in this version of the assembler, but there are a certain number of additions, differences and subtleties that we must carefully understand when we switch from the *ARM* universe to the *GNU* universe.

D.1.1. *Generalities*

These are not strictly the directives mentioned but the following syntactic rules must be respected in order to produce code that is acceptable to the assembler:

– the commentaries are, as is usual in *C*, the set of characters between the delimiters '/*' and '*/'. The user has a second chance to insert a comment by inserting an '@'. The rest of the line (until *carriage return*) will then be ignored. This second syntax is inevitably not very readable;

– symbols are made up of several "letter" characters (upper or lower case), "number" characters (with the exception of the first character) and the two special characters '.' and '_'. Please note that the '$' character, which is allowed in other processors, cannot be used here because (like #) it indicates the start of an immediate value;

– a label is a symbol followed by a ':';

– there are no differences when giving the expression of a numerical value other than for expression in any numerical base. Only bases 10, 16 and binary are allowed. For binary numbers, the value must be prefixed with *0b*. For example, the instruction *MOV R0, #0b100* would load the value 4 in *R0*.

D.1.2. *Memory management*

There is not a single directive to create sections. There are three directives that allow us to carry out openings (closings happen automatically with the opening of a new section). These are identified by the type of section that they create:

– *.text* lets us open a section of code;

– *.data* lets us open a section of initialized data;

– *.bss* lets us open a section of data initially set to zero.

These directives do not support certain options, unlike the ARM directive *AREA*. However, it is possible to add other directives to the section opening suite to specify specific properties:

– *.align n* allows us to impose an alignment on the instruction or datum that follows this directive. The alignment will be to an address divisible by 2^n;

– *.ltorg* allows us to specify that the contents of the *Literal Pool* must be placed in this section (which must be of the *.text* type).

D.1.3. *Management of variables*

The different directives that follow allow us to make various reservations. Do not forget that the symbols that will correspond to these reservations must, as for the labels, be followed by ':':

– *.ascii "string..."* makes a reservation of as many bytes as there are characters in the chain following this directive. Note that a *.asciiz* version exists and is set at 0 at the end of the chain;

– *.byte exp1{,exp2}{,...}* reserves a byte initialized by *exp*. There are as many reservations as expressions;

– *.equ symbol, expression* acts as a *find (symbol)/replace (expression)* in the current module. This directive therefore allows us to define constants;

– *.fill repeat {,size}{,value}* allows us to create *repeat* copies of the value *value* coded on *size* bytes. If *value* is not defined, the value will be zero. If *size* is not specified, the default size will be one byte;

– *.hword exp1{,exp2}{,...}* is equivalent to *.byte* for 16-bit reservations (a half-word);

– *.space size {,fill}*   reserves *size* bytes filled with *fill* (less than 255). The absence of *fill* leads to initialization at 0;

– *.word exp1 {,exp2}{,...}* is equivalent to *.byte* for 32-bit reservations.

D.1.4. *Conditional assembly*

The following directives allow us to carry out conditional assembly (see section 3.5.2):

– *.if expression* means that the lines that follow will be included in the section if *expression* is not false;

– *.endif* marks the end of the conditional part;

– *.else* allows us to include an alternative composed with *.if*.

D.1.5. *Miscellaneous*

There are other directives that can be necessary or useful:

– A module ends with *.end*. The assembler ignores the lines that follow this directive.

– The directive *.type* allows us to give additional information on a symbol. This information can be particularly useful with the use of a symbolic debugger. The most common use is *.type symbol,%function* to indicate that the label *symbol* corresponds to a procedure entry.

– There are no specific directives for indicating the importation of a symbol (see section 9.1.5). It is enough, in the module where the insertion of the directive *.global symbol* is declared, that *symbol* is shared with other symbols of the same name during link editing. This directive carries out the exportation of a symbol.

– *.weak name* marks the symbol *name* as *weak* in the symbol table. This means that another definition of the symbol will have a higher priority than this typed declaration.

– *.size name, expression* associates a size (*expression*) with a symbol (*name*). The dimension can be the result of a calculation, such as the difference between two symbols. This directive is typically used to calculate, for example, how much space a function takes up. For example, *.size Dim . – Deb_func* will assign the dimension corresponding to the difference between the current address (.) and the address of the symbol *Deb_func* to the symbol *Dim*.

D.2. Bootstrap program

The use of *GNU GCC* renders the use of *MicroLib* void. Compared to other projects developed in assembly language, the main function of this library that we must consider is the routine that allows us, following a *Reset* for example, to reinitialize the initialized variables (mainly in the *RW* or *.data* zones) as well as resetting the other zones to zero (the *ZI* or *.bss* zones).

The listing (see Example D.1) is therefore an example of a routine that carries out these initializations. The principle is quite simple, since it consists of making transfers from memory to memory (initialized variables) or resetting other zones (simple variables). What can be more obscure is the way in which it is possible to recover the addresses and sizes of these different zones. In our case, which incidentally is quite standard, the *Startup_constants* table that contains this information is made up from generic names created in the memory description files used by the linker. The names of these addresses are sufficiently significant to pass comment. The prefix *cs* means *CodeSourcery*.

EXAMPLE D.1.– *Variable initialization module (GNU environment)*

```
/*- - - - - - - - - - - - - - - - - - - - - - - - - - - - - - - - - -

Name : Startup.asm

Purpose : System stack initialization and initialized variables

Version : V1.1

Author : SDM (INSA de Toulouse)
/*- - - - - - - - - - - - - - - - - - - - - - - - - - - - - - - - - -

                .text
                .align 2
                .global Startup
                .type Startup, %function
Startup :                                      ;Stack initialization
                LDR R0, Startup_constants+12
                MOV SP, R0
/*- - - - - - - - - - - - - - - - - - - - - - - - - - - - - - - - - -
Initialization of initialized variables
R0 : @Destination, R1 : @Source, R2 : size, R3 : counter, R4 : time
/*- - - - - - - - - - - - - - - - - - - - - - - - - - - - - - - - - -
start_init_ram:
                LDR R0, Startup_constants+16
```

```
                LDR R1, Startup_constants+20
                LDR R2, Startup_constants+24
                MOV R3, #0
  loop_init_ram :
                CMP R3, R2
                BCS start_zero_ram
                LDR R4,[R1,#0]
                STR R4,[R0,#0]
                ADD R3, #4
                ADD R1, #4
                ADD R1, #4
                ADD R0, #4
                B loop_init_ram


/*- - - - - - - - - - - - - - - - - - - - - - - - - - - - - - - - -
Initialization at zero of uninitialized variables
R0 : @Destination, R2 : size, R3 : counter, R4 : time
/*- - - - - - - - - - - - - - - - - - - - - - - - - - - - - - - - -


start_zero_ram :
                LDR R0, Startup_constants+0
                LDR R2, Startup_constants+8
                MOV R3, #0
                MOV R4, #0
  loop_zero_ram :
                CMP R3, R2
                BCS call_main
                STR R4,[R0,#0]
                ADD R3, #4
                ADD R0, #4
                B loop_zero_ram
/*- - - - - - - - - - - - - - - - - - - - - - - - - - - - - - - - -
End of initialization routine, call main
/*- - - - - - - - - - - - - - - - - - - - - - - - - - - - - - - - -


call_main : BL main
/*- - - - - - - - - - - - - - - - - - - - - - - - - - - - - - - - -
```

```
Constants used by Startup
Stored in .text section, after the routine
/*- - - - - - - - - - - - - - - - - - - - - - - - - - - - - - - - - -
                .text
Startup_constants :
                .word __cs3_region_start_bss
                .word __cs3_region_zero_ram_loadaddr
                .word __cs3_region_zero_ram_size
                .word __cs3_stack
                .word __cs3_region_start_data
                .word __cs3_region_init_ram_loadaddr
                .word __cs3_region_init_ram_size
                .end
```

A second listing (see Example D.2) is an example of a bootstrap file. It corresponds and is comparable to that which we have already presented (see Appendix C). We have not described the whole module here. In fact, part of the interrupt vector table has been purposely excluded in order to make this listing lighter.

EXAMPLE D.2.– *Bootstrap file for a GNU assembler*

```
/***************************************************************/
/* STM32F10x.s : Startup file for ST STM32F10x device series */
/***************************************************************/
/* Version : CodeSourcery Sourcery G++ Lite (with CS3) */
/* Modified by SDM (call to Startup) */
/***************************************************************/


/***************************************************************/
/* Stack Configuration */
/***************************************************************/
                .equ Stack_Size, 0x00000200
                .data
                .align 3
                .globl __cs3_stack_mem
                .globl __cs3_stack_size
```

```
_ _cs3_stack_mem :
            .if Stack_Size
            .space Stack_Size
            .endif
            .size __cs3_stack_mem, . - __cs3_stack_mem
            .set __cs3_stack_size, . - __cs3_stack_mem
/*******************************************************************/
/* Heap Configuration */
/*******************************************************************/

            .equ Heap_Size, 0x00001000

            .data
            .align 3
            .globl __cs3_heap_start
            .globl __cs3_heap_end
__cs3_heap_start :
            .if Heap_Size
            .space Heap_Size
            .endif
__cs3_heap_end :
/*******************************************************************/
/* Vector Table */
/*******************************************************************/
            .section ".cs3.interrupt_vector"
            .globl __cs3_interrupt_vector_cortex_m
            .type __cs3_interrupt_vector_cortex_m,
__cs3_interrupt_vector_cortex_m :
            .word __cs3_stack              /* Top of Stack */
            .word __cs3_reset              /* Reset Handler */
            .word NMI_Handler :            /* NMI Handler */
            .word HardFault_Handler        /* Hard Fault Handler */
            .word MemManage_Handler        /* MPU Fault Handler */
            .word BusFault_Handler         /* Bus Fault Handler */
            .word UsageFault_Handler       /* Usage Fault Handler */
            .word 0                        /* Reserved */
            .word 0                        /* Reserved */
```

```
              .word 0                          /* Reserved */
              .word 0                          /* Reserved */
              .word SVC_Handler                /* SVCall Handler */
              .word DebugMon_Handler           /*Debug Monitor Handler */
              .word 0                          /* Reserved */
              .word PendSV_Handler             /* PendSV Handler */
              .word SysTick_Handler            /* SysTick Handler */
/******************************************************************/
/* External Interrupts */
/******************************************************************/
              .word WWDG_IRQHandler  /* Window Watchdog */
              .word PVD_IRQHandler   /* PVD through EXTI Line detect */
              ...
              Incomplete Table....
.size __cs3_interrupt_vector_cortex_m, . - __cs3_interrupt_vector_cortex_m
/******************************************************************/
/* Reset Handler */
/******************************************************************/
              .text
              .globl __cs3_reset_cortex_m
              .type __cs3_reset_cortex_m, %function
__cs3_reset_cortex_m :
              LDR R0,=Startup
              BX R0


              .size __cs3_reset_cortex_m,.-__cs3_reset_cortex_m


              .text
/******************************************************************/
/* Exception Handlers */
/******************************************************************/
              .weak NMI_Handler
              .type NMI_Handler, %function
NMI_Handler :
              B .
              .size NMI_Handler, . - NMI_Handler
/* - - - - - - - - - - - - - - - - - - - - - - - - - - - - -*/
```

```
                .weak HardFault_Handler
                .type HardFault_Handler, %function
HardFault_Handler :
                B .
                .size HardFault_Handler, . - HardFault_Handler
/* - - - - - - - - - - - - - - - - - - - - - - - - - - - - -*/
                .weak MemManage_Handler
                .type MemManage_Handler, %function
MemManage_Handler :
                B .
                .type MemManage_Handler, . - MemManage_Handler
/* - - - - - - - - - - - - - - - - - - - - - - - - - - - - -*/
                .weak BusFault_Handler
                .type BusFault_Handler, %function
BusFault_Handler :
                B .
                .type BusFault_Handler, . - BusFault_Handler
/* - - - - - - - - - - - - - - - - - - - - - - - - - - - - -*/
                .weak UsageFault_Handler
                .type UsageFault_Handler, %function
UsageFault_Handler :
                B .
                .type UsageFault_Handler, . - UsageFault_Handler
/* - - - - - - - - - - - - - - - - - - - - - - - - - - - - -*/
                .weak SVC_Handler
                .type SVC_Handler, %function
SVC_Handler :
                B .
                .type SVC_Handler, . - SVC_Handler
/* - - - - - - - - - - - - - - - - - - - - - - - - - - - - -*/
                .weak DebugMon_Handler
                .type DebugMon_Handler, %function
DebugMon_Handler :
                B .
                .type DebugMon_Handler, . - DebugMon_Handler
/* - - - - - - - - - - - - - - - - - - - - - - - - - - - - -*/
                .weak PendSV_Handler
```

```
              .type PendSV_Handler, %function
PendSV_Handler :
              B .
              .type PendSV_Handler, . - PendSV_Handler
/* - - - - - - - - - - - - - - - - - - - - - - - - - - - -*/
              .weak SysTick_Handler
              .type SysTick_Handler, %function
SysTick_Handler :
              B .
              .type SysTick_Handler, . - SysTick_Handler
/******************************************************************/
/* IRQ Handlers */
/******************************************************************/
              .global Default_Handler
              .type Default_Handler, %function
Default_Handler :
              B .
              .type Default_Handler, . - Default_Handler
```

Bibliography

[ARM 06a] ARM, *ARMv7M Application Level Reference Manual*, Arm Limited, Cambridge, 2006.

[ARM 06b] ARM, *ARMv7-M Architecture Reference Manual*, Arm Limited, Cambridge, 2006.

[ARM 06c] ARM, *Cortex-M3 Technical Reference Manual*, Arm Limited, Cambridge, 2006.

[ARM 10] ARM, *RealView Compilation Tools − Assembler Guide*, Arm Limited, Cambridge, 2010.

[COD] CODESOURCERY, http://www.codesourcery.com.

[KEI] KEIL, http://www.keil.com.

[YIU 07] YIU J., *The Definitive Guide to the Arm Cortex-M3*, Elsevier, Amsterdam, 2007.

Index